VISIONS OF WAR IN FRANCE

VISIONS OF WAR
IN FRANCE

FICTION, ART, IDEOLOGY

Catharine Savage Brosman

LOUISIANA STATE UNIVERSITY PRESS Baton Rouge

Designer: Glynnis Weston
Typeface: Cochin
Typesetter: Coghill Composition
Printer and binder: Edwards Brothers, Inc.

I am grateful to the following for permission to include in this volume material originally published elsewhere: the University of Delaware Press, for permission to reprint as chapter 1, with
some modifications and enlargements, my essay "Violence Justified? *Raison ∂'armée* in Early
Nineteenth-Century France," in *The Play of Terror in Nineteenth-Century France*, edited by John
T. Booker and Allan H. Pasco (Newark: University of Delaware Press, 1997); the *Sewanee
Review*, for permission to reuse portions of my essay "Reading Behind the Lines: The Interpretation of War," in vol. 100 (Winter 1992), which had originally appeared in a pamphlet of the
same title (New Orleans: The Graduate School of Tulane University, 1990); the *South Central
Review*, for permission to use material from my article "The Functions of War Literature," in vol.
10 (Spring 1992).

Library of Congress Cataloging-in-Publication Data
Brosman, Catharine Savage, 1934–
      Visions of war in France : fiction, art, ideology / Catharine
   Savage Brosman.
            p.   cm.
      Includes bibliographical references and index.
      ISBN 0-8071-2346-3 (cloth : alk. paper)
      1. French fiction—History and criticism.   2. War in literature.
   I. Title.
   PQ637.W35B76   1999
   843.009'358—dc21   98-50884
                                                              CIP

In memory of my father and my uncle

PAUL VICTOR HILL
(1907–1969)

—

JOHN ELLIOTT HILL
(1904–1944)

CONTENTS

ILLUSTRATIONS

following page 127

Antoine-Jean Gros, *Murat Defeating the Turkish Army at Aboukir,* ca. 1805

Horace Vernet, *Soldier on the Field at Waterloo,* ca. 1818

François Rude, *The Departure of the Volunteers in 1792* (La Marseillaise), 1835–1836

G. Guillaume, *Turks: Return from Sedan,* 1870

Smeeton, *Our Conquerors!* 1871

Honoré Daumier, *Promethean France and the Eagle-Vulture,* 1871

Maximilien Luce, *Patrie,* 1894

Gino Severini, *Cannon in Action,* 1915

Eugène Chaperon, *O Braves!* ca. 1880

Patriotic postcard, *On the Way to Victory,* 1916

Théophile-Alexandre Steinlen, *Sale Exhibition of Paintings by Artists for the Benefit of the Relief Department for the War Blind,* 1917

PREFACE

THIS STUDY TAKES as its topic certain written and iconographic expressions of one of the oldest recorded human phenomena: the sort of organized armed struggle among sizable groups of human beings called war. There could scarcely be a broader topic for investigation, or one of more general interest to the human species; it remains, sadly, extremely pertinent for the present age. My particular concern as a French literary historian is with literary and other artistic reflections of war in a period of roughly 160 years, from the Napoleonic Wars through World War II and some posterior developments.

I am not alone in investigating the topic of armed conflict in relation to aspects and products of culture; indeed, it has attracted considerable attention in the last few decades from critics, literary historians, cultural historians, writers on art, and other scholars who work on European or American topics. A brief glance at some of this scholarship may be useful to those unfamiliar with it. As early as 1967 Stanley Cooperman published his study of American fiction and World War I; Wayne Charles Miller brought out a history of the American military novel in 1970; in the mid-1970s Maurice Rieuneau did an extensive study of French writing about war and revolution, Holger Klein edited *The First World War in Fiction*, Paul Fussell produced his well-received study *The Great War and Modern Memory*, and Frank Field published his *Three French Writers and the Great War*. Chester W. Obuchowski brought out in 1978 a useful survey entitled *Mars on Trial: War as Seen by French Writers of the Twentieth Century*; the same year, Léon Riegel's *Guerre et littérature* appeared. In 1982 John Cruickshank published his *Variations on Catastrophe*, a study of French literature and the Great War. Brown University's exhibit entitled *All the Banners Wave: Art and War in the Romantic Era, 1792–*

1851 was held in 1982. British poets of World War I have been studied by a number of scholars in addition to Fussell, including Arthur E. Lane and Joseph Cohen.

More recently, the interest manifested in the Vietnam War by American historians and cultural critics, plus celebrations of certain World War II anniversaries, all taking place as the understanding of culture was changing and its study widening, may have played a role in drawing further attention to the topic of war writing and associated matters. The sense that the memory of World War I was dissolving, as its generation disappears, may have prompted a renewal in research. (Julian Barnes's novella *Evermore*, published in 1996, is evidence of the continuing effort to use the written word to memorialize that conflict.) Recent research on European wars includes three studies published in 1989: Margaret Atack's investigations into the literature of the French underground during World War II; David Bevan's *Literature and War*; and Alfredo Bonadeo's *Mark of the Beast: Death and Degradation in the Literature of the Great War*. Samuel Hynes's lengthy volume *A War Imagined: The First World War and English Culture* dates from 1991. M. Paul Holsinger and Mary Anne Schofield published in 1992 their *Visions of War: World War II in Popular Literature and Culture*. Evelyn Cobley brought out *Representing War: Form and Ideology in First World War Narratives* in 1993; Jay Winter's *Sites of Memory, Sites of Mourning*, a study of the theme and vision of mourning and its cultural implications during and after the Great War, appeared in 1995. An investigation of European war memorials by a research group at Stirling University in Scotland is under way, and the Group for War and Culture Studies, based at the University of Westminster in London, serves as an umbrella for various other investigations centered on war and culture in the twentieth century.

Numerous other recent and current investigations dealing with related topics suggest at once the remove at which critics can now place themselves with respect to war and the fascination that it continues to hold. The bibliography of the present volume includes additional studies of interest to those approaching this topic as cultural or literary critics or historians, including Michael Paris's bibliography of fiction either written in English or translated concerning World War II—an incomplete listing but still useful. It should be noted also that the Popular Culture Association and American Culture Association have included on the program of their joint convention for some years sections dealing with twentieth-century wars in which the United States was involved. It scarcely needs to be emphasized how much I am indebted to some of my predecessors and those currently dealing with aspects of the topic, whose particular contributions I shall acknowledge at the proper place. It will be observed, however, that among the books just cited, as well as other pertinent studies, none defines its subject precisely according to the chronological and national parameters I have chosen for the present volume.

The roots of this scholarly undertaking go back to my studies, in the early 1960s, of the midcentury French political novel, especially works by André Malraux, Jean-Paul Sartre, and Louis Aragon. Although I was then interested principally in fiction as a reflection or instrument of politics, the pertinent novels by these authors notably concern war or revolution. Obviously, politics and armed conflict are closely associated in any historical period marked by civil uprisings and revolutions, or when war either is used deliberately as an instrument of diplomacy or external politics, as Carl von Clausewitz understood it, or arises from the failure of other types of relations among powers. Such has been the case through much of the current century in Europe, as well as during certain decades of the previous century, and this repeated presence of war and other types of organized violence has affected French cultural products to a wide extent.

My work on the novels of Roger Martin du Gard and, again, Sartre, emphasizing the political and historical elements, was followed in the 1980s by studies of the writings of Jules Roy, of which many relate to midcentury warfare. These separate investigations prompted me finally to consider from more general perspectives the topic of war writing as a whole in France. The present volume builds on, and in some cases reproduces in revised version, certain previous studies that have resulted from this ongoing interest. I am grateful to the publishers, mentioned in the acknowledgments, who have allowed me to reprint here material that appeared previously.

What I examine in the following pages are written accounts of war in French of the sort ordinarily viewed as literary—involving deliberate shaping of historical material in the modes of imaginative discourse; in addition, I survey a body of nationalistic iconographic symbolism associated with war, in a range of sculptural and graphic examples. The focus is on French wars that took place in Europe, rather than those colonial ventures that began with the invasion of the Algerian coast in 1830 and ended only in 1962. Although, even with these chronological and geographical limitations, the field examined is vast, it can be seen to some degree as a historical whole and also as a literary and cultural one. This does not imply, of course, strict, unbroken continuity either of forms or attitudes, or unbroken historical development; to what degree the same assumptions are entertained in the war writing from different conflicts within this period, and what approaches should be adopted toward them, are matters for consideration.

Many aspects of war as fought by the French in the past two centuries are not examined in this study. The challenge of defining my undertaking more precisely can be met first by saying what this volume does *not* do. It is a project in literary history and criticism and, to a lesser degree, art history, but not history proper, although of course historical matters enter frequently into consideration. It is not a study of strategy or tactics or of particular wars, French warfare in general, or the French military establishment; my point of view is not and cannot be that of a military historian. Nor does this investigation focus primarily on social and political matters; questions of domestic revolution (even when it turns into armed conflict and thus takes on some of the character of warfare), partisan politics, political movements, social changes and clashes, and national attitudes are often germane but are not placed at the center of the study; even what can be termed the sociology of war is not a central concern, although it is a salient aspect of much war writing in the modern period, when armies increasingly have become cross sections of the national population and war has affected the civilian populations on a scale greater than in the past.

In addition, the topic of gender and war, which, with the recent development of gender studies, has become fashionable (*Arms and the Woman*, by Cooper, Munich, and Squier, gives various illustrations of how the topic can be treated), does not concern me as such, either in theory or as a focus of critical practice. I shall note, however, in part to explain my position, that — despite different attitudes toward the enterprise of war and combat sometimes displayed by men and women, if one judges by literary writing from Homer onward, in text after text and war after war — in those relatively few cases where, instead of appearing in men's texts, generally serving as mourners or critics or simply illustrating the effects of war, women themselves write of the war experience in their own voices, and not just of the fringes but of battle, the tropes and plot elements tend to be the same as those of men. This observation is exemplified in the similarities between Helen Zenna Smith's

World War I novel *Not So Quiet . . .* and much fiction of that war written by men: the same filth, rain, and cold, the bad food and lack of sleep—reduction to the animal state—the monotony of the guns, the sadistic officers, the terrible suffering and mutilation, the lack of comprehension on the part of those at the rear, the stupidity of the entire undertaking. As a rule, it would seem that to those of either sex or any ethnic or national group who undergo it, war becomes a common denominator; it is a universalizing experience. This seems true at least starting in 1914. There is, basically, only one plot to war, with few principal subplots and countless variations. It may be just this awful, tragic sameness of plot that appeals in war accounts; they stand so plainly as a paradigm of the human adventure.

To be sure, political reactions to certain wars appear to come only from marginalized groups, as Samuel Hynes has shown, and records such as letters often reveal, on the part of women perhaps more than men, opposition to warfare as such and particular wars. Nevertheless, although Virginia Woolf called the Great War "this preposterous masculine fiction," I would deny the essential specificity of the feminine response. One must remember that noble-women of the Middle Ages urged their knights on to battle—or at least this appears so from the preponderant written and graphic evidence; that John Ruskin spoke of "you tender and delicate women, for whom, and by whose command, all true battle has been," and doubtless basing his view on literary evidence chiefly, wrote: "All healthy men like fighting, and like the sense of danger; all brave women like to hear of their fighting, and of their facing danger."[1]

There are additional materials and aspects of the wide topic I do not propose to treat. Although France was a belligerent in the Crimean War, and a Paris boulevard bears the name of a famous battle from that conflict, its reflections in literature are too limited to be treated here. Similarly, while several major French novelists wrote about the Spanish civil war, they are not included, since the study is centered on wars fought by France. Notwithstanding an effort to understand the French experience as part of an inter-

1. Woolf's phrase is quoted in Panthea Reid, *Art and Affection: A Life of Virginia Woolf* (New York and Oxford: Oxford University Press, 1996), 193. The Ruskin quotations are from lecture 3, "War," in John Ruskin, *The Crown of Wild Olive: Four Lectures on Industry and War* (New York: C. E. Merrill, 1891), 109, 113.

national one, and some mention of literary reflections of war in English-speaking countries, this is not a comparative or cross-cultural study. Those among my readers who are students of Anglo-American war literature will recognize countless features in French writing that characterize English-language expressions of war; it is to be observed, however, that the French experience is different, perhaps essentially different, because the conflicts treated here were generally fought on French soil or adjacent territory.

While I recognize the importance of numerous war films, the interesting aesthetic questions that arise concerning them, and the value of cinema as a depository of war experiences whether contemporaneous with the events (as in André Malraux's film made during the Spanish civil war, *Sierra de Teruel*) or reenacted, I have deliberately omitted from this study the genre of the war film, about which John Whiteclay Chambers II, Jeanine Basinger, and Jay Winter have written with authority. Similarly, the recording of war by the press or by official observers will not be treated; it will be seen, however, that literary accounts assume certain characteristics of journalistic ones. With re-gret—especially in the case of Guillaume Apollinaire and the Resistance poets—I have as a rule left aside the genre of poetry, although the narrative poems of the nineteenth century and war lyrics of the twentieth have much in common with imaginative narratives. Nor is drama considered except in passing: of the chief imaginative genres, it is the least suitable, I suppose, for expressing war or the feelings inspired by war, simply because of staging dif-ficulties—although there have been "war dramas" since *The Trojan Women*, and splendid examples exist in the modern period, including Sartre's *Le Diable et le Bon Dieu*, which concerns religious and political wars in sixteenth-century Germany.

Questions of military ethics, in both theory and practice, and the broad philosophical and psychological questions of why wars are fought, their value if any, and the means of eliminating armed conflict in light of psychological and philosophical explanations offered for them, are of concern to me but not of primary interest in this study; readers will, however, discover that they arise frequently in connection with the works and authors treated. Issues per-taining to nuclear warfare are not examined, since, for the French, nuclear arms have so far remained on the level of policy, not that of practice or expe-rience, and thus have not led to much imaginative recording.

What, precisely, is the chief concern here, then? On the most immediate level, the aims of the study are to examine, in an historical framework stressing the development of nationalism and evolving views on warfare, how war has been depicted in France since 1800—the projects and products of authors and artists who took up the subject—and especially the distinctive ways of dealing with it in the subgenre called the "war novel." Individual and collective *attitudes* toward particular French wars, the military, and warfare in general as they are expressed in narrative and other texts will be examined diachronically, as well as the *ways* in which French writers have imagined war and undertaken to record it, perhaps in justification or condemnation. For example, included in my concerns is heroism—what is thought of as heroic by participants and observers, and how these views shape the literary expressions of war. Yet the primary focus is on a few critical moments of French history: one could say certain *hauts lieux* or high moments, except that disaster and defeat are involved more than triumph. The enormous cultural and mental effects of the major conflicts in which France was engaged after Napoleon—the Franco-Prussian War, the two world wars, and the post-1945 colonial wars (on which I touch only briefly and by way of conclusion)—will perhaps become clearer from this examination.

My study does not purport, however, to be a catalog or complete survey of French war writing. If some portions can serve as an approach to such a survey, I shall be gratified. While aesthetic judgments are not the main focus, the role and effectiveness of genre and style and other formal questions often concern me, and through narratological analysis I have aimed to offer at least a partial poetics of war writing, while acknowledging fully that it cannot pretend to completeness and that its applications are limited, even within this very volume. A parallel interest is with semiology: the common literary and graphic "vocabulary" of war and its relationship to subsequent national discourse and thinking. Some light may be shed thereby on an important strain in modern French literature.

The inclusion in this study of a chapter dealing with the body of nationalistic symbols and their graphic expression is appropriate in view of their tremendous importance, the overlapping of iconographic elements in written, pictorial, and sculptural art, and the semiotic resemblances among modes of expression. Graphic representations of war motifs are often particularly expressive. Drawn images frequently preceded corresponding written ones and sometimes had a much wider audience (as with cheap lithographs, called *images d'Epinal*, very common, and postage stamps and posters of World War I); the two can operate similarly, but the pictorial with more immediacy and less ambiguity. In surveying and analyzing this body of art, and the symbolism on which it often draws, I am greatly indebted to other scholars, and in particular to Pierre Nora and other contributors to *Les Lieux de mémoire*.

Several major figures in French literature of the last two hundred years, considered among the most important of their periods and known to many English-speaking readers, are treated in the following pages, sometimes in a different light from that in which they usually appear; among them are Vigny, Balzac, Stendhal, Hugo, Maupassant, Zola, Céline, Saint-Exupéry, Sartre, Beauvoir, and Claude Simon. There are also, however, numerous lesser figures, whose appearance here may lead to their attracting new readers. To emphasize several authors of the canon is to recognize the importance that the French themselves have traditionally accorded to certain writers above others, in whom they see, or wish to see, those qualities they prize especially: logic, critical spirit, intelligence, style and taste, and imagination. This is not to say, however, that these qualities are found uniformly in works examined below; in this connection, it is remarkable that the standards of style and taste, which long reigned over most French writing, were discarded or revised radically in the twentieth century partly under the influence of the very wars (chiefly the 1914 conflict) that authors proposed to depict.

While battlefield experiences are central to most of the texts featured here and clearly constitute the crux of any representation of war, I do not propose to limit my corpus to combat novels. The effects of war radiate into the entire national fabric, and the sometimes oblique relationships between present, past, or future wars and other cultural products and political processes, and the way war affects, and is affected by, other sectors of society, bear investigation. "The experience of war," write John Keegan and Richard Holmes, ". . . engulfs entire peoples. Its nature, too, is not specifically or wholly military. Warfare alters, sometimes transforms societies, and leaves no one who has been exposed to its turmoil unchanged."[2] I am concerned thus with the novel of *wartime* as well as the novel of war. I intend to emphasize the experiential dimension of warfare, which, precisely, literature (as opposed to statistics, reports, summary histories) excels at rendering—a fact that justified the

2. John Keegan and Richard Holmes, *Soldiers* (London: Hamish Hamilton, 1985), 259.

literary undertakings of so many who, having lived through battle, wrote about it subsequently.

Whether the contents and styles of works under examination are now fashionable is not a criterion for my interest, although the literary historian must of course register trends in reading, interpretation, and taste. My concerns differ greatly from those of radical cultural critics who examine literature and other cultural products (except willfully subversive ones) simply as products of power (racial, patriarchal, and so forth) intended to reinforce oppressive structures, and, taking them as oppressive instruments and signs rather than expressions of human free will and creativity, make no aesthetic distinctions among texts and other products. The critics I have in mind are, I assume, hostile to any sort of modern nationalism and wholly opposed, personally, to the institution of the military; they would be uninterested in seeing European wars in any light other than as strategies of power structures designed to oppress groups, and their reading of war narratives would presumably be entirely different from mine.

Certain questions arise in more than one connection in the chapters that follow — questions that derive from the very nature of imaginative literature as well as from the historical situations. I have already noted my focus on the narratology of war: relationships between types of war experience and their telling (for instance, individual versus group, full-scale battle versus prolonged trench and field experience, and so on); relationships between tactics and writing, if they can be identified; relationships between collectivities and individuals as they are structured into plot; sympathetic and antagonistic relationships among characters; and so on. Similarly, I am interested in a possible taxonomy, or classification, of war narratives, especially by the mid-twentieth-century, when a wider range of types appeared than had been seen before. While, as noted, military ethics are not the central focus here, literary expressions of moral judgments concerning war, especially as related to nationalism, are explored. Although a medical understanding of what the psyche experiences in war, especially in battle, is not within the purview of this study, the particular role of the imagination and its modes, or the *imaginaire*, in the experiencing of battle (according to literary accounts) as well as in the historical processes that bring about the events themselves will be considered, notably in such forms as soldiers' imagination and hallucinations and images in propaganda (written and graphic). I should hope, in fine, to contribute to an understanding of the functions and effects of war literature and images in French society during the past two hundred years, prior to, during, and after the conflicts.

I made a disclaimer above to the effect that this project in literary history did not aspire to, or wish to pass for, history. Yet, as E. D. Hirsch, Jr., wrote more than a quarter-century ago in *Validity in Interpretation*, "All serious students of texts from the past—texts of any genre—are historians."[3] There is no need, in my view, to apologize for an historical undertaking, either to historians or to literary critics. My position is neither the New Historians' nor the deconstructionists'. Those who reject diachronic understanding of literature are willfully blind to the obvious double fact that both change and continuity mark writing, as other cultural products, and that only acquaintance with the historical context in which change comes about and values are either discarded, reaffirmed, or invented can enable one to comprehend these products. In addition, the view that the meaning of a text cannot be recovered because of the circularity of reference or other undecidability cannot be supported.

With respect to the view that the past is unknowable, one could observe facetiously that such a position does not deserve further refutation beyond that afforded by the example of its adherents, as they remember what they did last year and pore over texts written at previous times. The historicists' position is not usually so ingenuous as this, to be sure; they argue typically that the recuperation of the historical context is problematical because the necessary evidence is originally so culturally conditioned as to be nearly irretrievable, and that, moreover, present ideologies, which filter and mediate the past, likewise interfere with access. That past and present conditions and attitudes are operative is one thing; that their relationship to cultural products is strictly determining and discrete is another. Hirsch's arguments concerning the possibility of valid interpretation of verbal texts remain sound even after thirty years of poststructuralist criticism. In short, to view literary products of the past as locked into particular worldviews for which the present has no key is carrying too far the acknowledgment that *certain* aspects of the past may escape later readers. Writing on behalf of traditional historians against the reduction of the historical project to "metanarratives," discourses of

3. E. D. Hirsch, Jr., *Validity in Interpretation* (New Haven: Yale University Press, 1967), 138.

power, and mythmaking, Wilfred McClay has reaffirmed that "history . . . when properly undertaken can supply us with reliable knowledge of the human world."[4] This observation holds for cultural and literary history alike.

As for these historians of the older school, their indulgence may be required on occasion because of my flagging command of the historical situation, but the following undertaking belongs in truth to their own: the project of assessing and understanding human beings' behavior, both individual and collective, in the past (and, by implication, perhaps in the present), by means of particular sorts of documents and artifacts available (contemporaneous or posterior)—documents that differ from archival evidence and other factual material, but which bring to bear their own sort of evidence. One need not agree with all the positions of Hayden White and others of his persuasion to see that both fiction and written history, by their normally linear construction, their concern with what happens in time, and their modes of discourse and rhetoric, have much in common; even their respective epistemological status, while different in the purest examples, tends to bleed into the other. Anthony Pugh is one of numerous critics who have brought out the role of encoding and mythmaking in historiography and fiction alike. As Herbert Lindenberger has observed, "Historical writing . . . imitates and expresses the characteristic gestures and practices of the artistic realm as surely as the latter feeds on what could once confidently be isolated as the historical realm. . . . The interactions we discern between history and art quickly compromise whatever dividing lines we set up between them."[5]

I am not, unlike some extremists, arguing that all history is myth, but rather that the fictional and other imaginative evidence of the past, including choice of material and manner of presentation, has historical value. Thus the novelist's task can justly be said to resemble the historian's, as Eugen Weber describes it: "To attain, beyond the manifest discourse of events, the elementary categories which unify, in a given period, the elementary ways of seeing

4. Wilfred M. McClay, review of *The Killing of History: How a Discipline Is Being Murdered by Literary Critics and Social Theorists*, by Keith Windschuttle, *Academic Questions* 11 (Winter 1997–98): 90.

5. Herbert Lindenberger, "Toward a New History in Literary Study," *Profession 84* (New York: Modern Language Association, 1984), 17. For an elaboration of Pugh's views, see Ian Higgins, ed., *The Second World War in Literature* (Edinburgh and London: Scottish Academic Press, 1986), 59–70.

and knowing." Claude Bonnefoy goes so far as to say that the novel alone can translate "the dimension of the individual and . . . this way in which we live our relationship to events."[6] There is no reason not to accord to a frankly fictional shaping of historical experience not only something like the higher poetic truth of Aristotle but truth of a historical order.

"War endures. . . . War was always here. Before man was, war waited for him. The ultimate trade awaiting its ultimate practitioner. That is the way it was and will be. . . . It endures because young men love it and old men love it in them." So speaks the judge in Cormac McCarthy's *Blood Meridian*. It is the supreme game, he argues, the one in which the stake is the highest: "All games aspire to the condition of war for here that which is wagered swallows up game, player, all. . . . War is the ultimate game because war is at last a forcing of the unity of existence. War is god."[7]

Without subscribing wholly to this analysis—which is qualified by the character of the judge, obsessed with the desire for unlimited power—I am obliged to acknowledge the near-universality of armed conflict in human societies and the failure of the most enlightened and determined attempts to eradicate it. If the present study elicits any further sensitivity in readers to the horrors of war and any greater understanding of its puzzling persistence among the species and of possible means to curtail conflict, it will be more rewarding than I presently dare hope. Despite the thirty or so wars that rage (according to reports) as I write this, one must look forward, as to a new golden age, to the time when men will "study war no more." Then armed conflict, which Charles de Gaulle called "the history of men," can be replaced by a united world, "the dream of the wise." In the meantime, the literature of war may be considered, in part, as a literature of triumph, to the degree that it expresses not only some understanding of the phenomenon it depicts, but also the desire of the spirit eventually to overcome it; as André Malraux wrote, "The difference between real life and its portrayal in the work of art consists in [the] subjugation of destiny."[8]

6. Weber's statement is quoted in Hope H. Glidden, "La Poésie du chiffre: Le Roy Ladurie and the *Annales* School of Historiography," *Stanford French Review* 5 (Winter 1981): 279. Bonnefoy's phrase comes from Claude Bonnefoy, "Quand le roman téléscope l'histoire," *Gulliver*, n.d., 37.

7. Cormac McCarthy, *Blood Meridian* (New York: Random House, 1985), 248–49.

8. André Malraux, *The Creative Act*, vol. 2 of *The Psychology of Art*, trans. Stuart Gilbert (Lon-

I should like to express my gratitude to numerous colleagues, institutions, and organizations. To the University of Sheffield, which appointed me the De Velling and Willis Visiting Research Professor for spring 1996 and thereby provided me with invaluable research time plus a congenial atmosphere in which to pursue this project, I am very grateful; my special thanks go to Professor David H. Walker for inviting me to lecture there in May 1995 and later nominating me for the professorship. To the Rutgers Center for Historical Analysis and Professor John Whiteclay Chambers II, of Rutgers University, then project director at the Center, I am grateful for being appointed as a Visiting Fellow in 1995 and for the opportunity to present some of my conclusions at the Center's round table. The program committees of the American Association of Teachers of French were kind enough to include on the program at three different meetings my papers connected to this research; similarly, the section chairmen of the Popular Culture Association conventions, where I spoke twice in the sessions on war, and the organizers of the 1993 Colloquium on Nineteenth-Century French Studies, who included on the program what became chapter 1, deserve thanks.

I appreciate likewise opportunities afforded or assistance offered by the following: Kenneth M. Price, former editor of the *South Central Review*, who invited me to contribute "The Functions of War Literature" to an issue of his magazine; George Core, editor of the *Sewanee Review*, who published some of my criticism on war literature and my own war poems; Drs. Peter Fawcett of the University of Leicester, Patrick Pollard of Birkbeck College, University of London, David Steel of Lancaster University, and Valerie Holman, then of the University of Westminster, who all invited me to lecture on aspects of this topic; Professor James Turner Johnson of Rutgers University, who very kindly gave me some of his time; Professor Henri Mitterand of Columbia University (emeritus Sorbonne-Nouvelle), who made useful suggestions; Jules Roy, who granted me numerous interviews and encouraged my scholarly investigation of his own writing and associated questions; President

---

don: A. Zwemmer, 1949), 148. The quotation from de Gaulle comes from Gordon A. Craig and Francis L. Loewenheim, eds., *The Diplomats: 1939–1979* (Princeton: Princeton University Press, 1994), 247.

Francis L. Lawrence of Rutgers University, who, when he was provost of Tulane University, appointed me Andrew W. Mellon Professor for Fall 1990 and thus gave me the opportunity to organize a series of lectures on war and revolution by colleagues and visitors and allowed me time to write two lectures of my own; colleagues at Tulane, including Drs. John D. Glenn, Jr., and Kathleen Turner, who participated in the Mellon lecture series and have furnished bibliographic information. It is a pleasure to acknowledge once again research and interlibrary loan assistance from the staff at the Howard-Tilton Library of Tulane University. My recent Tulane graduate students Drs. Frank A. Anselmo, Pascale Dhoop, Melanie Gordon Krob, and Sylvia Williamson graciously shared information with me. Dr. Thomas M. Biggs and Dr. Karlheinz Hasselbach assisted me in seeking locations of paintings. My thanks go also to Katherine Brosman Deimling, my daughter.

VISIONS OF WAR IN FRANCE

– 1 –

THE RATIONALE OF WAR
IN ENLIGHTENMENT AND
ROMANTIC LITERATURE

THE CONNECTION BETWEEN war and human culture is an ancient and powerful one, visible, among other ways, in the scientific and cultural developments that have grown out of offensive and defensive warfare—in medicine and architecture, for instance, as well as in military technology. This connection is not morally simple. On the one hand, no one needs reminding of the terrible toll of modern war; particularly in the last years of this century, it is viewed as so immensely destructive of human beings and their goods and achievements that many judge all recourse to arms as unconscionable. Yet the war phenomenon persists. In anthropological and psychological terms, it appears as an ancient curse and a perversion, and yet strangely necessary. In the preface, I quoted from Cormac McCarthy's *Blood Meridian* on the enduring attraction of war. Franco Fornari has argued that the war phenomenon is in the unconscious of every human being. John Keegan and Richard Holmes speak of the "strange and timeless fascination about warfare and the warrior" and suggest that there is something "inside the human psyche that lusts for and thrills to the clash of arms while enabling itself to blot out the shrieks of the maimed and dying."[1]

Moreover, a long-standing philosophical tradition stresses the positive value of warfare, which was implied in my opening sentence. Heraclitus called war "father of all, and king of all." The early eighteenth-century writer Vauvenargues viewed *gloire*—military honor and achievement—as the source

1. Franco Fornari, *The Psychoanalysis of War* (Garden City, N.Y.: Anchor Books, 1974), xxiii; Keegan and Holmes, *Soldiers*, 7.

of human virtue, the proof of merit, the highest reward, and wrote that peace, which "borne les talents et amollit les peuples" [limits talents and softens peoples] is not a good, either in morals or politics. "Il n'y a pas de gloire achevée, sans celle des armes" [There is no complete glory, without that of arms].[2]

Likewise, having observed that war "has something sublime in it," Immanuel Kant went on to assert, in his *Critique of Judgment* (1790): "Although war is an undesigned enterprise of men (stirred up by their unbridled passions), yet it is perhaps a deep-hidden and designed enterprise of supreme wisdom for preparing . . . a morally grounded system of those states. In spite of the dreadful afflictions with which it visits the human race . . . [war] is . . . a motive for developing all talents serviceable for culture to the highest possible pitch." Georg Wilhelm Friedrich Hegel likewise saw war as beneficial, specifically as a means of underpinning the state by creating a sense of community, through the exercise of individual freedom for a good surpassing the individual. "The health of a state is generally revealed not so much in the calm of peace as in the stir of war. . . . In war the power of the association of all with the whole is in evidence; this association has adjusted the amount which it can demand from individuals, as well as the worth of what they may do for it of their own impulse and their own heart."[3]

Some decades later, John Ruskin similarly recognized the connections between the militaristic cult and the impulse toward civilization, at least in its early stages: "All the pure and noble arts of peace are founded on war; no great art ever yet rose on earth, but among a nation of soldiers. . . . There is no great art possible to a nation but that which is based on battle. . . . War is the foundation of all the arts . . . all the high virtues and faculties of men." Friedrich Nietzsche wrote that "it is the good war that hallows any cause," and "you should love peace as a means to new wars."[4]

---

2. Heraclitus, *Fragments*, text and trans. with commentary by M. T. Robinson (Toronto: University of Toronto Press, 1987), 37; Luc de Clapiers, marquis de Vauvenargues, *Œuvres*, ed. D.-L. Gilbert (Paris: Furne, 1857), 128–37, 446. The word *war* in Heraclitus' text should perhaps be *strife*.

3. Immanuel Kant, *Critique of Judgment,* trans. J. H. Bernard (New York: Hafner, 1951), 282–83; Adam Nelson Krob, "Hegel's Community: Synthesizing the Romantic and the Liberal" (Ph.D. diss., Duke University, 1997), 98.

4. Ruskin, *Crown of Wild Olive*, 99, 105; Friedrich Nietzsche, *Thus Spoke Zarathustra*, in *The Portable Nietzsche*, trans. Walter Kaufmann (New York: Viking, 1954), 159.

This strand of thought reaches to the present century, when more than one Western society—not to mention Japan—has regarded war, as Modris Eksteins expressed it (in reference to Germany prior to 1914), as "the supreme test of spirit . . . a test of vitality, and culture, and life." War is seen as the school of civic virtue, the measure of a man. As the catalog of the 1900 Paris world exposition put it in the section on "Retrospective Exhibition of Land and Sea Armies": "It seemed indispensable to revive in all minds [the memory] of wars of the past"—not to discourage future belligerency, but rather because war is "a school of the highest qualities of man." Henry de Montherlant, while acknowledging that the Great War had been worse than most, argued in *Le Songe* [The dream], which John Fletcher calls a "rather tasteless panegyric of war," that one should "ramener dans la paix les vertus de la guerre" [bring back in peacetime the virtues of war]. Late in World War I, Winston Churchill, who nevertheless deplored the slaughter, said to Siegfried Sassoon that "war is the normal occupation of man," an instrument of policy and stimulator of individual achievements.[5]

Johan Huizinga, like Ruskin, related armed confrontation to play, itself a foundation of cultural development, and considered war a "cultural function" when it is waged according to principles and among equals, as a contest rather than as extermination. "Such an ideal of noble strife, fulfilled in myth and legend, is one of the strongest incentives to civilization," he wrote. Even if cultural evidence of warfare consists in part of fictions, "these fancies of war as a noble game of honor and virtue have still played an important part in developing civilization." The military writer Jules Roy, who had nothing of the warmonger in him, said in 1969, "Même juste . . . la guerre, c'est la malédiction de l'humanité. Et cependant c'est là que les hommes se révèlent dans leur vérité" [Even when just . . . war is the curse of humanity. And yet men reveal themselves there in their truth].[6]

5. The quotation from the Paris exposition catalog is from Eugen Weber, *France Fin de siècle* (Cambridge: The Belknap Press, 1986), 243. Other sources are as follows: Modris Eksteins, *Rites of Spring: The Great War and the Birth of the Modern Age* (Boston: Houghton Mifflin, 1989), 90; John Fletcher, "Henry de Montherlant," in *French Novelists, 1930–1960*, ed. Catharine Savage Brosman, vol. 72 of *Dictionary of Literary Biography* (Detroit: Gale Research, 1988), 279; Henry de Montherlant, *Le Songe* (Paris: Grasset, 1922); Winston Churchill, quoted in William Manchester, *Visions of Glory, 1874–1932*, vol. 1 of *The Last Lion: Winston Spencer Churchill* (Boston: Little Brown, 1983), 581.

6. Johan Huizinga, *Homo Ludens* (London: Routledge & Kegan Paul, 1949), 89, 102; Pierre Lhoste, "Jules Roy: Mes mots de passe," *Nouvelles Littéraires* 2201 (17 Nov. 1969): 1, 7.

In particular, from the days of the Greeks, the Romans, and the Hebrew chroniclers, epic poetry, drama, and historical accounts have repeatedly been inspired by, and often centered around, war: "Of arms and the man I sing." The role played by the Trojan War in the whole of ancient Western literature is so central that it can be considered the single most important topic of the body of writing inherited from early Graeco-Roman civilization. Likewise, in the large body of early European literature constituted by medieval sagas and epics, war is the central, indeed sometimes the only, theme; and although there were ancient influences, illustrated for instance in the French *Roman d'Alexandre* (twelfth century), most of this corpus, whether in the Germanic or the Romance languages, represented an autochthonous phenomenon. To note a similar association between much of the oral tradition of non-Western peoples and their armed conflicts with surrounding groups is then to affirm the near-universality of war as a subject for—and doubtless often an impetus to—song, drama, and narrative, oral and written.

It may be argued further that, except possibly for the theme of love (although it first became preeminent only in the *romans bretons* and troubadour texts of the twelfth and thirteenth centuries), no other literary rendering of human experience has exercised such an extensive influence on human behavior. For many of the most sensitive and reflective among young men, literary texts seem to have been a crucial factor in their love of the military and their enthusiasm for war. It should be remembered that, prior to the replacement of Latin by the modern languages in secondary schools, every year thousands of students read Caesar's *Gallic Wars*. Of Henry Fleming, the hero in Stephen Crane's *The Red Badge of Courage*, the author writes, "He had read of marches, sieges, conflicts, and he had seen it all." Paul Fussell has found abundant evidence among the British in World War I for an image of battle nourished by *The Oxford Book of English Verse* and other anthologies, and Samuel Hynes has stressed the role of the literary and cultural imagination, which saw war as heroic, in shaping contemporary attitudes toward World War I. Stanley Cooperman, examining the rhetoric of the Great War, identified in various texts innumerable references to the Biblical view of history as a vast struggle between God and Satan; Jay Winter has similarly identified among many World War I writers an apocalyptic spirit and belief in the supernatural. In France the enthusiasm for this same conflict had been fed for years by a literature of *revanchisme*, or revenge, to which writers as diverse as Alphonse

Daudet, Emile Zola, Maurice Barrès, and Charles Péguy contributed. After the American war in Vietnam, Michael Norman, who enlisted in the U.S. Marines in 1967, wrote, echoing Crane as well as revealing himself as a son of the age of television: "I had read the newspapers and watched television news; the sights and sounds of battle were irresistible. History was unfolding and I had an urge to be a part of it, a Henry Fleming hoping to 'mingle in one of those great affairs of earth.' "[7]

A thoughtful example of war literature's influence is offered by an American Navy captain who, after identifying the role played in his choice of a military career by the oral accounts of four uncles and by his superficial study of history, movies, and television films such as *Victory at Sea,* added a fifth factor: "a shallow and unsophisticated study of American literature." He explained: "Although it's difficult to sort out now what I read when, I think I had read *Red Badge of Courage, The Naked and the Dead, Battle Cry, The Young Lions,* and *From Here to Eternity.* . . . The writings of Hemingway influenced me. His notion of courage as 'grace under pressure' may have obscured deeper messages. . . . My limited sampling of mid-Twentieth Century American literature left the strong impression that war provides the quickest, sharpest, most dramatic, most public test of one's personal courage and character."[8]

This literary image of war as a proving ground, which is made possible by the power of language to convey experience, has often seemed tantamount to an invitation to the military life. André Chamson spoke of his belief, before he went to fight in Spain, that "j'allais pouvoir prendre ma mesure à l'occasion de cet événement" [I was going to be able to measure myself on the occasion of that event]—a belief of which he was subsequently cured. The image is connected to the ratification of personal and gender identity within small social groups such as the family and, by implication, with the collectivity and its ideas of manhood. War literature has its own, powerful version of such

7. Stephen Crane, *The Red Badge of Courage* (1895; reprint, New York: Modern Library, 1925), 6; Paul Fussell, *The Great War and Modern Memory* (New York: Oxford University Press, 1975); Samuel Hynes, *A War Imagined: The First World War and English Culture* (New York: Atheneum, 1991); Stanley Cooperman, *World War I and the American Novel* (Baltimore: Johns Hopkins University Press, 1967); Jay Winter, *The Experience of World War I* (New York: Oxford University Press, 1989); Michael Norman, *These Good Men: Friendships Forged from War* (New York: Crown Publishers, 1989), 76.

8. Warren Hudson, U.S. Navy, ret., written statement to the author, 7 December 1990.

themes as initiation and maturation, themes that reach far beyond the military context. This idealistic view of war as the test of oneself may also be connected to the question of national identity, particularly in Germany, both before and after World War I, but also in France. Ernst Jünger spoke in *Das Wäldchen 125*, his account of trench fighting in the Great War, of "the responsibilities that demand sacrifice of such corruptible treasures as life and property when a nation's greatness and its ideas are at stake. . . . War is not a material matter. . . . Values are tested in comparison with which the brutality of the means must . . . appear insignificant."[9]

This overview of the place of war in the Western literary tradition and its hold on the mind can serve as a reminder that, before the Napoleonic Wars, eighteenth-century readers would have been acquainted with, and often moved by, a substantial body of heroic literature featuring brave warriors and valiant deeds in battle. Furthermore, the question of justification for war was then generally preempted by the principles of the European political system. In both medieval and early modern times, prior to the period treated here, European dynastic wars were considered—by the ruling classes and the monarchies that engaged in them—inevitable and justifiable, willed by God. This conviction reflects the concept of divine omniscience and intervention in human affairs, and the belief in the divine right of kings. As Blaise de Monluc, or Montluc, wrote in the sixteenth century, "God Almighty raised up these two great princes [Francis I and Charles V] sworn enemies to one another." Allegiance to the monarch and God required acceptance of the cause; *raison d'état* was the equivalent of *raison d'armée*. "Be full of the love and loyalty we all owe our prince," he wrote. "And in so doing although his quarrel should not be just, God will not for all that withdraw his assistance from you; for it is not for us to ask our King if his cause be good or evil, but only to obey him." It might be supposed that these statements are an expression of the just war tradition in its classic form, which developed from Christendom's communal views in the late Middle Ages—although antecedents existed in Aristotle (who made the distinction between justifiable and unjustifiable par-

9. Ernst Jünger, *Das Wäldchen 125: Eine Chronik aus dem Grabenkämpfen 1918* (1926), trans. as *Copse 125: A Chronicle from the Trench Warfare of 1918* (1930; reprint, New York: Howard Fertig, 1988), ix. The Chamson quotation comes from John E. Coombes, *Writing from the Left: Socialism, Liberalism and the Popular Front* (New York and London: Harvester Wheatsheaf, 1989), 134.

ticipation in war) and Augustine—and which includes the concepts of both *jus ad bellam* (just cause) and *jus in bello* (just conduct). In fact, Monluc's views reflect the post-Reformation modification of *jus ad bellam* in the form of *compétence de guerre*—the doctrine that "each sovereign had the right and authority to decide when just cause for war existed."[10]

The old heroic tradition was maintained throughout the ancien régime, and it has been demonstrated that there was in the mid-eighteenth century an upsurge in military literature. One of the principal French military writers of the century, the Prince de Ligne, noted in his *Mélanges* (1795) that, since philosophy had not yet gained enough ground to put an end to war, "il faut chercher de la pratique où l'on peut. Si la Russie est en guerre il faut demander la permission d'y aller . . . S'il y a dans quelque autre pays des camps, de grands simulacres de guerre, et surtout des sièges, il faut tâcher de les aller voir" [One must look for practice where one can. If Russia is at war, one must ask permission to go there. . . . If there are, in other countries, camps, war games, and especially sieges, one must try to go see them].[11]

Yet the Enlightenment was also the period when, for the first time, warfare and national conflict became topics for extended debate, including considerable criticism of war and the policies that led to it. The possibility of peace was given prolonged philosophic and political consideration, in treatises by Pierre André Gargas, the abbé de Saint-Pierre, Jean-Jacques Rousseau, and Kant. (Parallel to this philosophic inquiry there developed a line of thinking, pursued by the maréchal de Saxe, the comte de Guibert, Puységur, and others, concerned with rationalizing and systematizing warfare according to universalist models.) Even Vauvenargues deplored a petty and disastrous war of alliances in which a young friend was killed, and in his *Traité sur le libre arbitre* [Treatise on free will] (1737), spoke of the "maladies épidémiques qui ravagent en tous lieux l'espèce humaine," seeing that "les hommes se détruisent eux-mêmes par les guerres, que le faible est la proie du fort," and denying

10. Blaise de Montluc, *The Hapsburg-Valois Wars and the French Wars of Religion*, ed. Ian Roy (Hamden, Conn.: Archon Books, 1972), 37, 231–32; Aristotle, *The Politics*, ed. and trans. Ernest Barker (New York: Oxford University Press, 1962), 285; James Turner Johnson, *Ideology, Reason, and the Limitation of War: Religious and Secular Concepts, 1200–1740* (Princeton: Princeton University Press, 1975), 8, 16.

11. Charles-Joseph, Prince de Ligne, *Œuvres choisies du Prince de Ligne*, ed. Basil Guy (Saratoga, Calif.: Anma Libri, 1978), 42–45.

that the "désordres" are really useful and beneficial. Kant, whose qualification of war as an "enterprise of supreme wisdom" was quoted earlier, nevertheless considered armed conflict as one of the greatest of human evils, the source of all moral corruption. This was true at least by 1795, the date when he published his pamphlet *Perpetual Peace*.[12]

In opposition to the principle of the divine right of kings, with its implied right to make war, which had been at the foundation of monarchal behavior and thinking, Enlightenment thought generally identified, as the foundation of sovereignty, social contracts and natural law, or what Montesquieu calls in *Les Lettres persanes* "le droit des gens, ou plutôt celui de la raison" [the rights of human beings, or rather that of reason]. Departing from the *compétence de guerre* principle, Montesquieu, who denounced holy or religious wars on the grounds that they spring from the spirit of intolerance, asserted in letter 95 that justice among nations is no different from justice among individuals; and, in a step toward a rationalization of war that departed from his predecessors' and emphasized the *relations* among social and physical factors, he asserted that there were only two cases of justice in warfare: self-defense against the aggression of an enemy (based, as he wrote in *L'Esprit des lois*, on the analogy of the right to self-defense in nature), and assistance to an ally who has been attacked. All declarations of war, he contended, should be acts of justice on one of these grounds. Conquest in itself confers no rights, but only obligations; peace treaties, which he calls "la voix de la Nature qui réclame ses droits" [the voice of Nature, which reclaims its rights], are sacred.[13]

Voltaire's statements on warfare, including the article "Guerre" in the *Dictionnaire philosophique*, indicate contrasting views, in a pattern of oscillation between what might appear to be bellicose monarchism or Hobbesian cynicism, on the one hand, and on the other a desire for a peaceful international order. In various early poems, including *La Henriade* (1723, 1728), and in "Poème de Fontenoy" (1745), he enthusiastically describes combats at length and evokes heroism and martial achievements—signs of his attachments to the classical

12. Vauvenargues, *Œuvres*, 146; Joachim Merlant, *De Montaigne à Vauvenargues* (Geneva: Slatkine, 1969), 362; Immanuel Kant, *Kant's Political Writings*, ed. H. Reiss (Cambridge: Cambridge University Press, 1970), 183; Immanuel Kant, *Perpetual Peace*, trans. Lewis White Beck (Indianapolis: Library of Liberal Arts, 1957).

13. Charles-Louis Secondat de Montesquieu, *Œuvres complètes*, 2 vols. (Paris: Gallimard/ Bibliothèque de la Pléiade, 1949, 1951), 1:174, 259, 271–72; 2:377.

tradition and to individual commanders. He saw dynastic wars as a political phenomenon, a deplorable one, but one that could at best be controlled, not eliminated, in the Europe that he knew; on the notion and prospect of international law, as set forth by Hugo Grotius and Baron Samuel von Pufendorf, he took a very cynical position. In particular, he argued that wars of defense were legitimate, and after the publication of the comte de Guibert's *Essai général de tactique* (1770), Voltaire wrote a poem, "La Tactique," in which he acknowledged that the art of war was, unfortunately, necessary.[14]

Yet he viewed most armed conflict as a foolish and burdensome expenditure for the state, undertaken "pour de très légers intérêts, et souvent pour de petits caprices" [for very insignificant interests, and often on small whims] — undertakings for which those least responsible often bore the heaviest burden; or, worse, wars were the product of religious intolerance, and thus totally unacceptable. What reader of *Candide* does not remember his satire of the wars of the Abars and Bulgars (that is, the Seven Years' War), a "boucherie héroïque" [heroic butchery] and of the so-called "lois du droit public" [public laws] that purport to justify violence? Only those conflicts having freedom as their object and result can be justified.[15]

Rousseau was repeatedly occupied with the question of war; he composed a "Jugement sur le projet de paix perpétuelle," referring to the scheme for European peace published by l'abbé Saint-Pierre in 1713 (which Voltaire had praised before criticizing). Rousseau took a stand elsewhere against Thomas Hobbes, the Western philosopher whose writings are most fundamentally concerned with war and who rejected the Just War tradition, contending that in the state of nature, or "this war of every man against every man," the notions of right and wrong had no place. To this position, Rousseau was thoroughly opposed, arguing, as his title puts it, "Que l'état de guerre naît de l'état

14. Voltaire, *La Henriade* and *Poème de Fontenoy*, both in *Œuvres complètes de Voltaire*, vol. 8 (Paris: Garnier, 1877). The Voltaire article on war can be found in *Political Writings*, ed. and trans. David Williams (Cambridge: Cambridge University Press, 1994), 7–11. See also Williams's introduction to *Political Writings*, xxviii, and Henry Meyer, *Voltaire on War and Peace*, no. 144 of Studies on Voltaire and the Eighteenth Century (Banbury, Oxfordshire: Voltaire Foundation, 1976), chap. 3.

15. Voltaire, *Essai sur les moeurs*, ed. René Pomeau, vol. 2 (Paris: Garnier, 1963), 811; Voltaire, *Œuvres complètes*, vol. 48 (Oxford: Voltaire Foundation, 1984), 126–27; Voltaire, *Mélanges*, ed. Emmanuel Berl (Paris: Gallimard/Bibliothèque de la Pléiade, 1961), 22.

social" [That the state of war springs from the social state]. According to his view of history, war was the result of the institution, in what had been the prelapsarian world, of property and civil society—not (as in Hobbes's view) of the state of nature. As he indicates in *Discours sur l'origine de l'inégalité*, "La Société naissante fit place au plus horrible état de guerre" [Rising society gave way to the most horrible state of warfare], a warfare both domestic— between the haves and have-nots—and national. In his view, the relation- ships among nations, constituting a sort of degraded state of nature, cor- rupted by the desires introduced by property and without the counterbalancing forces existing *within* society, produced "les Guerres Natio- nales, les Batailles, les meurtres, les représailles, qui font frémir la Nature et choquent la raison. . . . Les plus honnêtes gens apprirent à compter parmi leurs devoirs celui d'égorger leurs semblables" [national wars, battles, mur- ders, reprisals, which make nature tremble and shock reason. . . . The most respectable people learned to count among their duties that of slitting the throats of their fellows]. Rejecting the validity of conquest as a foundation of law ("Le Droit de conquête n'étant point un Droit n'en a pu fonder aucun autre" [The right of conquest not being a right could not be the foundation for any other]), Rousseau denies in effect the right to self-defense of all mod- ern nations, as based upon such conquests, while recognizing that as soon as one state was formed, others were obliged to constitute themselves similarly.[16]

The Revolution itself, then the Revolutionary and Napoleonic Wars, transformed military realities and attitudes toward armed conflict. "Eigh- teenth-century warfare, which, because of the political and social structure of the ancien régime, had been relatively limited in aims and scope, was now increasingly discredited and perceived as inadequate, if not absurd."[17] Under the ancien régime, even when dynastic warfare was criticized and its justifi- cation denied, the question of the proper relationship between the state and its military arm could remain, generally, unasked: if, in the monarch's view, "l'état, c'est moi," the army was simply an instrument of his authoritarian

16. Thomas Hobbes, *Leviathan*, ed. C. B. Macpherson (Baltimore: Penguin Books, 1968), 188; Jean-Jacques Rousseau, *Œuvres complètes*, vol. 3 (Paris: Gallimard/Bibliothèque de la Pléi- ade, 1964), 176, 178–79, 603.

17. Azar Gat, *The Origins of Military Thought from the Enlightenment to Clausewitz* (Oxford: Clarendon Press, 1989), 200.

statecraft, and the foundations of obedience and loyalty were not called into question except by implication in radical thinking such as Rousseau's. The Revolution and the Republic, with its principle of popular sovereignty and representative government, raised the issue of the relationship between an armed instrument of the nation—the *nation* being a new concept in political thinking—and both principles and practice of popular authority.

This development is illustrated as early as 1790 in the comte de Guibert's essay "De la force publique considérée dans tous ses rapports" [On public force considered in all its relationships], in which he explores, among other matters, the "rapports de l'armée avec la nation" [relationship between the army and the nation] such as the civil and political rights of soldiers and officers, the issue of taking oaths—to whom and of what nature—and the connection between the military and freedom.[18] Guibert was surely one of the first to recognize and assess the thorny question of the relationship between the military and the nation, on which Alfred de Vigny would meditate at length, as I show below.

As the purpose and character of warfare changed as a result of the Revolution, the army ceased being a dynastic tool, to become national and popular, the purpose of arming being no longer to support altar and throne, but principally to defend a people and a political philosophy that, to some degree at least, sprang from the people. David Thomson observes, "The *levée en masse*, or universal conscription for military service . . . revolutionized modern warfare. . . . The system led eventually to the modern citizen-army, and helped to turn war from a battle between armies into a conflict between whole nations." In other terms, warfare became an instrument of nationalism, which is, as William Pfaff writes, "a phenomenon of the European nineteenth century . . . a political consequence of the literary-intellectual movement called Romanticism [which becomes] the most powerful phenomenon of the twentieth century." The nationalism at issue here is a new national consciousness, sometimes a sort of spontaneous patriotism, sometimes highly ideological, and involving and appealing to a vast citizenry. Erckmann-Chatrian illustrated it, many years later, by imagining a new invasion by the allied monarchies in 1815: the people would arise in mass, the nation would be declared in danger, and it would no longer be a war of soldiers, but a war of all the

---

18. [Jacques] Comte de Guibert, *Écrits militaires, 1772–1790* (Paris: Copernic, 1977), 256ff.

French against those who would oppress them. "Le temps des soldats est passé . . . un peuple qui veut se défendre ne craint pas les meilleurs soldats du monde" [The time of soldiers, or mercenaries, has passed . . . a people that wishes to defend itself does not fear the best soldiers in the world].[19]

This new attitude toward war, though of pragmatic origin, represented a synthesis of certain philosophic positions displayed in the previous century, while constituting an enormous watershed. "According to the legacy of the Enlightenment," writes Michel Delon, "militant action is fully justified by [the] gap between progress proposed and the vicissitudes of chance." Universal military service was a sign of the change of warfare from dynastic to nationalistic origins and purposes; soldiers were no longer just hirelings. Military commanders of the nobility were replaced in some cases by self-made men, of whom the Little Corporal is the most striking example. Revolutionaries came to see war as a *civic* undertaking, necessarily an extension of revolution, to which the military code no longer applied. Robespierre stated the view in the extreme when he wrote, in articles to be appended to the Declaration of Rights, that "those who make war on a people to arrest the progress of liberty, and to destroy the rights of man, deserve to be attacked by all, not as ordinary enemies, but as brigands, rebels, and assassins."[20] Warfare within the state, whether against individual or collective enemies of the Revolution (such as the royalists in the Vendée), was of a piece with that waged against enemies beyond French borders. Similarly, for *émigrés* and other royalists, war turned into a desperate battle against not a territorial rival but an enemy at home, sacrilegious, destructive—thus a battle of and for the soul.

The nationalism at issue was, to be sure, a heterogeneous phenomenon, given the complexity of politics in early nineteenth-century France— legitimist, Bonapartist, republican—and other factors that worked against its homogeneity. Nor was it, of course, felt elsewhere in Europe as early as in

19. David Thomson, *Europe Since Napoleon* (London: Longmans, 1957), 22; William Pfaff, *The Wrath of Nations: Civilization and the Furies of Nationalism* (New York: Simon & Schuster, 1993), 3; [Emile Erckmann and Alexandre Chatrian] Erckmann-Chatrian, *Le Conscrit de 1813; Waterloo* (1864, 1865; reprint, Paris: Jean-Jacques Pauvert, 1962), 331.

20. Michel Delon, "Germaine de Staël and Other Possible Scenarios of the Revolution," in Madelyn Gutwirth, Avriel Goldberger, and Karyna Szmurlo, eds., *Germaine de Staël: Crossing the Borders* (New Brunswick: Rutgers University Press, 1991), 26; J. M. Thompson, *Robespierre* (Oxford: Basil Blackwell, 1988), 353.

France. As John Lukacs has written, "As late as the early nineteenth century, in most of Europe national sentiments (as we know them today) did not really exist, except here and there among the middle classes; surely not among the peasantry—that is, among the mass of the population and the bulk of the foot soldiery when needed by the rulers of states."[21] Yet whether one is justified in stressing more the continuity or the discontinuity of political and cultural forms between the early nineteenth century and later periods, certainly it is clear that the new sense of nation and the military changes wrought in the Republican and Napoleonic campaigns had far-reaching consequences.

Looking back, one sees that the philosophic rationalization of warfare was certain to be reconsidered. In the previous century the philosophes could condemn dynastic violence easily, in the name of liberal principles, since it bore little positive relationship to what they considered the national welfare; they had no conception of how violence would be installed at the center of their nation and of a "liberal" society by the Revolution and its subsequent wars. Moreover, in Rousseau's case at least, no consideration had been given to the value of the moral energies associated with military achievement. The thinkers of the nineteenth century, by contrast, had to deal with what Jeanne Bem calls "l'enchaînement de la violence" [the chain of violence] from 1789–1793 to midcentury—a nationalized, institutionalized violence—which in its Napoleonic form represented a new heroism, a noble counterpart to the military cult of the Roman Empire.[22] Moreover, this violence was romanticized through its association with other features of thought and art in the early nineteenth century: not the *mal-du-siècle* sort of Romanticism, which comprised or sprang from worldweariness and inertia, but that strain of Romanticism which drew on and emphasized energy, individualism, self-expression, and expansion of boundaries (literary and other), and is associated with a new understanding of the sublime. Paradoxically, this period of great vitality also witnessed the development of increased fascination with the destructive power of nature (storms, torrents) and humankind (grandiose battles)—all appealing to and revealing of the soul—and with death, the supreme moment, especially in its violent forms.

21. John Lukacs, *The End of the Twentieth Century and the End of the Modern Age* (New York: Ticknor & Fields, 1993), 244.

22. Jeanne Bem, "*Châtiments* ou l'histoire de France, comme enchaînement de parricides," in Michel Grimaud, ed., *Victor Hugo 1* (Paris: Lettres Modernes/Minard, 1984), 43.

James Turner Johnson, in assessing the attitudes toward war displayed by modern writers, especially those post-1918 authors whose disillusionment has been studied closely by Paul Fussell and others, suggests that the way war is perceived began to change well before the Great War. Johnson is correct, I believe, in identifying the change as beginning under Napoleon and in stressing the subjective dimension of disillusionment and irony.[23] This shift is not incompatible with the Romantic fascination with power and violence; indeed, modern irony was developed in large part from the worldview that observed the sweeping power of history (the Revolution and Napoleonic Wars, followed by repeated domestic upheavals) and the grandeur of nature, on the one hand, and on the other, the petty scale of the individual and his inability to prevail against these enormous forces.

To what use did writers of the period propose putting organized violence? Could it be rationalized and justified in post-Revolutionary terms? Could it be made more tolerable or should it, as Clausewitz was to suggest when he was composing his work in the 1820s, be pushed *à outrance* by its own logic? These questions must be seen, of course, in the context of the Restoration and the July Monarchy, especially in light of the repression of revolutionary movements in the 1820s and 1830s.

The views of Germaine de Staël, a transitional figure between Enlightenment thought and Romanticism, were formed by her close acquaintance with and espousal of liberal philosophic thought, her observations of the disorders of the Revolution, its consequences, and its sequels, and her powerful dislike of Napoleon. She did not attempt to justify or rationalize in Enlightenment terms what she had seen. In her *Considérations sur les principaux événemens de la Révolution française* (1818), she concluded that the revolutionary conflicts that she witnessed, like the previous dynastic wars, all sprang from both religious and political fanaticism, but especially from the need to dominate and the desire for property. As for Napoleon, she was convinced that he needed and used war as a means to extend his tyranny and rally support through military glory.

For Joseph de Maistre, violence is a necessary arm of the state, whether in the form of the executioner or that of the army, both "executions" of the

---

23. James Turner Johnson, *Just War Tradition and the Restraint of War: A Moral and Historical Inquiry* (Princeton: Princeton University Press, 1981), 33–34.

monarch's will, expressing divine will. This ultraconservative position, expressed in the first and seventh "Entretiens" of the *Soirées de Saint-Petersbourg* (1821), reflects the rabid fear of Jacobinism that characterized certain French governments after the First Republic, and singularly the extreme reactionism of the Bourbon Restoration. But de Maistre was not satisfied with adopting violence as a political tool; for him, it had to be rationalized in opposition to the liberal Enlightenment tradition, which, although it did not by itself cause the Revolution, certainly underlay it—a tradition by which, as I noted earlier, authority for government was recognized as coming from the governed, implying that the use of armed force was a prerogative only of the latter. While de Maistre has recourse to terminology and notions from the ancien régime, his view of the state has a great deal in common with that of Hegel and other thinkers of the German school, for whom the state—not the individual—is the supreme expression of rationality and morality, the true masterpiece of man; for them, force is a necessary and justified arm of the state and cannot be evaluated according to humanistic or "rights-of-man" ethics.

De Maistre's rationalization went further than that of some earlier thinkers in the direction of divine determination: whereas Monluc had held that God willed the conflicts of his age—that is, war was necessarily justified because it was either decreed or allowed by God (a position that left open the question of theodicy)—de Maistre stated bluntly that "la guerre est divine." He implied that it is not because God wills it that war is divine, but rather that God wills war because it is already divine—violence hypostatized to the level of a manifestation of the Omnipotent, or, as de Maistre calls him, following the Old Testament, the DIEU DES ARMÉES [God of the Armies].[24]

De Maistre's dialectic on this topic bears examination. When, in the seventh "Entretien," the Sénateur claims that war cannot be explained humanly, the Chevalier retorts by expressing a common-sense view, which is Monluc's argument, in its pragmatic form: "Les rois vous commandent, et . . . il faut marcher" [Kings command you and you must march]. The Sénateur objects that such explanations are simplistic; even the supposed love of glory does not suffice to explain war, since military renown is available only to leaders,

---

24. Joseph de Maistre, *Œuvres complètes*, vol. 5 (Lyons: Librairie Générale Catholique et Classique, 1892), 21, 26.

not the ordinary soldier, and anyway such an explanation merely begs the question. Rather, says the Sénateur, the soldier's functions are by their nature spiritual, part of a divine scheme both *in* the world and *beyond* it. Man, the creature "qui tue pour tuer" [who kills in order to kill], is part of a chain of being, similar to that envisioned by the Enlightenment thinkers, but without the same foundation or implications. "C'est l'homme qui est chargé d'égorger l'homme. . . . Ainsi s'accomplit sans cesse, depuis le ciron jusqu'à l'homme, la grande loi de la destruction violente des êtres vivants" [Man is charged with slitting the throats of men. . . . Thus is ceaselessly accomplished, from the mite up to man, the great law of violent destruction of living beings].[25]

This is a sacrificial, religious destruction, part of an eschatological vision, for which de Maistre cited the authority of Saint Paul (1 Cor.: 15, 26), but which sounds more Hegelian. "La terre entière, continuellement imbibée de sang, n'est qu'un autel immense où tout ce qui vit doit être immolé sans fin, sans mesure, sans relâche, jusqu'à l'extinction du mal, jusqu'à la mort de la mort" [The whole earth, continually soaked with blood, is but an immense altar where everything that lives must be immolated endlessly, without measure or interruption, until the extinction of evil, until the death of death]. Man as a species is particularly marked out by the exterminating angel, who circulates around the globe, raising nation against nation everywhere, but especially where unspecified crimes have been committed. War is divine, in short, for transcendent reasons, as its results "échappent absolument aux spéculations de la raison humaine" [escape absolutely the speculations of human reason].[26] (Thus, in his *Considérations sur la France* [1796], de Maistre treated the Revolution as divine purification.)

De Maistre concluded by asking at what period of time the *moral power* of war had played a more crucial role than during his own—a question that reveals his understanding of the integral role of the Napoleonic Wars and others in modern history. It should be noted that Robespierre had a similar view of violence as a necessary and indeed laudable instrument to bring about the consolidation of republican power and the salvation of the state. The war of liberty against tyranny, as he termed it, was justified as long as it was needed. Similarly, François-Emile (called Gracchus) Babeuf exorted his followers to sweeping, indeed total violence as a means to an end. The oratory of these

25. *Ibid.*, 2, 23, 25.
26. *Ibid.*, 25, 27.

figures, Babeuf in particular, was of considerable importance in the formation of mid-nineteenth-century socialism, including the thinking of Marx and his followers, whose eschatological communism offers obvious parallels with the eschatological Christian view of de Maistre.

De Maistre's reflections on armed conflict considered only wars between states, not civil unrest; he had no need to posit the army as an instrument of social order, since the *bourreau* (executioner) functioned in that way. His view of the army was, moreover, static: recognizing no legitimacy in the revolutionary upheavals and liberal institutions of his age, he saw warfare as a timeless undertaking, not one whose nature has been modified by historical change; it is a manifestation of divine law like those seen in the past.

The position of Vigny vis-à-vis the historical situation around him was exactly the opposite; he could have agreed with the recent statement of Terrence Des Pres that "after 1789 the individual knows no armistice with history," changes in kind having taken place from the Revolution onwards. After having served as a career officer for a restored Bourbon government concerned with reacting against the Napoleonic legacy, Vigny—the author of what has been called "the most important attempt during the century to describe the soldier's life"—saw all too well that the role of the army had been radically changed. His own dream of military glory having been dashed by the peace that followed the Congress of Vienna and the end to French expansionism in Europe, he lamented, "la Destinée m'a refusé la guerre que j'aimais" [Destiny denied me war, which I loved]. Like his liberal opposite Stendhal, he continued to admire the moral energies associated with military achievement and to nurture nostalgic visions of war; after his resignation, he harbored great disappointment, and he called his *Servitude et grandeur militaires* (1835) part of "une sorte de poème épique sur la désillusion" [a sort of epic poem about disillusionment]. Although he spoke also of his "guérison pour cette maladie de l'enthousiasme militaire" [being cured of this sickness of military enthusiasm], he continued to look upon the soldier as he did the poet, a representative of a superior way of being, yet marginalized, as illustrated in *Stello*—the other of his "deux thèses sur le désenchantement" [two theses on disenchantment].[27]

27. Terrence Des Pres, *Praises and Dispraises: Poetry and Politics, the 20th Century* (New York: Penguin, 1988), 12; *All the Banners Wave: Art and War in the Romantic Era 1792–1851* (Providence: Department of Art, Brown University, 1982), 9; Alfred de Vigny, *Œuvres complètes*, ed. Fernand Baldensperger, 2 vols. (Paris: Gallimard/Bibliothèque de la Pléiade, 1948, 1950), 2:1050, 1037;

What is more significant, Vigny saw that the moral foundations of the army were threatened by the political uses to which military power was being put in the post-Napoleonic period and by lack of fiber in the army itself. He observed what his later editor Fernand Baldensperger termed "obéissance passive soumise souvent à un commandement inepte, détérioration des chefs, en raison d'un embourgeoisement progressif des sociétés, favoritisme en haut lieu, et, parmi les intellectuels, dépréciation correspondante du métier 'soldé' des armées" [passive obedience often subjected to an inept command, the moral decline of commanders, through a progressive *embourgeoisement* of society, favoritism in high places, and, among intellectuals, a corresponding loss of respect for the "paid" profession of arms]. From the military point of view, Vigny thus belongs less to what Isaiah Berlin calls the "Counter-Enlightenment" than to the Enlightenment itself, with its ideal of orderly battles as an expression of rational statecraft; one must not forget that his father told him about seeing Frederick the Great on the battlefield. At the same time, he examined the relationship between military discipline and *le libre arbitre* or freedom of conscience—a notion that, in the form it took for Vigny, is foreign to de Maistre's essentially theocratic view of the *polis*. Vigny was, moreover, concerned with the moral problem of killing. Yet some of his views, especially on discipline and *gloire* and the contribution of military life to forming a man's character, are not dissimilar to those of the author of *Du Pape*, whose influence he denied, but which subsists in *Servitude et grandeur militaires*.[28]

What, then, constituted military right for Vigny? He denied explicitly the proposition of "un sophiste" [a sophist], that is, de Maistre—whom he had already combated in connection with the same topic in *Stello* as an "esprit falsificateur . . . et menaçant" [falsifying and threatening mind]—that war is divine. "La guerre est maudite de Dieu et des hommes mêmes qui la font et qui ont d'elle une secrète horreur" [War is cursed by God and even by the men who wage it and who secretly loathe it]. Recognizing, however—in a view

---

Alfred de Vigny, *Servitude et grandeur militaires*, ed. Auguste Dorchain (Paris: Garnier [1955]), 93, 334.

28. The Baldensperger quotation and de Maistre's view come from Vigny, *Œuvres complètes*, 2:517. On Frederick, see Vigny, *Servitude et grandeur militaires*, ed. Dorchain, 11–12. Berlin's phrase is quoted in Gat, *Origins of Military Thought*, 142. On de Maistre's influence, see also Stirling Haig, "The Grand Illusion: Vigny's *Servitude et grandeur militaires*," in Stirling Haig, *The Madame Bovary Blues* (Baton Rouge: Louisiana State University Press, 1987), 47.

that anticipates the optimism of his poem "La Bouteille à la mer"—that although "les armées et la guerre n'auront qu'un temps" [armies and war will last only for a while] their end has not yet come, he examined their principles and justification. The principles of operation are strict. The function of officers is to command, that of men, to obey; both demand discipline and sacrifice, *dévouement* and *abnégation*. This structure of authority makes of the army the creature of the supreme civil power that commands it. "L'armée est aveugle et muette. Elle frappe devant elle du lieu où on la met. Elle ne veut rien et agit par ressort. C'est une chose que l'on meut et qui tue; mais aussi c'est une chose qui souffre" [The army is blind and mute. It strikes out from the spot where it is put. It desires nothing and acts like a spring. It is a thing that is moved and that kills; it is also a suffering thing]. Soldiers are, morally speaking, slaves, since their freedom of conscience is subordinated to the will of others; Vigny compared them to Caesar's gladiators. As recognition, they receive scorn and *malédiction*.[29]

Accordingly, the army is an encounter of two sorts of violence: that exercised by the state on its soldier-servants, and that exercised by one army against another. Justification of the first needs to conciliate the good of the state with freedom of conscience, a principle that Vigny strongly believed to be a natural right, whether because he was influenced by the vein of Enlightenment thought that emphasized natural reason or as a result of his personal (perhaps innate) moral vision. That is, ideally a soldier will, in the name of a higher good, renounce freely his right to exercise his own judgment, thus willing his abdication of will. Only then, if I read Vigny correctly, is the military condition less than tragic. But this can happen only when the army is truly at the service of the nation—meant in its fullest sense. It can no longer be a question of devotion to a man, as during the Napoleonic period and during the feudal wars up to the Revolution; rather, the army belongs "à la Patrie et au Devoir" [to the fatherland and to duty], and this duty is to "un Principe plutôt qu'à un Homme" [a principle rather than a man].[30]

What, then, is the nation? The question, implicit in Vigny's text, would be asked in different terms and circumstances in the following hundred years

---

29. Alfred de Vigny, *Stello; Daphné*, ed. Annie Prassoloff (Paris: Gallimard, 1986), 180; Vigny, *Servitude et grandeur militaires*, ed. Dorchain, 24–25, 100.

30. Vigny, *Servitude et grandeur militaires*, ed. Dorchain, 174, 284.

and more—indeed at least until 1958 and the creation of the Fifth Republic. Its transposition into literary terms, in the form of fiction (including Vigny's own narratives in *Servitude et grandeur militaires*), constitutes a new cultural development and an important generic one, on which I touch in chapter 3. Vigny pointed out that governments in the post-Revolutionary period change from one year to the next and govern by caprice. Furthermore, they ask of the military tasks that are improper: for example, the absurd order to the ship's commander in "Laurette ou le cachet rouge" [Laurette or the red seal] to execute a young man who had mocked the Directory, or the order in "La Canne de jonc" [The reed cane] to put down civil unrest—to behave as a *gendarmerie*. As the old commandant says, "Jamais le capitaine d'un bâtiment ne sera obligé d'être un bourreau, sinon quand viendront des gouvernements d'assassins et de voleurs" [Never will a ship's captain have to be an executioner, except when governments of murderers and thieves appear]. Hence, "en regardant de près la vie de ces troupes armées que, chaque jour, pousseront sur nous tous les Pouvoirs qui se succéderont, nous trouverons bien . . . que l'existence du soldat est . . . la trace la plus douloureuse de barbarie qui subsiste parmi les hommes" [looking closely at the life of these armed troops which, every day, the successive powers will thrust onto us, we discover indeed that the soldier's existence is the most distressing trace of barbarity that subsists among men].[31]

Even when properly seen in the context of the fatherland, the soldier's duty is to exert violence on those of an opposing army—a duty hard to reconcile with Vigny's horror of bloodshed, which had been reinforced by readings of Félicité-Robert de Lamennais's *Paroles d'un croyant* and other authors. "Laurette ou le cachet rouge" offers as a point of reconciliation the concepts of abnegation and honor ("l'union de la force et de la bonté" [the union of strength and goodness]): obeying, the soldier, through honor, accepts what would be dishonor (that is, killing), renounces clean hands, and, like other victims, does expiation for the wrongs that he takes upon himself in the name of society. "Le soldat est un pauvre glorieux, victime et bourreau, bouc émissaire journellement sacrifié à son peuple et pour son peuple, qui se joue de lui" [The soldier is a poor hero, victim and executioner, a scapegoat daily sacrificed to his people and for his people, who make light of him].[32] One is

31. Ibid., 75, 100.
32. Ibid., 22–23.

struck by the word *bourreau*, the very term used by de Maistre to elevate to a sacred status the role of *civil* destruction. Vigny's solution opposes, to the dilemmas of violence, a position that does not eradicate them, much less the violence itself, but goes beyond them to a mystique of moral stoicism that allows the individual to achieve grandeur and redeems the individual *and* the army—an aristocratic position to be expected from him.

The contrasting positions of de Maistre and Vigny—the one rationalizing institutionalized violence in the name of an absolute (divine reason), the other, partially, in the name of honor—adumbrate thinking discerned in subsequent decades in varied forms. For convenience, their positions can be labeled respectively *absolute militarism* and *moral militarism*. Both are connected to nationalism, varying according to the author's view of the state in general and of France in particular. Even some socialist thinkers displayed a variety of moral militarism—as chapter 4 shows, in connection with the idealization of Napoleon as suffering hero.

A less idealistic, more pedestrian expression of it can be found in the novels of Erckmann-Chatrian (written under the Second Empire) dealing with the Napoleonic Wars. Insisting repeatedly that, whether on the part of the emperor personally or a lesser warrior, *la gloire* is no longer a defensible ground for armed conflict nor a just measure of a man, the authors of these popular novels held up as the sole justification for war the defense of the democratic nation against tyranny and ambition, whether from within or without. "Toutes les grandes idées de gloire ne sont rien, car il n'y a qu'une chose pour laquelle un peuple doit marcher . . . c'est quand on attaque notre Liberté, comme en 1792. . . . Voilà . . . la seule guerre juste" [All the great ideas of glory are nothing, for there is one thing only for which a people should go to war . . . It is when our freedom is attacked, as in 1792. . . . That . . . is the only just war]. The way Napoleon was portrayed by Erckmann-Chatrian supports this position: for all his successes (which, of course, the common fighters paid for dearly), he is shown merely as a man, "une grosse tête pâle et grasse, une touffe de cheveux sur le front" [a large head, pale and fleshy, with a clump of hair on his forehead]. It is implied, moreover, that the proper understanding of the nation demands equality: for the common citizens to be massacred so that a few may live in idleness and luxury is unjust. Whereas the Revolutionary generals led their people in defense of freedom and bivouacked with their men, under the late empire leaders sought personal glory.

"Maintenant, il leur faut des canapés, ils sont plus nobles et plus riches que nos banquiers. Cela fait que la guerre, la plus belle chose autrefois—un art, un sacrifice, un dévouement à la patrie—est devenue un métier." [Now, they want couches, they are nobler and richer than our bankers. That means that war, formerly the finest thing—art, sacrifice, devotion to the fatherland—has become a trade].[33]

A third position—radical rejection of militarism, including all warfare, hence all standing armies—can likewise be identified in the decades succeeding the Revolution, not as a direct legacy or development of Enlightenment thinking on the possibility of perpetual peace, but rather as a product of early, radical socialist thought. Perhaps the most extreme and original thinkers in early nineteenth-century France on *raison d'armée* are those radical socialists, in the wake of Babeuf and Charles Fourier, who saw that militarism, being inexorably bound to and an arm of the state, could not disappear until the state itself was remade from top to bottom, with the new social bond of *equality* replacing the primary republican value of *liberty*, and the organized oppression exercised by privileged governing classes (as in the scenes from "La Canne de jonc") brought to an end. This could be only a product of a fully developed class consciousness. But even remaking the state would not be enough, since, in practice, a state exists only in contradistinction and competition with other states; the very idea of statehood would need to be replaced by an international order in which *raison d'état* would disappear. As a neo-Babouviste wrote in 1839, French workers should cease expressing hostility toward foreign workers: "Prenez-vous-en au privilège qui vous écrase, et non pas à des frères qui souffrent autant que vous" [Go after the privilege that crushes you and not your brothers who suffer as much as you]. There remains, of course, the problem of the relationship between the Utopian dream of ending the state and the violence that, both in theory and in practice, accompanies it, from Rousseau's imagined state through the Soviet Union, each time that "le peuple exigera, les armes à la main, que ses biens lui soient restitués" [the people, arms in hand, demand that their goods be restored].[34] Ironically, Babeuf, like numerous other socialists, exhorted his

33. Erckmann-Chatrian, *Le Conscrit de 1813; Waterloo*, 8, 39, 90.

34. Maurice Dommanget et al., *Babeuf et les problèmes du babouvisme* (Paris: Editions Sociales, 1963), 251, 261.

followers to sweeping violence as a means to an end. Whereas, as a later chapter shows, some war novelists after 1914 were led by the war experience to envisage and espouse such an international order founded on nonviolence, the power of the literary mind to imagine fully such an order showed itself, like that of philosophic minds, to be limited; the question of violence as a means to investing nonviolence would be dealt with thoughtfully by few novelists.

2

ICONS WITH A SWORD
French Nationalistic and Military Symbolism

BEGINNING WITH THE Revolutionary Wars, one finds in France an extensive visual and verbal iconography associated with the successive campaigns in which the nation was or had been embroiled, including a vast corpus of painted reflections. Military art was a major subgenre of nineteenth-century art. The editors of *All the Banners Wave* remark that in the first half of the nineteenth century in France an artist could be known as a military painter, the way others were portraitists or landscape painters. In this chapter I examine, in the general framework of French nationalism, the principal veins of these images from the Revolution through the Great War and later, including arbitrary republican and revolutionary symbols; the representation and symbolic value of equipment, landscape, and the body; the role of the female icon, including the figure of Joan of Arc, which had different values according to the period and the user; and the image of Napoleon, whose iconic value is studied below while his appearance in fiction is surveyed in chapter 3.

By iconography I mean the "art of representing by pictures, images" and so forth (*Webster's New World Dictionary*) and, by extension, a body of such pictures and images, including verbal equivalents by means of description and figurative language. Hence I shall cite various written parallels to graphic work, although emphasis here will be on graphic art and the symbolic value of certain icons. That there were connections between the written and the painted image will be clear. Even though static in the material sense, graphic art is often narrative: whether directly so—a picture telling a story by means of juxtaposed panels, sections, planes; or indirectly—the literal pictorial elements leading the viewer to reconstruct what has happened or is happening; or allegorically and symbolically—as in the power of the *tricolore* flag to evoke the Revolution as story in addition to republican values. As for written narrative, a copious vocabulary used by readers and critics alike points to its powers to "paint" scenes, although in the twentieth century the place given to full description, as opposed to suggestion, declines, and the set piece nearly disappears, replaced by fragments, peripheral glimpses, subjective visions, and even hallucinations.

National iconography is broadly cultural, involving what is known and what is believed by a nation or segments of it; it is connected to history in general, politics and government, war, literature, graphic arts, religion, and what Maurice Halbwachs and others have called "collective memory." According to the historical perspective I adopt here, meaning is a process, not a stasis, and hermeneutics must be synthetic. To assess as precisely as possible the role that images and codes played in consolidating patriotism is a major task of cultural historians, far beyond my scope here; but the question of their importance arises as one notes their abundance, persistence, penetration through French class divisions, and reappearance at successive generations. I assume in any case an interrelationship between politics and culture. When one realizes that by early 1914 "almost every fit European male of military age had a soldier's identity card among his personal papers," as John Keegan points out, and that shortly entire, enormous nations were fighting each other, one must inquire what role war iconography played in developing, maintaining, and altering the practice, course, and meaning of war for the French.[1]

While the performative value of imagery is generally recognized, assessing it is very difficult. As Rima Drell Reck has written, "The question of emphasis is crucial: art as effect, or art as cause." If the history of the United States is, following Lewis P. Simpson's argument, embodied in a text—the Declaration of Independence—the idea and history of post-1789 France is certainly embodied, to a great degree, in *images*, from those of the storming of the Bastille to those of the Great War and then of resistance against the Nazis a generation later. Heinz Gollwitzer has observed how nationalism "documented [its] desire for historical perpetuation and the creation of a mass conscious-

---

1. John Keegan, *A History of Warfare* (New York: Knopf, 1993), 22.

ness of history" by erecting architectural and other public symbols.[2] For the literary and art historian, other issues arise also, such as the relationship between graphic and verbal expression and also the transmission and role of inherited iconography. Most of the militant iconography to be considered below, principally graphic but also literary, proclaims the necessity, even the glory, of arming and fighting, the spirit of battle. Some, however, is critical, and the gradual appearance of icons that denounce war is noteworthy.

War iconography was not new, of course, in the nineteenth century; in verbal form, it goes back to Homer, and in graphic and architectural form, to the Egyptians and Mesopotamian peoples. In medieval France it was illustrated by the Tapisserie or Broderie de la Reine Mathilde in Bayeux (late eleventh century) and, in written form, was central to the medieval epic. It similarly appeared in works of the Renaissance and thereafter, as in d'Aubigné's *Les Tragiques* and poems by Voltaire mentioned in the previous chapter. But, beginning with the Revolution and Napoleonic Wars, there developed new styles of images, whose appearance coincided with and expressed a different sense of the nation and its aspirations, including the need to defend itself *qua* nation. As a new, popular nationalism, both political and military, was built on the foundation of the Revolution and in France and, later, elsewhere replaced the monarchal structures of feudal origins, a popular patriotic iconography arose, largely associated with revolution and war, since war had become an instrument of national policy as well as an expression of collective consciousness. As Ernest Renan wrote in "Qu'est-ce qu'une nation?" (1882): "Un passé héroïque, des grands hommes, de la gloire (j'entends de la véritable), voilà le capital social sur lequel on assied une idée nationale" [An heroic past, great men, glory (I mean the genuine sort), that is the social capital on which one establishes a national idea].[3] Yet war iconography, especially painting, was also connected to the turbulence of the Romantic movement, in some of its broadest characteristics, including the fascination with terror and violence and those feelings known as the sublime, some of which were antisocial and destructive, the contrary of a rational use of force.

2. Rima Drell Reck, review of *Impressionism: Art, Leisure, and Parisian Society*, by Robert L. Herbert, *French Review* 67 (May 1994): 1090; Lewis P. Simpson, *The Fable of the Southern Writer* (Baton Rouge: Louisiana State University Press, 1994), 16; Heinz Gollwitzer, *Europe in the Age of Imperialism 1880–1914* (London: Thames & Hudson, 1969), 147.

3. Ernest Renan, *Discours et conférences* (Paris: Calmann-Lévy, 1887), 306.

The construction of this iconography was purposeful. James Clifford has written, "The collection and preservation of an authentic domain of identity cannot be natural or innocent. It is tied up with nationalist politics, with restrictive law, and with contested encodings of past and future."[4] Some of its icons became so important that they can be considered as national myths — not just a single coherent one, as with the monolithic monarchy and church, but rival and politically contrasting myths, all the more militant for being contested. The replacement of a single national myth by competing ideologies and symbolisms may have been responsible (along with developments in technologies of production and distribution) for the nineteenth-century expansion of iconographic and emblematic material. Variously, the monarchy of the ancien régime, Roland, hero of the most famous *chanson de geste*, Joan of Arc, the Revolution and its sequels, Revolutionary heroes, Napoleon, the republic (personified), and republican figures became invested with emblematic, almost sacred qualities.

Their ultimate product was the cliché, which Keegan defines as "the art of the freeze-frame . . . a moment of apparent realism literally plucked from an entirely contradictory reality." As Vaheed Ramazani has noted, while the use of the term in the sense alluded to is a development of the second half of the nineteenth century, it was made possible by the Revolution and the breakdown of a single, collective symbolism.[5]

Yet, even in their opposition, the different veins of mythmaking contributed to a French consciousness. Robert Gildea here underscores this point: "What matters is myth . . . in the sense of a construction of the past elaborated by a political community for its own ends."[6] From the Revolution onward through de Gaulle, at least, regimes cultivated an image of offensive military achievement, on which they relied largely for their domestic and foreign prestige. This bellicose image was, of course, buttressed by the famous cultural patrimony inherited from the ancien régime and enlarged and promoted in spectacular ways by Napoleon (for instance, the building of public

4. James Clifford, "On Collecting Art and Culture," in Simon During, ed., *The Cultural Studies Reader* (London and New York: Routledge, 1994), 61.

5. Keegan, *History of Warfare*, 53; Vaheed Ramazani, "Historical Cliché: Irony and Sublime in *L'Education sentimentale*," *PMLA* 108 (January 1993): 133n3.

6. Robert Gildea, *The Past in French History* (New Yaven and London: Yale University Press, 1994), 12.

monuments and the collections of art removed from various sites to France), then developed anew in the latter half of the nineteenth century—as evinced by the redesigning of Paris under Baron Georges-Eugène Haussmann and world's fairs of 1889 and 1900—as, much later, under the Fifth Republic.

French war iconography is highly allusive: recycled, or, to apply Mikhail Bakhtin's term, dialogic, incorporating many allegorical images that are quotations from the past. In written material, these allusions to past images can be called *intertextual*, in Julia Kristeva's terminology, or *prefigurative*. The supreme model for such prefiguration and intertextuality is, of course, the Bible, with the books of the Hebrews constituting, for believers in the New Covenant, an elaborate prefiguration of Christian scripture. It is not fanciful to identify, in conservative French minds of the late nineteenth and early twentieth centuries, a view of history whereby the past would prefigure a future more or less messianic, since it would involve a restoration, as yet unrealized, to which the republic acted as a Luciferian obstacle. In 1914, notes Samuel Hynes, representation of war conveyed *ideas* of war by means of images of the past. The past and its quoted images serve as ways of reading the present; but the present, with *its* images, is also a way of reading the past. "L'homme moderne," wrote Pierre Drieu La Rochelle, "est rongé par des rêves du passé" [Modern man is devoured by dreams of the past]. In each generation, there are numerous symbolic elements, some of which are inherited, and among which the juxtapositions are revealing. While some were an explicit denial of the old (as the *tricolore* replaced the white flag of the Bourbons) and thus indicated to contemporary viewers a deliberate break with the ancien régime, others explicitly revived the old, to indicate continuity with the past despite historical disruptions, and to affirm France's historic greatness.[7]

Beginning with the Revolutionary period, with its juxtaposition of symbols, such as a Sèvres plate dating from 1789–1790 that combines the royal emblem with the red cap of liberty, there is increasing eclecticism, attested by the copresence of images of Joan of Arc, the revolutionary and republican *cocarde*, and Napoleonic references. The historian Adolphe Thiers illustrated such synthesis by interpreting the July regime as the reconciliation of monar-

7. Hynes, *War Imagined*, 34; Pierre Drieu La Rochelle, *La Comédie de Charleroi* (Paris: Nouvelle Revue Française, 1934), 27.

chy and revolution. This nationalistic synthesis foreshadowed the politics of reconciliation or *union sacrée* that emerged at the start of the Great War, despite the deep divisions within the Third Republic from its inception, dramatized by the Dreyfus Affair. There remained, of course, throughout the nineteenth century deep discords about the usage of cultural material. Gildea explains, "As one community sought to impose a collective amnesia about certain events, rival communities sought to resurrect their memory in order to disqualify or delegitimise their opponents. . . . The same event or figure was often the subject of different constructions by different communities. . . . Napoleon, Joan of Arc, and Proudhon were the victims of tugs-of-war between rival political communities, each seeking to legitimize its cause by making its own presentation of these figures prevail."[8]

The elements or vocabulary of military iconography can be categorized as symbols (more or less arbitrary), personifications and allegories, metaphors (based on in difference), and metonyms (based on similarity), notably synecdoche. I am not concerned, however, with such technical classifications, nor with questions of medium, although one can observe that choice of medium points to the intended audience, often popular: in literature, sentimental stories, singsong verse, stirring rhetoric; in graphics, *images d'Epinal* and other semiprimitive styles. (These latter were widely circulated lithographs, cheap, melodramatic, and without subtlety or depth, produced in great numbers in the nineteenth century by the Pellerin factory in Epinal; often they featured patriotic or military motifs. In one of his World War I lyrics, Guillaume Apollinaire refers to the "guerriers d'autrefois / que Georgin gravait dans le bois" [warriors of long ago / whom Georgin engraved in wood], Georgin being one of the best-known Pellerin engravers).[9] As for compositional features — foreground versus background, center versus border, inherence versus arbitrariness, directness versus indirection, full identification versus suggestion or allusion, singularity versus plurality, univalence versus polyvalence — the artist's or writer's treatment of these elements and their combination, which can be as revealing as the elements themselves, will be considered in appropriate cases.

8. Gildea, *Past in French History*, 11.

9. Guillaume Apollinaire, *Œuvres poétiques*, ed. Marcel Adéma and Michel Décaudin (Paris: Gallimard/ Bibliothèque de la Pléiade, 1965), 281. On *images d'Epinal*, see Jay Winter, *Sites of Memory, Sites of Mourning* (New York: Cambridge University Press, 1995), 122–32.

One can identify first of all arbitrary, conventional elements, nonhuman, known to all French, which preside over war symbolically on a general and almost abstract plane, from the Revolution onward: these include the three-color flag and *cocarde* (cockade or other small insignia), the red Phrygian bonnet (a sartorial symbol of freedom, derived perhaps from the American Revolution), and the *coq gaulois*. They appear in fiction, cartoons, book illustrations, paintings, posters, and other graphic material. In the most immediate, concise way possible, these images evoked for viewers and readers—and favorably, for all those sympathetic to the Republic—the heroic past of the Revolution, that is, the self-consciousness of a modern people that had overthrown its oppressors and defended itself against a European coalition of monarchies. Some of these emblems were also associated with Bonapartism. That Napoleon was finally defeated made little difference, ultimately, in the national consciousness, as the following chapter illustrates. In Keegan's words, "The French, by some strange translatory process, managed to make an epic out of the defeat."[10]

The *tricolore* appears everywhere, in songs, fiction, and graphic work, often joined to other images, sometimes as the cockade, sometimes as an unfurled flag, elsewhere as a banner or bunting. Although the *bleu-blanc-rouge* of bunting and flag were already utilized somewhat under the Bourbons, their designation as the revolutionary color symbolism is often explained by the addition to the Bourbon white of the red and blue of the city of Paris; the two colors of Paris were combined with the Bourbon white as early as 16 July 1789. There is, moreover, the model of the red-white-and-blue of the young American republic. In verbal form, the red of the *tricolore* is often explicitly associated with blood spilled for the fatherland (as in Paul Déroulède's poem of the Franco-Prussian War "La Cocarde"). To evoke these symbols was thus to consolidate faith in the nation and its power to endure and finally to overcome its enemies. Speaking of the nineteenth-century flag, Raoul Girardet observes that "le mémorial militaire français et l'éthique qu'il sous-entend lui accordent une place de plus en plus large . . . le drapeau que l'on plante sur

10. John Keegan, *The Face of Battle* (New York: Viking, 1976), 118. On the cockade and the Phrygian bonnet, see J. Godechot, "Nation, patrie, nationalisme et patriotisme," *Annales Historiques de la Révolution Française*, no. 206 (1971): 495–96; and Raoul Girardet's discussion in Pierre Nora, ed., *Les Lieux de mémoire*, 3 vols. (Paris: Gallimard, 1984–1992), 1:5–35, 3:521.

la position arrachée à l'ennemi, que l'on défend, que l'on sauve, que l'on serre dans les bras, au pied duquel on meurt" [French military memorials and the ethics that they imply grant it a wider and wider role. . . . the flag that one plants in a position taken from the enemy, that one defends, that one saves, that one presses in one's arms, at whose foot one dies]. Daudet's short story "Le Porte-drapeau" illustrates the powerful affective magnetism of the colors: after twenty-two flagbearers have been killed in a battle against the Prussians, the tattered silk of the company is finally assigned to an old sergeant, otherwise undistinguished; when, following Bazaine's capitulation in October, he is obliged to surrender it to the enemy, he is struck by apoplexy.[11]

During World War I, the *tricolore* was similarly ubiquitous, in songs, fiction, and graphic work, often joined to other images. It is featured, for instance, along with bottles and cards, in a Cubist still life by Picasso, dated 1914–1915, unusual by reason of this nationalistic touch. In World War II, under the Occupation, when there were two views (at least) on patriotism, the Pétainist and the Gaullist, the Cross of Lorraine—de Gaulle's colors— came to replace the *tricolore* as the emblem of choice for those who sympathized with the Free French and clandestine opposition; they displayed it proudly at the time of the Liberation.

An associated image is the laurel crown or garland, often in the form of twinned branches. Going back to antiquity, with suggestions of heroism (Greece) and republican or imperial grandeur (Rome), and used conventionally in literature under the Bourbon monarchy as a symbol of valor and grandeur (as in Pierre Corneille's *Horace*), it persisted through the Revolutionary era, appeared on the seal of the Republic, and was adopted under Napoleon. Indeed, the emperor is shown wearing a laurel crown in the Jacques-Louis David canvas "Le Sacre," in "Napoléon sur le trône impérial en costume du sacre" by Jean-Auguste-Dominique Ingres, and in Pierre Paul Prud'hon's "Triomphe du Consul Bonaparte," in which the First Consul, riding a Roman chariot, appears crowned with laurel and watched over by a winged angel. The laurel then was used in numerous drawings connected to the Franco-Prussian War and to the war of 1914. Its association with antiquity persisted, as in "Le Triomphe de la République" (1889), in which, as the woman com-

11. Nora, *Lieux de mémoire* 1:10, 26, 3:538 n.28; Alphonse Daudet, *Œuvres*, ed. Roger Ripoll, vol. 1 (Paris: Gallimard/Bibliothèque de la Pléiade, 1986), 659–64.

poser and performer Augusta Holmès recites her triumphal ode, the witnesses are draped in Graeco-Roman tunics and chlamyses. In honor of Italy's entry into the war on the Allied side in 1915, Jean Cocteau, in "Dante avec nous," showed the great poet—who of course is a link with Virgil, the poet of "arms and the man," and thus with antique grandeur—wearing a Phrygian cap decorated with laurel.[12]

The laurel is often associated with another classical emblem, that of the *fasces* or *faisceaux de licteur*, that is, either a bundle of arrows, always stylized, or the even more stylized image of twisted columns with a hachet, or "verges liées avec une hache qui les surmontait" (*Petit Littré*). The sign of power among the Romans, the emblem of stylized arrows, which also appears in American public iconography, was adopted by Napoleon and then widely used in republican iconography as an emblem of fraternity, although discredited in the mid-twentieth century because of its association with fascism. The hatchet often crowning the *faisceaux* is the *francisque*—the Frankish war hatchet, Marshal Pétain's emblem in the 1940s, hence now in public disfavor in France.[13]

The *coq gaulois* appeared on standards and flags for the first time during the Revolution. It may be connected to the medieval Chantecleer. The origin of its political symbolism is murky and complex, as Michel Pastoureau has shown in his essay in Nora's *Les Lieux de mémoire*. The identification between France and the cock, first made by the Romans, is due to the double sense of the Latin *gallus*, meaning *coq* and *gaulois*. At that period, because of its mythological symbolism, it already had strong associations with war. Widely used in Revolutionary iconography, though not usually with official sanction, the

---

12. For reproductions of many of the paintings, drawings, and other objects mentioned, as well as similarly characteristic ones, see Norman Hampson, *The First European Revolution: 1776–1815* (New York: Norton, 1969); John Laffin, *The Western Front Illustrated, 1914–1918* (Wolfeboro Falls, N.H.: Alan Sutton, 1991); Wolfgang Leiner, *Das Deutschland Bild in der französischen Literatur* (Darmstadt: Wissenschaftliche Buchgesellschaft, 1989); Jean-Jacques Lévêque, *L'Art et la Révolution française, 1789–1804* (Neuchâtel: Ides et Calendes, 1987); Kenneth E. Silver, *Esprit de Corps: The Art of the Parisian Avant-Garde and the First World War* (Princeton: Princeton University Press, 1989); Alan Wintermute et al., *1789: French Art During the Revolution* (New York: Colnaghi, 1989). *All the Banners Wave* and Nora's *Lieux de mémoire* likewise include many illustrations. Numerous Franco-Prussian War lithographs are reproduced in Emile Zola, *La Débâcle*, in *Œuvres complètes*, vol. 6, ed. Henri Mitterand (Paris: Cercle du Livre Précieux, 1967).

13. See Michèle C. Cone, *Artists Under Vichy: A Case of Prejudice and Persecution* (Princeton: Princeton University Press, 1992), 38, 76, for objects featuring the *francisque*.

cock was featured along with the three colors. Subsequently, it lost ground under Napoleon to the eagle, which had begun to be used shortly after 1789, as in Joseph Chinard's allegorical sculpture "L'Autorité du peuple," and was greatly favored for its imperial associations. The Restoration government eliminated all official use of the cock, but it endured in the popular imagination as a sign of resistance to the Bourbons. It then reappeared under Louis-Philippe, as both a semiofficial emblem, frequently used, and a sign of protest to the Orléans monarchy; and, under the Second Republic, it finally appeared on the Great Seal.

Following another eclipse under Louis-Napoleon, who restored the eagle to prominence, the cock became after 1870 a symbol of republican militancy (against Bonapartists and monarchists) and of the desire for national revenge against Germany. The eagle, meanwhile, was banished or deconstructed, as in several drawings by Honoré Daumier, who transformed the Napoleonic emblem into a vulture. An example is his powerful *Promethean France and the Eagle-Vulture* (1871), which shows France chained to a rock while the huge bird gnaws at her vitals. Some thirty years later, in Marthe Fiel's 1911 *revanchiste* novel *Sur le sol d'Alsace* [On Alsatian soil], a German in Alsace "crut à l'aube et au chant d'un coq. . . . Oui . . . c'était le coq gaulois qui s'éveillait" [thought that it was dawn and that he heard a rooster crow. . . . Yes, it was the Gallic cock awakening].[14] The icon persisted throughout the two world wars. Raymond Duchamp-Villon used it in a bronze casting designed in 1916. In Lucien Métivet's twin illustrations for the story "Marianne et Germania: Histoire d'un bonnet et d'un casque" (1918), the cock appears at the apex of one frame, depicting Marianne in her Phrygian bonnet, while on an adjacent frame appears a rather puny, un-imperial eagle above a helmeted Prussian woman. Similarly, in Raoul Dufy's 1915 drawing "La Fin de la Grande Guerre," an iconographic mixture reminiscent of an *image d'Epinal*, the dominant figure is the French rooster, who is trampling on the imperial eagle, *terrassé*. The position is, it will be noted, that of St. George and the Dragon. (The drawing incorporates other patriotic icons also, lightly-sketched, including Joan of Arc, a *gisant* [supine figure on a medieval tomb], a military execution, a French marshal—perhaps Joffre—and Rheims cathedral burning.)

In addition to these conventional or highly stylized images there are

14. Marthe Fiel, *Sur le sol d'Alsace* (Paris: Charpentier, 1911), 143.

graphic elements that are either inherently associated with war, such as weapons, or so traditionally connected that their mere presence in a drawing invokes by metonymy the military world to which they belong; they serve both literally and figuratively in innumerable war texts and pieces of graphic art. Among them are paraphernalia, notably headgear, boots, drums, and trumpets, the latter two symbolizing the call to arms. It stands to reason, of course, that soldiers should be pictured or described in their gear; but sometimes the equipment, separated from its wearer, is metonymic, standing either for the presence or the absence of a soldier (for instance, in monuments to the dead that show a widow grieving over the helmet). The Revolutionary *bonnet phrygien* or *bonnet de la liberté*, mentioned earlier, the imperial three-pointed hat, and the other headgear of the Napoleonic Wars all had a political as well as a military message. In the Franco-Prussian War appeared on the enemy side the hated *casque pointu* or spiked helmet, which from then on was highly charged semiotically. In an illustration for a collection of Déroulède's militantly patriotic poems, showing the execution of two French civilians, the latter have thrown their soft hats onto the snow, a sign of their utter vulnerability (and perhaps as homage to the heroes they invoke); facing them is a firing squad of helmeted Prussians. In French fiction as in drawings, the helmet alone is sufficient to identify the enemy, as this remark by one of Emile Zola's narrators illustrates: "C'étaient enfin des Prussiens, dont ils reconnaissaient les casques à pointe" [Finally, there were Prussians, whose spiked helmets they recognized]. The helmets also serve in synecdoches: Daudet writes of "casques pointus sur les routes" [spiked helmets on the roads], that is, Prussians marching. In his story "Le Siège de Berlin," it is the sight of Prussian helmets on the Place de l'Etoile that kills a frail old man whose daughter had lured him into believing that the French were winning the war. Helmets reappear in graphic art of the Great War, as in a caricature by Cocteau published in *Le Mot* showing grotesquely obese, helmeted Prussian officers conspiring. It should be noted that the spiked helmet, like boots (discussed below), had great positive value for the Prussians, as examples of their patriotic painting of the period reveal.[15]

15. Paul Déroulède, *Chants du soldat*, with illustrations based on watercolors by Eugène Chaperon and Charles Morel (Paris: Modern-Bibliothèque/Arthème Fayard, 1909), n.p.; Zola, *Œuvres complètes*, 6:860; Daudet, *Œuvres*, 1:614, 635. The caricature from *Le Mot* is reproduced in

The *képi* (military cap), a militant emblem as well as a practical item, is featured in innumerable graphic works from the Franco-Prussian War on. In graphics of the Great War, it is often replaced by the characteristic basin-shaped helmet, which reflects the predominance and intensity of artillery, but also distinguishes officers at the rear from those at the front; thus, while eclectic in political terms, the *képi* acquired class meaning, as did, of course, the Phrygian bonnet. Its patriotic symbolism is often unmistakable; however, in 1871 it became for some French the symbol of foolish resistance. In Daudet's "Mon képi," the initial positive value of the old cap the narrator finds in his closet, reminding him of his service in the Garde nationale during the siege, is transformed through his reminiscences into negative value, standing for "toutes les folies, tous les délires d'un peuple emprisonné" [all the follies, all the delirium of an imprisoned people].[16]

As for boots, after their positive value in Romantic art—as in portrayals of Napoleon and his generals, and Théodore Géricault's drawings of cavalry (and, much later, in Picasso's 1914 drawing of Apollinaire)—they came frequently to assume, with the Franco-Prussian War, a negative value, heavily darkened in drawings of Prussians. However, boots are emphasized also in drawings of French soldiers, as if in answer to the metaphoric suggestion of crushing by the enemy—a figurative use into which the image slips more and more frequently after 1870, as in Zola's "cette grosse botte poussant le corps" [that big boot pushing the body]. In literature, the metaphor of the Prussian boot crushing Alsace and Lorraine is so frequent as to be a cliché; one instance of many is, in Erckmann-Chatrian's *Le Brigadier Frédéric*, the image of the crushing heel. The jackboot, like the helmet, reappears in texts and images from the Great War, then in writing concerning World War II, still representing German military oppression; among others who use it are Vercors (pseudonym of Jean Bruller), Pierre-Henri Simon, and Elsa Triolet. Triolet, for example, wrote that the German boot was trampling French hopes.[17]

William A. Emboden, *The Visual Art of Jean Cocteau* (New York: International Archive of Art/ H. N. Abrams, 1989), 91.

16. Daudet, *Œuvres*, 1:687, 1556.

17. Zola, *Œuvres complètes*, 6:891; [Emile Erckmann and Alexandre Chatrian] Erckmann-Chatrian, *Le Brigadier Frédéric* (Paris: J. Hetzel, 1874); Vercors, *Le Silence de la mer* (1942; reprint, Paris: Albin Michel, 1951), 37; Pierre-Henri Simon, *Histoire d'un bonheur* (Paris: Editions du Seuil, 1965), 280, 301; Elsa Triolet, *Le Premier Accroc coûte deux cents francs* (Paris: Egloff, 1945), trans. Francis Golffing as *A Fine of 200 Francs* (New York: Reynal & Hitchcock, 1947), 238.

The tunics and trousers of uniforms, graphically portrayed, carry a great deal of weight, indicating the rank of the wearer, perhaps participation in battle, even the success or failure with which he has met (clean, fresh uniforms, as opposed to torn and dirty ones, indicate variously stylization of war images, rear versus front, inexperience versus experience, fierce fighting, victory, defeat). In military iconography of the Napoleonic period, uniforms of officers and especially of high-ranking ones are given full treatment, with their plumes, sashes, contrasts in colors, and imperial touches; they seem to adhere to the person, constituting his essence. Throughout the period under examination, regimental badges and colors of clothing signified past glories, rivalries with other branches, and ultimately schools of thought with respect to warfare. The red trousers of the infantry persisted through the beginning of World War I—a telling sign of ossified military thinking; dragoons were identified by the egret plumes on their helmets. Anonymous drawings published in *L'Illustration* in Paris and others in the *Illustrated London News* in 1870 seem clearly intended to inform readers about styles of French and Prussian uniforms and headgear. The dress of colonial soldiers (the North African Zouaves and Turcos, or *tirailleurs algériens*, who participated in considerable numbers in the war of 1870–1871) conveys the image of French territorial unity and refers obliquely to the Napoleonic period (the Egyptian element). Daudet's story "Le Turco de la Commune" uses this motif. In Dufy's "Les Alliés: Petit panorama des uniformes" (1916), the intention is clearly to underline the common Allied cause. Marcel Proust, in *Le Temps retrouvé*, describes the picturesque uniforms of colonial soldiers on leave in Paris during the Great War, and the current fashions, in which the colonial tradition is quoted by means of Egyptian motifs.[18]

Then there are weapons, including rifles, sabers, swords, bayonets, arrows (always stylized), and lances (the latter often draped with the *tricolore*). The arrows are clearly anachronistic but exert an appeal perhaps by their classical associations. The stylized *faisceaux* are represented, it was noted, crowned with the Frankish hatchet—both a military and a historical symbol. In the hands of a soldier or officer, weapons ordinarily bespeak military readiness; alone, they can have the same meaning, but can alternatively be used to sug-

---

18. Daudet, *Œuvres*, 1:688–91; Marcel Proust, *Le Temps retrouvé*, in vol. 3 of *A la recherche du temps perdu* (Paris: Gallimard/Bibliothèque de la Pléiade, 1954), 763; cf. 760.

gest defeat. One of the oldest symbolic traditions in the Western world, the sword remained part of an officer's dress uniform, sometimes even battle gear, into World War II (a cavalry officer in Claude Simon's *La Route des Flandres* dies with his sword raised). In Picasso's drawing of Apollinaire, the poet holds one, incongruously juxtaposed with an artillery piece.

The caisson, or field artillery piece, also appears frequently from the Napoleonic period onward, sometimes with decorative Roman chariot touches for the First Empire, more functionally rendered in works of the Franco-Prussian War. Artillery is often scattered, compositionally speaking, amongst groups of infantry and cavalry, the horse and caisson, footsoldier and large guns, complementing each other. In World War I, artillery assumed an enormous iconographic role, befitting the battles fought. In Apollinaire's war poems—the best French poetry of any twentieth-century war, said André Gide—artillery is both backdrop (he wrote his poems on the field) and actor. A striking graphic example is found in the work of the Italian Futurist, Gino Severini, living and exhibiting in Paris in 1916: a cubist-style painting, "Canon en action," combines verbal elements, superimposed planes, multiplied trajectory patterns, and mechanical elements in addition to the centrally placed main artillery piece—but with only a minimized human figure—to suggest the dehumanization of warfare, the multiplication of the mechanical. Among the verbal elements in this canvas are references to gas, the term "soldatsmachines" (one word, suggesting perhaps the German language), the words "éventrement de la terre" (evisceration of the earth), and lexical elements suggesting the anxiety of warfare. References on the lower plane to "puissance" (strength) and "France" have been taken as patriotic, but need not be—the power displayed is a destructive one, shaking earth itself. In another, even less human painting, Severini featured an armored train: a speeding machine, all angular planes, from which cannons and rifles fire, manned by barely perceptible, stylized human figures. The theme of war as an antihumanism, rather than a heroic venture, is carried out even more explicitly in his painted collage "La Guerre," where the word "Antihumanisme" dominates a harsh tableau featuring chemical names, mathematical formulae, a factory chimney, a telegraph pole and wires, a half-map of Europe, and, on a dotted line, as on a map, the words "Gaz asphyxiants."

The landscape itself plays an important role as a nationalist and military icon. In the Napoleonic period, it was the landscape of military conquest (Napoleon crossing the Alps—an imposing figure dominating an imposing land-scape, with his troops miniaturized behind him) and defeat (the Grande Armée crossing the Berezina—again, a vast landscape, befitting the huge army and the immensity of retreat and suffering). After the conquest of Algeria in 1830, Algerian scenes by Horace Vernet and others, whether of land-scape alone or some military skirmish, served as symbols of the new French colonialism in Africa. Cold, rain, and mud (mentioned by Stendhal's Fabrice, by Zola's characters in *La Débâcle*, in stories by Daudet, and by nearly all of the writers of World War I) are suggested in graphic renderings of the retreat from Russia, Waterloo, and other campaigns—as in Ernest Meissonier's "1814"—and subsequently appear in both pictorial and written art through-out the following wars. Associated with the muddy landscape in the Great War are barbed wire and tree stumps—the natural landscape disemboweled and disfigured, a parallel to the mutilation of soldiers. But even then, the landscape can also be suggestive of the true France, with its vineyards and wheat: images of vines and sheaves in the field, for instance (foreshadowed by grain imagery in Charles Péguy's poetry antedating 1914), suggest bread and wine, thus home and hearth, France itself, and, explicitly or otherwise, the sacredness of the struggle by association with the Eucharist symbolism. In the following conflict, Resistance poets used widely the term *terre* and vari-ous landscape images as signifiers of the patriotic struggle.

Ecclesiastical motifs, whether painted, sculpted, or written, likewise served to reinforce the nationalist, sometimes the military message, with the implication of divine protection and justification. Often the cross is featured: cruciform tombstones or those engraved with a cross; roadside or village steles and *calvaires*; military medals that include cross motifs. The symbolic suggestions of the cross—arguably the most widespread image known to his-tory—include sacrifice, divine favor, holiness, salvation, and reminiscences of the Crusades, with an implied identity between Christendom and the French cause in modern times. Pointing to the traditional role of France as "fille aînée de l'église" [elder daughter of the church] and thus favored by God, is the village church, which appears in the background in many drawings and is used by Proust, in *Le Temps retrouvé*, in the form of Saint-André-des-Champs, to personify the authentic patriotic spirit. Even more imposing is the cathe-dral, notably Chartres, in Péguy's patriotic poetry, and Rheims, where Joan led Charles VII for coronation. The cathedral of Rheims appears, for instance, in the Dufy *coq gaulois* drawing; in photograph form, on a postcard of 1914, taken during bombardment; and in a commemorative stamp, "Rappelez-vous 1914," on which a draped female figure, standing on a garland, gestures toward the burning edifice; the legend reads, "Français: Ne consommez aucun produit allemand" [Frenchmen: Do not consume any German product].

I have so far concentrated on nonhuman war imagery, although some of it, such as uniforms, is generally represented in direct connection with human figures, and the landscape paintings mentioned have human elements. The iconography of the body in relation to war and nationalism deserves some particular attention. The use of human beings in France to represent the military or national ideal goes back to medieval iconography—the knight, or the king and his armies—and to the postmedieval monarchy, chiefly through royal portraiture, although there were battle paintings also. This earlier body of portraiture did not presumably play so great a role in national consciousness as that of human figures after the Revolution because the means of production and distribution were much more limited. In addition, the monarchy relied more on abstract, conventional images: the sun emblem for Louis XIV, the royal flag, and others. In the nineteenth century, military images were generally connected to the idea of the individual and the citizen, who is the source of political authority (government by consent of the governed) and who is also, through his acknowledgment of his civic responsibility, the instrument for carrying out policy—which, from 1792 through 1815, and again in the early 1830s, after the invasion of Algeria, meant waging war. Hence the importance of human iconography, developed early in the century as an aspect of the individualism envisioned and promoted by Romantic art and literature. The genre painting of the eighteenth century, with its domestic scenes and its use of ordinary figures—even if aesthetically idealized—was doubtless a contributing factor in the growth in the early nineteenth century of a patriotic art using representative but anonymous figures. After all, it was against the background of citizen armies and popular government that Napoleon rose, a populist and truly popular figure but also a mythomaniac, who promoted himself through military skill into a position of supreme power, with all the trappings of empire—an individual above all others and recognized as such in iconography.

The human body is iconographic in and of itself, carrying meaning imme-

diately, through its humanity. (There is no one, except the blind or the imbe-
cilic, who does not recognize a drawn body for what it is and respond to it as
such, irrespective, initially, of what it is supposed to stand for beyond itself,
such as sanctity.) Because, even under the lay republican regimes, France retained strong ties to Christian tradition, belief, art, and institutions, the Christian overtones of the body's value were never distant, and sometimes were
explicit: a suffering body (Christ, and His imitators, the saints and martyrs)
that ultimately transcends its passion to achieve a higher end (on this model,
even the body of the Church, used in the mystical Pauline sense, is pertinent).
In Péguy's vision, French soil is a great body, to whom its members belong
and for which they will fight a just war and suffer a triple martyrdom, as individual, nation, and Church: "Heureux ceux qui sont morts pour la terre char-
nelle" [Happy those who have died for the carnal earth].[19]

The body as signifier has two messages: body as means, body as end.
While, by its very nature, the human project (that is, activity, whether labor
or play) ultimately transcends the body, it always refers back to the enabling
instrument on which it depends. In graphic depictions of the body, one sees,
or asks: What is it *doing*? In art, in mysticism, in love, this instrumentality can
be minimized, the body either ignored, or, in contrast, adulated *as body*; but
in combat, on the contrary, men are only functional: they bear weapons—and
not in their own name but in that of a state or group of which they are in turn
arms.

Yet the body is also, implicitly, the end; national warfare is carried out in
the name of other human beings (the body politic), who, in written and
drawn renderings of war, are often symbolized by visible figures (figures
on the margin of drawings, wives and children of whom fictional combatants
think, and so on). In the narratological terms I use in the following chapter,
the body is at once the *sender* of action in the form of a national will or other
authority, expressed by the bodies of a parliament, ruler, or other group; the
subject carrying out this will, by means of the instrumentality of men's bodies
in combat; and the *receiver* of the action, which transcends the war toward the
après-guerre and its material purposes. Only in those understandings of *state*
by which the abstract state transcends all individual values and projects

19. Charles Péguy, *Œuvres poétiques* (Paris: Gallimard/Bibliothèque de la Pléiade, 1957),
1026.

would the body not be felt as subject. A pure Hegelian (that is, abstract) political art is hard to imagine, although it may be most nearly conceivable in architecture (here one thinks of Nazi constructions); in socialist realism, such as the paintings of Diego Rivera, the Marxist project of remaking the state is conveyed crudely, but in concrete, immediately recognizable terms of human bodies and the work they perform.

Both aspects of the body, means and end, are implied in war art and writing, though instrumentality is usually stressed. Moreover, the human figure can be mimetic—a soldier, for instance, to be taken as such—or it can be chiefly figurative, symbolic or allegorical, as in the representation of the army and republic as a woman. Even in figurative renderings, however, the immediate meaning of the body *qua* body cannot be overlooked.

Human figures in war iconography are generally combined with other elements, either inherently military, such as gear and armaments, or symbolic objects. The figures can be static or shown in action, allegorical or mimetic, and can appear singly or together. In the Revolutionary and Napoleonic periods, graphic depictions of battles, derived considerably from eighteenth-century models, were characteristically collective: a set piece with units disposed around the battlefield, corresponding roughly to the type of warfare being carried out, as Jean Duplessis-Bertaux's "Victoire remportée à Fleurus" and Denis-Auguste-Marie Raffet's "Carré enfoncé" illustrate. Crowds appearing in such scenes express political unity. However, depictions of Napoleon always highlight his unique presence and individuality, by centering and foregrounding him against much smaller middle-ground and background figures or against a dramatic landscape. Characteristic is David's "Bataille d'Austerlitz" (1806), which shows the general in the left foreground, on a rearing horse, overlooking from a Romantic height the battlefield, including tiers of soldiers reaching far into the distance; foregrounded with him, though lower, is a smoking cannon and an *artilleur*, along with a fallen soldier and an officer.

In somewhat later Romantic painting, importance is given to the individualized soldier, centered on the canvas but anonymous and viewed as a type. The complex question of generality versus individuality arises in this connection. On the one hand, the citizen soldier is singled out by the aesthetic composition, in keeping with the emphases on individualism, noted earlier, and on the idea of equality; on the other, his uniform, his function, and even characteristic poses and expressions mark him as one of many, a representative but not singular character. The political implications are clear: although the ultimate source of sovereignty, this power is abstract only; the citizen still belongs to the nation and his individuality is subsumed in his function on its behalf. Examples include Vernet's "Le Soldat de Waterloo" (ca. 1818), Nicolas Charlet's "Le Soldat français" and "Cuirassier français portant un drapeau" (1818–1819), and many canvases by Géricault, who often concentrates on a single warrior, especially a horseman. Perhaps it is owing to the dominant image of Napoleon in other canvases that even the common, anonymous soldiers depicted in painting of the period tend to assume heroic proportions by virtue of their central position, the emblematic details, and the powerful strokes of Romantic brushes.

Regarding the Franco-Prussian War, one finds two veins in painting of human figures. In one, small groups or single figures predominate: Marshal Mac-Mahon, a hussar, a few soldiers, scenes and vignettes from the field — such as soldiers sleeping, or a camp with tents and fires, or occasionally the rear. In the other, there are sweeping battle scenes dependent upon landscape and reminiscent—intentionally so—of battles of the First Empire: for example, G. Giostiang's lithograph "Bataille de Wissembourg, 4 août 1870" and V. Tull's lithograph "Prise de Sarrebruck, 2 août 1870." In the latter, there is close fighting in the foreground, the German helmets indicating clearly the enemies; smaller figures appear in the center and upper planes, becoming crowds and reaching to a hillock; a village and bridge are visible in the distance. Only Napoleon I is missing, although that absence may strike modern eyes more than those that viewed the work originally. That most of these graphic works of the Franco-Prussian War were done after the Second Empire had ended and it had become clear that the reverses of August and September 1870 had led to defeat sheds an ironic light on them. Drawings and paintings of the Great War, in which the word *battle* no longer had the same meaning, thanks to trench warfare, tend, in contrast, to focus on individuals, dispersed in trenches or in desolate landscapes with tree stumps and wire. Yet, like much war fiction of the corresponding period, there is some combining of the collective and the individual, with the latter foregrounded. Images from the rear and from lulls in fighting contrast with those of battle: inns, cafés, done in genre-painting style, as in a drawing by Antonio Ugo, or in the cubist manner, by Fernand Léger.

The represented body can appear and convey meaning *as a whole*—simply a wounded soldier, for instance, or men marching in order toward battle; and in literature, of course, as contrasted to painting, the reader normally imagines human beings in this way, even when a particular bodily action (running, reaching) is emphasized. In addition, as the previous survey of such parts of military accoutrement as headgear and boots suggests, discrete parts of the body, usually covered by the appropriate gear but sometimes bare, and normally shown connected to the whole but sometimes graphically detached or isolated in description (occasionally intended as real physical disconnection), can carry considerable meaning: feet, head, sometimes hands and arms, raised in salutes and other gestures or simply carrying weapons. This appearance stresses the *use* of the body (function or dysfunction) more than its meaning as *end*. Certain poses and gestures become conventional, starting with Romantic art: shooting with muskets or rifles, offering drink (to give nourishment or courage, or perhaps as a kind of last rite) or otherwise ministering to the wounded, carrying wounded, discovering dead comrades, collapsing, lying prone. A component of some scenes is the gesture of the raised arm and clenched fist—a gesture that became also part of the working-class and anarchistic revolutionary vocabulary, thus tying war and revolution. This connection was particularly strong in works from the aftermath of the Franco-Prussian War and the Commune, and again on the eve of World War I; it disappeared from general sight when war actually broke out. In 1937 Louis Aragon used the image of the raised arm in a tableau uniting landscape, armaments, and human actors, figuring national revolution but also war, since devasted countryside appears: "vos villes et vos campagnes dévastées, où des bras maternels lèvent vers le ciel des petits cadavres innocents au milieu des héros farouches qui serrent leurs fusils dans leurs poings de travailleurs" [your cities and countryside devastated, where mothers' arms lift toward heaven little innocent corpses in the midst of fierce heroes who hold their rifles tightly in their laborers' fists]. The body may be significant also in terms of *its* metaphors, as in this example from a World War II story composed in 1984: "Un gros lard se penchait vers lui" [A big fat bacon leaned down toward him]—a phrase that conveys the girth, diet, and vulgarity of the Germans.[20]

20. Léon Mercadet, *La Brigade Alsace-Lorraine* (Paris: Grasset, 1984), 277. Aragon's phrase is quoted in Coombes, *Writing from the Left*, 112.

The value of wounded bodies, body parts, and corpses depends upon which side they belong to (indicated by insignia and uniforms). In some cases, the wounded or mutilated body is removed from the battle context and set apart as an icon in itself: the role of dressings, crutches, and blindfolds is significant. In literary texts and graphic works from all wars of the period treated in this study, tremendous place is given to the mutilated: in narrative, for example, Georges Duhamel's sketches of World War I; in art, a Théophile-Alexandre Steinlen poster of 1917 for a sale of paintings benefiting the war blind. Cocteau's famous drawing of Apollinaire with a bandage over his head—dating from 1921, it is believed, although the poet died in 1918—gives predominance to the dressing and wound it implies. By the midpoint of World War I, mutilated bodies had assumed in many representational forms a supranational value, no longer standing for the French or the German side, but rather conveying the universality of suffering. Wounded horses also play an iconographic role, from the Napoleonic period through Claude Simon's novel *La Route des Flandres* (1960).

Among the human figures that carry the message of war both symbolically or allegorically, and directly, women occupy a preeminent position. In the period under examination here, their role as receiver of action (it is in the name of the hearth and home that so many battles are fought) is inseparable from their cultural position, a position of political and social subordination tied to their very high valuation as sexual creatures, at once to satisfy male desire and to produce and nurture progeny. Emphasis on the female breast, to which I shall return, underlines both functions. Women can also be seen as senders of the action, in the form of the nation personified. The question of the relationships among men's political power, women's attitudes toward war, and female iconography should be kept in mind, although I do not subscribe to the belief that if women ruled there would be no armed conflict. The iconographic use of the female is extremely rich, especially allegorically, incorporating often more than one symbolic component. (I construe the term *allegorical* somewhat narrowly, in reference to narrative expression, even if truncated; thus, while allegory may incorporate symbols, I do not equate it with symbolism, although critics often use the terms interchangeably, a practice justified in part by the fact that much symbolism often refers obliquely to a narrative *behind* the symbol.)

The term *la Marianne* to indicate the republic appeared as early as year II on the Revolutionary calendar and was first used pejoratively before it came to stand for France itself. The figure was a development of the female representation of liberty, dating from the earliest Revolutionary days but echoing symbolism from antiquity and Gaul: a representation of Gaul in Roman times showed a woman bearing the insignia of a boar—a frequent symbol for the Gauls. This feminine personification of liberty appeared on the seal of the new republic in 1792, with Phrygian bonnet and *faisceau d'armes*. The feminine personification contrasts with the masculine nexus of king and ancien régime. A contributing factor to the feminization of the national ideal may be the active role played during the Revolution by women of the lower classes in civic and political matters, at least in the streets; their presence is brought out in period drawings of *sans-culotte* costumes and in other representations. (Women were, by decree, "to make tents and clothing, and serve in hospitals.") Presumably their activity encouraged the association between female and republic. Moreover, the birth of popular nationalism, which invited those of all classes to identify and feel unity with the nation, put a new stress on the soil; this would encourage feminine identification, since women were viewed as the keepers of the hearth, the matrices of the future. The feminine gender of the abstract nouns in the Revolutionary triad and of such words as *nation*, *république*, and *France* may also have reinforced the connection. Moreover, one should note the graphic resemblance between numerous representations of Marianne and the Revolutionary apotheosis ceremonies and paintings involving "la déesse Raison" and "la déesse de la Liberté." While "revolutionary," these works and their motifs are very close in style to earlier eighteenth-century neoclassical sculpture. Iconographic styles under the Directory and Empire subsequently reinforced this neoclassical element. Etienne Quatremère's designs for representations of the republic (for instance, with a Minerva figure), Chinard's representation of the republic as a female, and Simon-Louis Boizot's similar allegorical drawings illustrate the graphic variations on the female identification of France.[21]

There are many famous renderings of Marianne in her Phrygian bonnet,

21. Nora, *Lieux de mémoire*, 3:508; Maurice Agulhon, *Marianne au combat: L'Imagerie et la symbolique républicaines de 1789 à 1880* (Paris: Flammarion, 1979), 21, 29, 44–45; the decree of 23 August 1793, quoted in Bruce D. Porter, *War and the Rise of the State: The Military Foundations of Modern Politics* (New York: Free Press, 1994), 131.

and other works abound in which the republic assumes a similar feminine identity. In Eugène Delacroix's "La Liberté guidant le peuple" (1830), among weapons and corpses a bare-breasted female figure on the upper plane, with an unfurled flag, leads the freedom fighters into the foreground; on the Arc de Triomphe, François Rude's "Le Départ des Volontaires en 1792," more commonly known as "La Marseillaise" (1835–1836), puts on the upper plane a bellicose feminine figure with a Phrygian bonnet; in Georges Montorgueil's 1890 drawing of a military parade, the republic is represented as draped in the flag and with laurel in her hair, but with the lines, gestures, and coiffure of a woman of the upper classes. Sainte-Geneviève, the female patron saint of Paris, is sometimes featured. In some of these scenes, there is slippage between the allegorical and nonallegorical: the female personification, though stylized and sometimes larger-than-life, nevertheless occupies the same pictorial ground as the other human figures. In Gustave Doré's "La Marseillaise" (1870), she participates with soldiers in the charge (if implausibly, since she is dressed in flowing robes, most unmilitary).

The nonallegorical, literal function of women in war iconography is less developed than that of men, since they did not take a direct part in battle. Yet although historically marginalized, they are often central in war painting and other representations. In art of the Romantic period that deals with combat, women are featured as *vivandières*—those women who, with their carts, followed the troops to sell them food and drink during the Revolutionary and Napoleonic wars (one plays an important role in the Waterloo section of Stendhal's *La Chartreuse de Parme*). They are often shown weeping over the dead or assisting the wounded. In a Vernet painting (1826) that probably represents a scene from the campaigns of 1814, a handsome, almost noble-looking though barefoot peasant woman defends her farm and cattle against pillaging cossacks, while protecting her wounded husband and her child. Although the figure is not allegorical, her association with liberty and the republic and her resemblance to Delacroix's Liberté a few years later are clear.

After the Napoleonic period—that is, wars of conquest, on foreign soil—the iconographic role of women appears to increase with fighting taking place on French soil during the Franco-Prussian War and the subsequent loss of territories. Continued use of female emblems in patriotic, especially republican, symbolism surely reinforced this iconographic presence. Later in the century, in the abundant body of military and other nationalist graphic work,

46

women are shown in a range of practical roles: mothers, daughters, wives, sometimes widows of soldiers; women innkeepers or others who receive soldiers hospitably (later incarnations of the *vivandières*); nurses; knitters and other women shown working in other supportive industry (foreshadowing female industrial workers of the twentieth century); pretty girls who greet passing troops or wait for them (Déroulède spoke of "mères, filles, soeurs, épouses, fiancées" [mothers, daughters, sisters, wives, fiancées]). A striking literary use of a woman in connection with the Franco-Prussian War is found in one of Guy de Maupassant's most famous stories, "Boule de suif" [Suet ball] (1880), in which a female—significantly denoted by a culinary term—is sacrificed, in essence, to the Prussians by her compatriots, whose hostility toward her reflects the power of caste judgments even in the face of occupation by an enemy.

Whether or not women are iconographically associated with the land—by being shown in a pastoral or agricultural setting or being connected to a product such as wheat or wine—both metonymically and metaphorically they stand for France, associated with the feminine gender, and for its posterity. In many incarnations, it is they whom the soldiers must protect, they for whom *revanche* must be sought. In other cases, woman represents the true military spirit—which will prevail over the enemy—or a tutelary presence protecting men. Both these functions are frequent in graphic symbolism of World War I. In a 1915 engraving by Louis-Charles Bombled entitled "Les Zeppelins passent, Paris a le sourire," a smiling buxom woman in military dress, armed with a rifle and bayonet, lolls in a reduced cityscape including the Seine, the Eiffel Tower, and the Sacré-Coeur, as if lying in wait for the zeppelins, caught in the searchlights. In Amédée Ozenfant's "Le Front—le collier de la victoire" (1915), a female face is imposed on a map of Europe, her bead necklace coextensive with dots marking the front lines. A publicity poster for sewing machines (post-1918) shows a female figure, with a cock at her feet, who is sewing Alsace and Lorraine onto the map of France.

Female figures with the characteristic headgear of Alsace and Lorraine appear frequently in the early decades of the Third Republic, unmistakably a summons to duty. In a drawing by Dufy, a peasant girl dances surrounded by symbols of the lost provinces. Even the Venus de Milo appears, arranged to support military propaganda. Sometimes the vulnerability of women is heightened by such characteristics as extreme old age, maternity (infants at the breast), or handicaps (notably, male figures, such as *mutilés de guerre*, can appear in these images also). Numerous steles and other monuments to the dead of the Great War feature a woman gazing at a burial cross or a discarded helmet. Yet females can suggest the enemy also: "La Vertueuse Germania" by Léo d'Angel (1917) depicts a vulgar Teutonic peasant woman with a brutish face, carrying a torch—not the symbol of illumination, but rather of arson. Similarly, they can be associated with anarchism or antiwar movements (as indeed women were in fact): in Henri Rousseau's "La Guerre" (1894), war is depicted as a depraved woman with a sword and torch, surrounded by bodies littering the ground. Woman, thus, sometimes served to condemn unjustified violence. Similar is a Goyaesque anarchist figure by Maximilien Luc (1894) showing a female figure, identified as "Patrie," devouring an infant and surrounded by skulls of others; the caption reads, "The abominable ghoul is never satisfied! Rough Bitch, Madame Patrie: she devours her children."[22]

The question of sexuality arises in connection with female representations. The Marianne figure representing the republic is commonly shown stylized, usually with only head and bust, the latter with flowing classic lines. Other female iconographic figures associated with nation are either asexual (Joan of Arc, treated below) or both sexual and asexual. The sexuality is of two kinds, maternal and erotic, indicated by the bare breast—as in "La France républicaine ouvrant son sein à tous les Français" ca. 1792—suggesting both a nourishing mother, helping to repopulate France, and a desirable woman aroused from her bed; the latter suggestion implies rape by foreigners or internal enemies of the republic as well as an erotic quality, which, according to tradition, will excite men to displays of strength and valor. As Maupassant wrote, "Mais la femme, voyez-vous, on ne l'enlèvera pas de nos coeurs. Elle y est, elle y reste. Nous l'aimons, nous l'aimerons, nous ferons pour elle toutes les folies" [But, you see, they won't take woman away from our hearts. She is there, she remains there. We love her, we will love her, we will commit every folly for her]. The seminudity of female figures representing France has, like the singularity of soldiers who occupy the center of a canvas, two sides: while the individuality of the person is laid bare by being disrobed,

22. John Hutton, *Neo-Impressionism and the Search for Solid Ground: Art, Science, and Anarchism in Fin-de-Siècle France* (Baton Rouge: Louisiana State University Press, 1994), 233.

since she is no longer shielded by the layers of protective and semiotically charged clothing that signal her as a member of the social order, at the same time, nudity proclaims its universality.[23] Both types of sexuality support or are supported by the feminine suggestions of the nouns from the nationalist vocabulary noted earlier. The iconographic figure's sexuality also offers a reminder of the participation of women in the streets under the First Republic and, later, the Commune; she is the *common* woman, not an idealized figure.

At the same time, any female figure representing war may be asexual, her femininity (signified by breast, hair) offset by her assuming the role of warrior—not just a victim (as in much iconography of the Franco-Prussian War and World War I), but an agent. An early Revolutionary text called "Prière des Amazones à Bellone" reads as follows: "Et nous aussi, nous savons combattre et vaincre. Nous savons manier d'autres armes que l'aiguille et le fuseau" [And we also can fight and conquer. We know how to handle arms other than needles and spindles].[24] In Rude's "Le Départ," the allegorical war figure wears a coat of mail over her (very obvious) breasts and presides over the phalanx of volunteers, rousing the men to action. This militancy is exercised for the *nation*, to whom she belongs.

Joan of Arc is a complex icon, historical yet tending toward symbol and myth; she constitutes the fullest personification of France as a female. In view of her immense role as a symbol for militant France, a survey of her fortunes in literature and art during the period under examination is warranted. Considerable syncretism in her cult is visible from the Revolution onward in historical accounts, literature, and drawings. The two principal strains were republican, on the one hand, and Catholic, royalist, and conservative on the other—her banner being *tricolore* or her traditional white, accordingly; but shadings can be identified. Gilbert Zoppi observes, "Pour les uns . . . elle symbolisera d'abord le surnaturel s'incarnant dans l'histoire, et pour les autres la naissance du sentiment national, et même de l'esprit démocratique" [For some she will symbolize first of all the supernatural becoming incarnate

23. James A. W. Heffernan, ed., *Representing the French Revolution: Literature, Historiography, and Art* (Hanover and London: University Press of New England, 1992), fig. 21; Guy de Maupassant, *Contes et nouvelles*, ed. Louis Forestier, vol. 1 (Paris: Gallimard/Bibliothèque de la Pléiade, 1974), 162.

24. Hampson, *First European Revolution*, 77.

in history, and for others the birth of national sentiment and even of the democratic spirit]. Because Joan had insisted upon the authority of her voices, she could be viewed as the victim of superstition and oppressive institutions, and the representative of conscience and free thought. She was adopted for Revolutionary purposes as early as 1792 in a work printed in Orléans entitled "Complainte historique sur la Pucelle d'Orléans," with the subtitle "Portrait de Jeanne d'Arc la Pucelle d'Orléans, ressuscitée en esprit chez les sans-culottes" [Portrait of Joan of Arc the Maid of Orléans, resuscitated in spirit among the *sans-culottes*]. This engraving combines graphics with inscriptions of a song to be sung to the "Air de Marlbroucke": "Vaillante sans-culottes, guide les coeurs français. Que l'on purge la France des partisans des rois" [Valiant *sans-culottes*, guide French hearts. May France be purged of the kings' partisans]. Napoleon, for his part, attempted to draw authority from her example, reestablishing in 1802 the feast (which the revolutionaries had abolished) of 8 May (date of the liberation of Orléans from the English), in homage to her military feats.[25]

In contrast to republican female representations, Joan of Arc is unvaryingly asexual—*la pucelle*. (Voltaire's view of her as a sexual being whose virginity is at issue is exceptional.) Her body is shown encased in armor, no breasts are visible, and her femininity is sublimated into the role of warrior. The opposition that some critics have seen in war narratives and iconography between the male principle of aggression and the female principles of suffering and passivity does not obtain in her case. Joan is above the ordinary vocation of women; her ultimate canonization results from and proves it. She is depicted either as solitary or *above* the troops; her eyes are often lifted toward heaven.

In the nationalistic, republican vein there were two types of written texts concerning the Maid: violently anticlerical in the manner of Voltaire, whose *La Pucelle*—the most famous Johannine work of his century, though far from the best—had as its sole aim the discrediting of church and dogma; and "objective," in which examination was based on rationalistic principles and erudition. The latter trend, visible already in a few documentary studies at the end of the eighteenth century, blossomed as the following century pro-

---

25. Gilbert Zoppi, "Jeanne d'Arc et les républicains," in *L'Esprit républicain; Colloque d'Orléans, 4 et 5 septembre 1970* (Paris: Klincksieck, 1972), 314; Nora, *Lieux de mémoire*, 3:704.

gressed, as in Vallet de Viriville's *Jeanne Darc, sa vie, son procès, sa mort* (1867), where the spelling reflects the author's desire to separate Joan from the ecclesiastical and royalist axis and identify her with the people. Whether the approach was partisan and anticlerical, or objective, Joan served as a nationalist icon. As Jules Quicherat wrote in 1850, "Jeanne représente à la fois le Tiers-Etat sauvant la patrie, et la libre pensée écrasant le dogme par la logique, la bonne foi et la raison. La France n'a qu'une sainte" [Joan represents both the Third Estate saving the fatherland and free thought crushing dogma by logic, good faith, and reason. France has only one saint].[26]

Generally speaking, the Romantic writers, with their interest in the Middle Ages and also a nostalgic royalism, found Joan an appealing figure, whatever their religious and political persuasion; among them is François-René de Chateaubriand, who spoke of her in "Sur l'histoire des ducs de Bourgogne." Alphonse de Lamartine, in his *Jeanne d'Arc* (1852), called her "l'inspirée, l'héroïne, et la sainte du patriotisme français" [the inspired one, the heroine, and the saint of French patriotism]; George Sand placed her in the pantheon of those who underwent ecstasy, along with Socrates, Jesus, Saint John, and Dante.[27] Studies of the trial in Rouen multiplied around midcentury, with sundry political shadings. The most famous and influential partisan of Joan in the century was, of course, Jules Michelet, whose three chapters on her in the fifth volume of his *Histoire de France* (1841, published separately in 1853) conciliated the Romantic, lyrical view of his heroine as pure, believing in her mission, with the republican, antiroyalist view. (After all, the king did nothing to save her.) At the same time the Church attempted to use her to combat anticlerical positions, and to that end worked from midcentury onward for her beatification. She was declared venerable in 1893, beatified in 1909, and canonized in 1920—events which would act as an attestation of divine and miraculous intervention in French history.

In the shadow of the 1870–1871 defeat, the Third Republic was generally well disposed toward Joan, yet the struggle over who and what she was and to what part of the French and their history she belonged continued; in fact, she was claimed by all, including Catholics besieged by anticlericalism. She

---

26. Quoted in Zoppi, "Jeanne d'Arc," 317.

27. Egide Jeanné, *L'Image de la Pucelle d'Orléans dans la littérature historique française depuis Voltaire* (Liège: Vaillant-Carmanne, 1935), 50.

appeared as "la patronne des envahis" [the patron saint of the invaded] in literature concerning the Franco-Prussian conflict. In Déroulède's *Chants du soldat*, the earliest of which date from 1872, the Catholic and Republican poet emphasizes the *idea* of the soldier; Jeanne rises from the tomb to inspire the French to chase out the Germans:

> Et vouant notre espoir, consacrons notre haine
> Consacrons nos coeurs recueillis
> A Jeanne la Française, à Jeanne la Lorraine,
> La patronne des envahis!

[And nursing our hope, let us consecrate our hatred / Consecrate our reverential hearts / to Joan of France, to Joan of Lorraine / The patron saint of the invaded!]. Déroulède also read a poem at the 1875 inauguration of the statue of Joan by Emmanuel Frémiet, Place des Pyramides. On the 1878 centenary of Voltaire's death and the day of Joan's execution, a celebration was held in the Théâtre de la Gaîté, emphasizing *republican* Joan, martyred by the Church. In Maupassant's "Les Idées du colonel" (1884) she is held up as a heroine and leader because of her femininity: "Rappelez-vous ce que Jeanne d'Arc nous a fait faire autrefois. Tenez, je vous parie que, si une femme, une jolie femme, avait pris le commandement de l'armée, la veille de Sedan, quand le maréchal de Mac-Mahon fut blessé, nous aurions traversé les lignes prussiennes, sacrebleu!" [Remember what Joan of Arc made us do long ago. Say, I bet you that, if a woman, a pretty woman, had taken command of the army, right before Sedan, when Marshal Mac-Mahon was wounded, we would have crossed the Prussian lines, by heaven!].[28]

At the time of the 1889 centennial celebrations, Joan was pointedly hailed by republicans. A motion was made at the Congrès Universel des Libres Penseurs held that year that there be a national holiday in her honor, since she was seen as the supreme patriot. (This holiday had already been proposed in 1884. After several intermediate steps, it was finally instituted after World War I began.) In 1890 and 1891, at the Paris Hippodrome, a mimed spectacle was devoted to her, with music and poetry by Auguste Dorchain, claiming her as a nationalist figure. At the Porte-St.-Martin Theater, Jules Barbier's

---

28. Gildea, *Past in French History*, 156; Maupassant, *Contes et nouvelles*, 163.

successful play about Joan, originally presented in 1873, was revived to great acclaim, with Sarah Bernhardt. A contemporary art nouveau poster by E. S. Grasset (1894) shows the great actress accoutered as Joan above a sea of sharp-pointed spears and lances, bearing a banner decorated with fleur de lys motifs and Mary and the Christ Child. In 1894 Freemasons appeared at the Place des Pyramides with a wreath calling Joan "abandoned by the monarchy . . . victim of the clergy."[29]

Yet during the Dreyfus Affair, the figure of Joan was easily harnessed to anti-Dreyfusard thought and movements — seen as military defender of France and the army; as defender of the Christian faith; as defender of *terre* and traditions, opposed to foreigners, formerly the English, now Jews, viewed as international and nomadic; as defender of spiritual values against material ones, in the form of international (Jewish) finance; and finally, as defender of the *race*. At the turn of the century, her figure remained popular; it was in 1902 that Antonin Mercié's statue "Jeanne recevant son épée de la France meurtrie" was erected in Domrémy. At the Salon of 1906 a Joan in armor was exhibited. Increasingly, she was connected with *revanche* against Germany, as her double status as patriot and religious personage became confirmed. Péguy, at the beginning of the twentieth century, made Joan central in his work as the supreme image of an authentic France built on the medieval past but reevaluated in the context of his socialist republicanism. This mixed iconographical and ideological use persisted throughout World War I. A 1916 postcard, "Sur la route de la victoire," shows Joan, on a white steed and surrounded by banners and flags (some with Christian motif, others the *tricolore*), riding beside a column of soldiers in winter gear, including a *turco*.[30]

Yet at the same time a split widened between the historic Joan, whom critically minded writers such as Anatole France would continue to investigate in their studies, and the almost mythological Joan, celebrated by Georges Bernanos and Charles Maurras, who continued to hail her heroism or sanctity. Bernanos, who married a collateral descendant of Joan, is a particularly interesting case. He joined the Action Française and its youth guard, the

29. Maurice Barrès, *Autour de Jeanne d'Arc* (Paris: E. Champion, 1916), 43–44; Gollwitzer, *Europe in the Age of Imperialism*, 172; Gildea, *Past in French History*, 158.

30. Régine Pernoud and Marie-Véronique Clin, *Jeanne d'Arc* (Paris: Fayard, 1986), 192–93.

Camelots du Roi, and was listed on its honor roll of those wounded and imprisoned as a result of street battles; along with others, he was jailed for demonstrating against the skeptical and anticlerical treatment of Joan by Sorbonne historian Amédée Thalamas. In *Jehanne relapse et sainte* (1934) Bernanos argued that she represented "la fine fleur de la chevalerie" [the fine flower of chivalry], the spirit of childhood, and the true France.[31]

Joan's graphic presence, like her verbal presence, suggests triumph over the enemy who occupies French soil, a triumph willed by God. It may suggest also the return to the genuine past of France, away from the skepticism and destruction of the modern age. The same sort of conflicting claims and interpretations would characterize the political use to which Joan was put in the 1930s and during World War II, when she was claimed by Vichyites and Resistance writers alike, and notably by the communist atheist Aragon. In *Le Fils du peuple*, the collectively composed "autobiography" of the Communist leader Maurice Thorez, one reads: "Le patriotisme des humbles, le patriotisme de Jeanne d'Arc, paysanne de France abandonnée par son roi . . . marque chaque étape de l'émancipation de notre peuple" [The patriotism of the humble, the patriotism of Joan of Arc, a French peasant abandoned by her king, marks each step of the emancipation of our people].[32] Well after the end of the war she was still being hitched to political wagons, chiefly those of the extreme right.

The Napoleonic cult constituted the third major historical vein of French war iconography of the nineteenth century, enduring well into the twentieth. Napoleon's case is different from Joan's: there was no question of the accuracy of historical claims, no real issue of miraculous works or divine mission (despite a literary rhetoric that tended toward deification), so that his actions were not disputed; even the hermeneutics of his generalship remained stable, with only the political value being open to contest. Despite enormous iconic value, moreover—he was the great idol, to whom neither the republicans nor the royalists could provide any rival—he remained a human figure, both *of*

31. Georges Bernanos, *Jehanne relapse et sainte* (Paris: Plon, 1934), 12, 33.

32. Cited in Coombes, *Writing from the Left*, 110. See "Richard II Quarante," in Louis Aragon, *Le Crève-coeur* (London: La France Libre, 1944), 44. See also Gabriel Jacobs, "The Role of Joan of Arc on the Stage of Occupied Paris," in Roderick Kedward and Roger Austin, eds., *Vichy France and the Resistance: Culture and Ideology* (London and Sydney: Croom Helm, 1985), 106–22.

and *beyond* the common man, whereas she, though springing from the people, moved beyond ordinary human achievement toward saintliness. Napoleon differed also, obviously, from the monarchs of the ancien régime, having achieved his greatness by himself, as an individual, rather than by the grace of God: thus, despite the coup d'état of 18 brumaire 1799 and the establishment of the empire, his image could be exploited in the democratic rhetoric of his century.

There were three principal interpretations of his achievements: Napoleon the military hero (never successfully contested); Napoleon the political hero, viewed positively, as savior of the Revolution and of France, then as emperor; and Napoleon the monster, destroyer of liberty—the view, for instance, of Germaine de Staël. But even those who took this last view had to recognize his prowess. Adolphe Thiers, in his *Histoire du consulat* and *Histoire de l'empire*, condemned Bonaparte's despotism and one-man rule, but praised his military genius and excused Waterloo as the doing of Grouchy. To these three principal interpretations can be added another, the messianic view, by which, as chapter 4 shows, Bonaparte appears as greater-than-life, the representative and savior of a hypostasized ideal nation. Léon Bloy's *L'Ame de Napoléon* (1912), for instance, considers the emperor as the source of *gloire* and *énergie*, whose decline led to "la putréfaction universelle" [universal putrefaction]— even more, as the instrument of God, "le préfigurant de CELUI qui doit venir" [the forerunner of him who is to come].[33]

During his own reign, Bonaparte saw to it that his image, as military leader and sovereign, was widely depicted and distributed, beginning with paintings by Antoine-Jean Gros in 1796, and including works by major painters such as David, Ingres, and Géricault. Architectural monuments, often imitative of the Romans, were part of his personal cult: the triumphal arches in Paris, that of the Carrousel and the Arc de Triomphe, both begun in the first decade of the century (the latter monument was finished under Louis-Philippe); bridges named after his battles—Iéna, Austerlitz; and the Vendôme column, decorated with military scenes and a spiral in metal made from the 1,250 cannons captured at Austerlitz. Napoleon developed an imperial iconography featuring Roman emblems such as the eagle, chariot, laurel crown, Roman hachet, and *faisceaux*, which were noted above as being repub-

33. Quoted in Maurice Bardèche, *Léon Bloy* (Paris: La Table Ronde, 1989), 367.

lican symbols also. Though many of the graphic representations of Napoleon, particularly during his reign, reflect his imperial ambitions and the grand scale of his achievements and aspirations, after his death there developed an enormous vein of popular iconography—including *images d'Epinal*—featuring him, generally in less lofty poses and sometimes with a strong republican motif. Typical is "Napoléon au siège de Toulon": when a cannon-server is injured, he steps in to help. This is the people's Napoleon, the hero worshiped by Julien Sorel in Stendhal's *Le Rouge et le noir*, and by Goguelat in Honoré de Balzac's *Le Médecin de campagne*, the leader who fought against the royalists before assuming imperial authority and who ultimately was recruited for purposes of a rather eclectic, but nonroyalist, patriotism.

Under the restoration of 1815, Napoleonic images were officially replaced by Bourbon ones. Nevertheless, such products as P. J. Béranger's "Le Vieux Drapeau" (1820) and *Souvenirs du peuple* (1828), Emile Debraux's song on "la colonne" (Vendôme), 1818, Charlet's lithograph, "Le Grenadier de Waterloo" (1818), Victor Hugo's "A la colonne de la place Vendôme" (1827) and "Lui" (1829), and Auguste Barthélemy's epic poem *Napoléon en Egypte* (1828), for which the author was imprisoned, revealed nostalgia for Napoleonic grandeur and energy and kept the cult of the empire before public eyes. The return of the emperor's companions in exile in 1821 contributed similarly. Napoleon reappeared in art under the July Monarchy, when paintings of his battles were encouraged, presumably in connection with the resumed imperial aspirations, illustrated in the occupation of Algeria—which also gave rise to its own vein of war painting, in scenes by Horace Vernet and others. Indeed, it may be said that the July Monarchy found the Napoleonic cult useful; it provided a grandeur otherwise missing. Napoleon's statue on the Vendôme column, which had been removed under the Restoration, was replaced by a new one, and in 1840 the emperor's remains were brought back from St. Helena to lie in the Invalides. Bonapartist and royal iconography was succeeded briefly under the Second Republic by republican emblems, only to be replaced in turn, in 1852, by Napoleonic ones again, which Louis-Napoleon cultivated to the maximum, making Bonapartism an orthodoxy.

In texts by detractors and enemies of the Second Empire, Napoleon III appeared often in contradistinction to his uncle, as in Victor Hugo's *Châtiments*. In texts of the Franco-Prussian War, such as Zola's *La Débâcle*, the emperor was a shadowy, lofty figure, in contrast to Louis-Napoleon or "Badinguet," responsible for the defeat. Although in the aftermath of the war, there was discreditation of Bonapartism, especially on the part of radical republicans, such as Jules Vallès, even the Third Republic needed the Napoleonic legend. One of the statues of the emperor was brought up from the Seine, where Communards had thrown it in the spring of 1871, and a replica of the first statue of the emperor on the Vendôme column was placed there. Around the great emperor's image hung a complex of heroism that could be evoked simply by the name of a Napoleonic battle or general. The illustration mentioned earlier showing an execution scene bears the caption: "O braves dont je viens saluer la mémoire / Vous que Hoche ou Desaix eût pris pour compagnons" [O brave ones whose memory I come to salute / You whom Hoche or Desaix would have taken as companions]. Similarly, a painting by Édouard Détaille, "Le Songe," shown in the Salon of 1888, depicts soldiers bivouacking during the Franco-Prussian War, while in the skies above them ride the soldiers of Napoleon's Old Guard, occupying the position of angels in Christian iconography. Whereas Joan of Arc connected French military efforts to the Middle Ages and the forcible removal of the English occupant from France, Napoleon evoked, by the imperial motifs, the wars of conquest of antiquity — hence France as the modern heir of classical grandeur; in this view, the Prussians and other Germans correspond to the barbarians who destroyed the Roman Empire.

Although Napoleon's descendants (principal members of the family) were expelled from France in 1886, starting about 1890 there was tremendous development of Napoleonic motifs, with the emphasis on Napoleon as the architect of French grandeur. Much material appeared concerning Bonaparte: memoirs, letters from Napoleonic generals, histories, novels. One of the best-received creative works of the period was the play by Victorien Sardou and Emile Moreau, *Madame Sans-gêne*, staged in 1893, which gave the emperor himself a central role. Edmond Rostand's stunningly successful play *L'Aiglon*, a historic drama concerning Napoleon's son (the duke of Reichstadt), was produced in 1900. (The cock, Chantecler, in his unsuccessful play of the same title and the figure of Cyrano de Bergerac, who personified the heroism of the past, round out the pantheon of patriotic figures in Rostand's work.) Barrès, in his novel *Les Déracinés* [The uprooted] (1898), at once aggressively regionalistic and nationalistic, called Napoleon a "professeur d'énergie." In a famous passage, seven students take an oath at his tomb, "viennent lui demander de l'élan, lui apportent aussi leur tribut. Sous tous les Napoléons de l'histoire, qu'ils ne contestent pas, mais qui ne les attacheraient pas, ils ont dégagé le *Napoléon de l'âme"* [come to ask him for impetus, come to bring him their tribute also. Under all the Napoleons of history, whom they do not challenge but whom they would not serve, they have discovered the *Napoleon of the soul*].[34]

During the Great War, in *Les Traits éternels de la France* (1916), Barrès noted that Napoleon and his republican generals, like Joan, appealed to the glory of the past, the valor of those soldiers and people who made France; this same spirit was shown by those rushing forward out of the trenches singing "La Marseillaise."[35] Even Hitler, shortly after the fall of France, made use of the Napoleonic legend; in an attempt to appease the French and stress the ties between France and Germany, and possibly to project an imperial vision of himself, he ordered the return of L'Aiglon's ashes from their burial site in Vienna to be reunited with those of his father in the Invalides (December 1940).

To the iconic figures of Joan of Arc and Napoleon, one must add another, that of Roland, long associated with God and monarch but, with the Revolution, turned into a nationalist hero. Harry Redman, Jr. has shown how widespread the Roland legend was in literature and other arts — songs, paintings, opera — from Claude-Joseph Rouget de Lisle's patriotic song composed in 1792 through Lucien Bonaparte's epic *Charlemagne ou l'église délivrée* (1815), sections of Victor Hugo's *La Légende des siècles* (1859), Auguste Mermet's opera *Roland à Roncevaux* (1864), René Fabert's historical drama *Charlemagne* (first performed in 1878, and later turned into an opera), and a story by Anatole France (1893). Even before 1800 Roland "came to be viewed as a militant patriot battling to preserve or extend France's boundaries and rid her soil of enemies."[36] The same use of the paladin as a nationalist, militant hero would reappear in the aftermath of the Franco-Prussian War and before and during the Great War, when Péguy, Barrès, Rostand, and others invoked Roland in their rhetoric and verse.

These figures and strains of imagery — republican, Napoleonic, Johannine,

34. Maurice Barrès, *Les Déracinés* (Paris: E. Fasquelle, 1897), 262–63. On patriotic symbols in Rostand, see Alba della Fazia Amoia, *Edmond Rostand* (Boston: Twayne, 1977), 16, 123.

35. Maurice Barrès, *Les Traits éternels de la France*, ed. Fernand Baldensperger (New Haven: Yale University Press, 1918).

36. Harry Redman, Jr., *The Roland Legend in Nineteenth-Century French Literature* (Lexington: University Press of Kentucky, 1991), 29.

and more generally military—in drawing, painting, sculpture, songs, drama, history, and fiction were an integral part of nineteenth-century national self-consciousness and an ingredient of both defensive and offensive national militarism. They served as a sort of guarantor of French continuity, the outward and visible signs of an inner identity, whose proper government could be disputed but whose cohesion and grand destiny rarely were. They shaped and guided the French imagination throughout the nineteenth cenury and for much of the twentieth; reliance on them was, in some ways, incommensurate with the facts of France's comparative military and economic disadvantages and political heterogeneity. The idea of an authentic French past points to the essentialism that underlay much French thinking throughout the nineteenth and twentieth centuries and that gave rise to the notion of "eternal France."[37] The continued appearance of these symbols, both written and drawn, during the decades following 1900 has constituted a kind of civic and nationalistic text, a constant intertext and self-quotation in products of the imagination and political discourse alike—available to all, cited by those of opposing camps, and affording artists and orators a shorthand route toward moving audiences. Opposed to it, especially after 1918, was the symbolism of refusal: literature and art that was antiwar, antination, often pro-working class, whereby antiestablishment artists rejected the role of spokesman for the national traditions and institutions and sought to redefine the relationship among art, the citizenry, and the world.

37. For an extended analysis of this idea, see Melanie Gordon, " 'Leben wie Gott in Frankreich': German Identity and the Myth of France, 1919–1945," Ph.D. diss., Tulane University, 1998.

3

NARRATIVES OF WAR
Structures and Types

WAR NOVELS AND related works such as short stories, novellas, and personal accounts dealing with battle or wartime may be studied from a number of different perspectives, including the historical one by which they are considered principally as one or more of the following: (1) conveyors or mirrors of events, whether directly or indirectly—usually intended and informed by deliberate subjective judgments, though I do not discount the dimension of the unintended (the author being unaware of implications, biases, subtending ideology); (2) products of events, like other cultural products but more closely related since they take history as their topic and are directly connected to events; (3) "events" themselves that become normative and shape, or are intended to shape, subsequent developments or products. This historical approach, at least in its wide construction, is adopted frequently in the chapters to follow and is implied throughout this study. External questions such as circumstances of production, relation of author to the events in question, and distribution and readership as well as internal matters, including scope of war material and manner of presenting it, are part of the historical picture.

One can adopt, in addition or instead, aesthetic and generic considerations like those one would adopt for study of any other narrative, as well as some internal criteria pertaining especially to the subgenre of war narrative, such as the relationship of the narrative voice to the moral question of war. Interpretation and criticism must take into account such considerations if, in contradistinction to being treated reductively as a vehicle of information, the work is to be dealt with as *literature*—a treatment that recognizes both aesthetic intentions and the validity of subjective experience and its communication through imaginative constructs.

The above manifold approach can be systematized in a taxonomy of the genre, and one of my concerns here is to draw up tentatively such a classificatory structure, without, however, devising names for all the subtypes. While definition and classification are not essential to the appreciation of individual works, they underlie any discussion of the genre as such and any study of its evolution. What in practice distinguishes war fiction from other types of imaginative narrative is a question taken up in the following pages, in addition to a consideration of what characteristics of French war fiction derive from the peculiar circumstances of French history in the mid-twentieth century.

Even when contemporaneous to the event, war fiction is, of course, a subgenre of historical fiction, itself a subgenre of fiction in general, and thus shares features that have been generally, though not uniformly, characteristic of novels, novellas, and short stories in the Occidental tradition from the eighteenth century onward and especially from the mid-nineteenth century. The twentieth-century evolution of fictional modes from inherited realism through modernism—as illustrated, in France, by André Gide, Marcel Proust, certain surrealists, and others—and into postmodernism, with the New Novelists, has been paralleled by developments in war fiction.

The status of historical fiction has not occupied critics in proportion to its interest. It at once lays claim to reality, founded as it is on known events (which are singled out from what precedes, follows, and underlies them and from other components of the historical process), and lays claim also to the absolute of story, which cannot be challenged on factual grounds. (I discount fantasy for purposes of this discussion.) Its structure conventionally depends upon the assumption that history has an ascertainable order, which can be expressed linguistically and to which human action, whether at the center or on the fringes of the event, is related. The tests of truth that apply are of two kinds: the truth of fact (more or less objective and verifiable) and the truth of fiction (however the latter is to be defined and thus tested: persuasiveness, inventiveness, emotional power, moral rectitude, as one wishes). The truth of fact has, or can have, a cognitive dimension: for instance, a recent reader, who can have no experience of trench warfare in the Great War, presumably learns a good deal from reading novels about it, which act as histories. This type of cognitive material does not belong to the truth of fiction, where "cognition" is a matter of understanding and judgment. How far a war novelist, for instance, should undertake to convey fact must be a matter of artistic practice: reproaches for not telling enough about the reasons for a war or the progress of a battle can be made only on the grounds that the reader needs more for comprehension and appreciation; to expect otherwise is to expect the novelist to act like an historian. The work must, however, be grounded in fact ultimately; and how far the novelist can go in ignoring this claim of fact is a question not only of practical aesthetics but of theory, since the question of what distinguishes historical fiction is begged if the author ignores, opposes, or otherwise casts doubt on the historical grounding. The tendency among most writers is not to minimize history but instead to err in the opposite direction: among French war novelists, Honoré de Balzac in *Les Chouans*, Emile Zola (toward the end of *La Débâcle*), and Jules Romains, whose *Prélude à Verdun* is, for many pages, indistinguishable from historical summary, have tended toward bird's-eye panoramas and straight historical narrative.

In historical fiction, the order of imaginative truth coordinates with and interpenetrates the order of fact, as microlevel plot fits into the war, the macroplot. *Micro* and *macro* as used here do not refer to the amounts of invented and historical material that an author uses or to their presence in foreground versus background of narrative, but to particulars, usually invented, as opposed to wholes, normally factual. It may be, of course, that the microplot or invented material is situated on the most global level of the war: for instance, the plot may revolve around major historical figures and actions on which the novelist embroiders the invented particulars. Imaginative truth includes individual experience and the resulting subjective interpretation of history, normally resulting from this experience. What is sometimes called the "worm's-eye view" (in Romains's term, *côté moléculaire*, as opposed to *côté astronomique*) coordinates with or replaces global summaries; abstractions and generalities that would characterize a historical survey are replaced by the concrete; and there is stress on experiential understanding, human process, and subjectivity, the way it shapes and even creates reality, and the manner in which events are experienced from the inside.[1]

1. Jules Romains, *Prélude à Verdun*, vol. 15 of *Les Hommes de bonne volonté* (Paris: Flammarion, 1938), 30.

Whether a narrative consists of mostly invented material or is a memir.... or other semifactual narrative in which the recounting *I* or other subject is quasi-identical to the historical being who lived the experience, it offers a means of seeing not only the raw event but also its reflections and repercussions on the mind. By its traditional double role of looking into the interior workings of human behavior—thought, feeling, motivation—and recounting the doings of human beings in the exterior world through imaginative construction or reconstruction, fiction re-creates the confrontation of person and world. Elsa Triolet, speaking of her own fiction, said that "the novel is the intermediary between man and history."[2]

War fiction deals with a particular type of event, common to every century but also highly conditioned by the material, social, economic, and political facts of the respective periods. It is of necessity concerned with both individual and collectivity: whether or not the collective experience is related in detail, it is implied; there is no such thing as the war of a single man. In this respect, war fiction simply illustrates particularly well a property of fiction in general: except for solipsistic novels—the enclosed, introverted world of exaggerated French Romanticism, as illustrated by Etienne de Senancour, or that of Samuel Beckett's fiction and certain even more extreme postmodernist creations—the purview of fiction is precisely that juncture where individual experience and collective experience converge or conflict. Even in panoramic depictions of wars that deal mostly with actions of groups and masses, there must be some imaginative rendering of human reactions of one or more characters in such a way that the reader feels them. Otherwise, the work fails as literature, or should properly be considered as logbook, chronicle, or other type of historical record or summary.

As I use the term, war fiction appears only after the advent of Romanticism. Although, in France, the term *roman* (novel, as distinguished from the earlier *roman* meaning medieval romance) is used for invented narratives from the seventeenth century on, and in the eighteenth century the genre developed greatly in both types and numbers, its application to either the individual or collective experience of war did not take place until the first part of the nineteenth century. This is almost surely not coincidental: it required the Romantic reshaping of the genre from the psychological novel and novel of

2. Triolet, intro. to *A Fine of 200 Francs*, trans. Francis Golffing.

manners into two new types: the historical novel, under the influence of Walter Scott and then Balzac, as well as the novel governed by subjectivity.

Not every fictional work that alludes to war necessarily should be termed *war fiction*; such mentions can be incidental. Conversely, as I argued in the preface, it does not require battlefront scenes or extensive military considerations for fiction to deserve at least in some manner the label *war novel*, since the war experience has direct and indirect repercussions on virtually all other areas of national life, overflowing the spatial and chronological bounds of the fighting to color what comes before, after, and elsewhere. Thus, to take an obvious example, Roger Martin du Gard's *L'Eté 1914*, a narrative focusing chiefly on the approach of war, belongs in the wide sense in the category under examination, although very little military action, very few scenes from the front, are included.

My choice is to adopt a pragmatic approach toward classification. Simply put, the term *war fiction* should be used for stories and novels whose plot involves, in a manner other than incidental, episodes from war itself, war's imminence or aftermath, or the fringes of war as affected by the conflict. The question of quantity arises. Although one should be cautious in extending the label to works where the war episodes are only part of a plot that is generally directed elsewhere, such works still may deserve consideration, if the episodic material is substantial or presents original ways of viewing or recounting war. The Waterloo episode in Stendhal's *La Chartreuse de Parme* is only a small portion of the plot, and seems only obliquely relevant to the rest; yet it is a significant piece of war writing. Similarly, Victor Hugo's Waterloo section in *Les Misérables* is at once a small portion of the novel and a major reconstitution of the battle. Proust's pages on Paris during World War I, while constituting only a small percentage of his long opus, in fact comprise an extensive piece of writing about wartime and a revealing one.

The central problem of the self, both in relation to others and in its existential autonomy, its identity, and its isolation—so often the source of meaning and values, as well as of anguish, from the Romantics on—can be focalized in its starkest terms in fiction that deals with modern warfare. "Great literary works related to war touch the innermost existence of man and defy the nothingness of human life," wrote Joseph Remenyi. Unlike the social context of the novel of manners, which already exercises considerable pressure on the individual, in the military context opponents hold the potential power of death over the subject, whence the seriousness of every action. Thus what marks war fiction especially is the sense of urgency and ultimate importance of events to individuals, and sometimes the converse—an urgency that the novel of manners cannot furnish, even when dealing with its own types of finality (mainly marriage and property), and that the novel of individual development provides less strikingly, since the circumstances are not so extreme. John Ruskin, writing in 1865, saw the importance of the death threat when he called war a serious game in which a man's true qualities are revealed: "You cannot test these qualities wholly, unless there is a clear possibility of the struggle's ending in death. It is only in the fronting of that condition that the full trial of the man, soul and body, comes out." In other terms, although armed conflict is a collective problem, war fiction lends itself to those limit situations that existentialists favor because they demand difficult and radical choice.[3]

Unless they are very short—vignettes, brief stories—and sometimes even then, war narratives are inevitably shaped and colored by either affirmation or denial of a collective purpose or meaning that presides over the conflict. Even when a purpose is affirmed, there is usually an explicit, but always an implicit, opposite purpose or adversarial position qualifying the first. Heroes may ultimately affirm or deny the nation's dominant purpose. This quality is both teleological and ideological; at the extreme, it is theology or mythification. Hayden White is one of numerous modern historians who have argued that narrative discourse, far from being a neutral medium for the representation of historical events and processes, is the stuff of what he calls a "mythical" view of reality.[4] I shall return later to this question.

Fiction is not alone, of course, in seeing or providing purpose and ideology; to narrate anything is to interpret, and all literary and journalistic language must reflect personal choices. Even when historical readings seem to rely on objective data about the past, they also are charged with assumptions, although, as I indicated in the preface, I do not go so far as to accept the radical position of certain New Historicists to the effect that present ideologi-

3. Joseph Remenyi, "The Psychology of War Literature," *Sewanee Review* 52 (1944), 147; Ruskin, *Crown of Wild Olive*, 114.

4. Hayden V. White, *Tropics of Discourse* (Baltimore: Johns Hopkins University Press, 1978), 124–25.

cal interferences prevent all genuine contact with the past and distort every attempt to retrieve it. The writing of history, also, has always involved the imaginative and the emotional. As James Olney puts it, "The writers of history organize the events of which they write according to, and out of, their own private necessities and the state of their own selves."[5]

The creative vision that joins event to individual experience is the same vision that controls the work's form. Like all artistic forms, however, the vision that shapes the datum and governs its imaginative recreation is historically conditioned, even as it may go beyond historical fact. That relationships can be found between the historical and cultural facts of wars and the ways in which wars are recounted should surprise no one; I spoke earlier of fiction as product of history. Among these facts are not only those of the global event as well as particulars concerning the war's characteristics, purposes, and the means of waging it, but also popular and official attitudes toward the conflict, the concept of the nation behind it, and the entire cultural context, including the literary forms available for the writer. As an example of the relationship to which I am alluding, one has only to consider, for instance, Balzac's understanding of and judgment on historical event—and his consequent use of the historical novel—as illustrated in *Les Chouans*, where the governing vision is a coherent, recuperable understanding of France and its destiny. (When the novel first appeared, under the title *Le Dernier Chouan*, this vision was a republican one, tinged with admiration for Napoleon, the strong man who could consolidate republican achievements and put an end to social turmoil and guerrilla warfare. By 1834, the date of the revised version, Balzac had turned away from republican liberalism to adopt legitimist principles, although he never lost his fascination with Napoleon.) One can then compare Balzac's treatment of war and nation with twentieth-century ones, such as Henri Barbusse's *Le Feu* and Claude Simon's *La Route des Flandres*, in which traditional understandings of novel, war, and nation are simultaneously called into question.

One development warrants special attention. The rise of the individual under the great impetus of Romanticism and liberal revolution at the end of the eighteenth century and throughout the following decades—and the con-

5. James Olney, *Metaphors of Self: The Meaning of Autobiography* (Princeton: Princeton University Press, 1972), 36.

current creation of new literary modes and forms—were paralleled by changes in battle tactics that brought this new individual into a different position. Keegan and Holmes elaborate: "Regulations designed to keep dull-witted conscripts together on the shoulder-to-shoulder battlefields of the blackpowder era are inappropriate in an age when weapons and tactics demand dispersion on the battlefield, and when initiative may be more important than blind obedience."[6] This development of the individual's role in battle had further military and cultural consequences, including the need and opportunity for greater personal intitiative in war, greater isolation of the fighting men, and the tendency for them to act and judge with self-reliance. World War I trench fighting, with its dispersion on the one hand and its immensity on the other, then foxhole and other individual combat of the sort carried out in World War II and the ensuing conflicts in Asia—a style that created small groups of two or three and discrete actions—produced extremes of behavior: courage, heroism, difficult moral choices in the name of the collective purpose or, just as frequently perhaps, for the sake of "buddies"—the few who share space with each other, the few among whom there is a sense of solidarity. In contrast, these modern modes of warfare gave rise equally to alienation from and rejection of collective purposes and military codes in the name of this same atomization and isolation, and sometimes moral and military abuses. Guerrilla warfare—in its modern form, partly a product of the Napoleonic Wars, during the occupation of Spain—and other types of irregular combat are extreme examples of this development: the single guerrilla fighter or small band makes its own judgments, often going against standard military practice and authority. Civil insurrections involve, by definition, such irregular fighting. No better illustrations can be found than during the German occupation of France in 1940–1945, when individuals took it upon themselves to attack what they considered the occupying enemy, and armed bands in the maquis waged guerrilla warfare. In fiction, the associated developments can be seen in both content and form, with individual and often semi-isolated combatants occupying the center of the narrative, and a single and direct linear narrative thread being replaced often by multiple plots and types of fictional incoherence.

A similar breakdown occurred, starting after Napoleon, in the relationship

6. Keegan and Holmes, *Soldiers*, 56.

between leader and men: that is, between national authority and will in its outward and visible signs, and those assigned to carry it out. Whereas the emperor on the battlefield had overseen the whole and established visually a tie between himself and his troops—"Chef suprême . . . joueur d'échecs que son génie illumine devant les figures instantanées du jeu" [Supreme chief . . . chess player whose genius enlightens him before the instantaneous patterns of the game]—after the defeat at Sedan in September 1870 and the abdication of Louis-Napoleon, the tie began to loosen.[7] Zola shows well in *La Débâcle* how the ailing ruler made pointed appearances in the villages around the area of engagement and attempted pathetically and futilely to exercise leadership from behind a curtain. During the two world wars generals did not ordinarily appear on the battlefield, and "château-general" became a bitter joke.

This distancing is in part, of course, as much an effect of changed technology as of a different order of human participation. Speaking of the impossibility for an officer to view the entirety of a World War I battle area, Romains wrote: "Le chef le reconstituait péniblement—paisiblement—dans le salon désaffecté d'une villa provinciale, à l'aide d'une grande carte épinglée au mur, et de télégrammes abstraits qu'un officier venait de temps en temps jeter sur une table" [The commander reconstituted it with difficulty—calmly—in the unused parlor of a provincial house, with the help of a big map pinned to the wall and abstract telegrams that an officer came to throw onto the table from time to time]. The commander can grasp neither the whole, which he cannot see, nor the detail: "le fait de guerre lui-même, vécu par l'homme, antérieur aux télégrammes et aux rapports . . . Plus l'action sur le front même devenait intense, plus il devenait difficile de la percevoir dans sa particularité véritable" [the fact itself of war, experienced by men, prior to telegrams and reports . . . The more intense action at the front became, the harder it became to perceive it in its true particularity]. An order given in such circumstances sets in motion an invisible and immeasurable series of actions: "Le chef pouvait déclencher la bataille. Mais ensuite il se faisait un peu l'effet de l'homme qui vient d'ouvrir un barrage énorme au-dessus d'une vallée habitée. . . . La bataille, une fois allumée, fulgure, serpente, crépite, moitié comme on a voulu, moitié comme elle veut" [The commander could set off the battle. But then there was something like the effect of a man who has just opened an enor-

7. Romains, *Prélude à Verdun*, 36.

mous dam above an inhabited valley. . . . Once lit, the battle moves like light-
ning, winds, crackles, halfway as one wanted, halfway as it wants].[8]

Those even farther removed from the conflict—the contemporary political
leaders and bureaucrats in the capital, the strategists who pressed the button,
as it were—were so alienated from the war, or from the way combatants perceived it usually, that their sense of nation and national purpose and values
could be entirely different from those of the participants to whom their decisions were transmitted. This remoteness had likewise been the case, to be
sure, during the dynastic warfare of the pre-Revolutionary period; but the
soldiers of the past two hundred years, as citizens, have been in a position to
perceive and reject the official rationale for war as their forerunners were not.
The result was often epistemological and narrative difficulty like that I
stressed earlier and a moral gulf, reflected in fictional form. War narratives
of the twentieth century, from Jean Giono's *Le Grand Troupeau* through Tim
O'Brien's *The Things They Carried*, express this division between nation and
agents; characteristically, they are decentralized works in which such devices
as enumeration, repetition, rhetorical denial, dispersal of plot, rejection of
character (as fictional function or human concept), and disarticulation of syntax correspond to the changes in fighting techniques and the absence of authority.

———

Although it is doubtless risky to propose a distinctive structural model for the
war novel, I should like to explore its possibilities, using some of the notions
of narratology. This model can serve as a guide for reading war fiction in general and certain examples of the subgenre in particular, and for identifying
radical departures from the model. I do not propose, however, to apply the
model rigorously and mechanically throughout the rest of this study, since
there is no need to do so and many aspects of the works to be examined over-
flow the structural skeleton.

Narrative is a form of understanding and explanation; one constantly tells
stories to oneself and to friends, arranging the past in an attempt to grasp it.
Imagination—not gratuitous embroidering, but picturing to oneself through

8. Ibid., 29–30.

mental, hence verbal, images—is a part of this telling. Fictional (that is, fictitious) narratives of events, which may have a substantial basis in fact but do
not, I have said, occupy the status of information, are constructed by the author from the start to constitute a reconstruction of event and an assigning of
meaning (explicit or implicit ideology) by means of invention and manipulation of characters and plot. By ideology I mean a body of common beliefs,
usually political, religious, ethical, or economic, as a system of referents and
a foundation for action. Plot—the "logic and dynamic of narrative," in Peter
Brooks's phrase—is not just an organizing structure; it is goal-oriented, and
the goal is to make the events recounted available, in the fullest sense possible, to consciousness.[9] This plot logic need not be, of course, linear or otherwise rigid; "logic" in aesthetic construction is not identical to analytical thinking and exposition. In any historical narrative, plot structuring, added to pre-
given historical events, highlights some facts and eliminates others, in view of
producing a conclusion that fits the historical context but also has its own
teleology, according to the author's conscious or unconscious ideological bias
(more on this distinction later). It is, of course, the historical novelist's role to
re-create the past—the plot of fact, or macroplot—on its own terms as well
as his, unless the presumption of authenticity is to be sacrificed, a strategy
that will elicit from readers an entirely different response.

   War texts—including chronicles and histories—have generally been structured on a basic pattern of opposition: a dualism fundamental to the undertaking of war itself, which opposes one group to another violently, but fundamental also, it would seem, to the very idea of narration, and thus singularly
fitting, even exemplary. In the psychological novel, such as *La Princesse de
Clèves*, opposition and conflict are chiefly internal. In the social novel and
novel of manners, although there may be ideological conflicts, oppositional
patterns arise generally from the interference between subjects, acting individually, on the one hand, and opponents, sometimes representing social ob-
stacles, on the other. Since, however, the novel of war (and of revolution) is
defined by such opposition, contextual conflicts are even more crucial, always
involving confrontation between one's own cause and the enemy's, and nearly
always, conflicts between individuals in the same camp; and the confrontations are acted out in violent ways. Moreover, the teleology is not just an indi-

   9. Peter Brooks, *Reading for the Plot: Design and Intention in Narrative* (New York: Knopf,
1984), 10, 12, 34.

vidual one (the aim of making one's fortune, or marrying well) or a social one (such as to restore threatened institutions); it is collective, national, and thus historical.

Narration is, of course, sequential, at least in some sense: one follows (or subverts but acknowledges) a sequence, fixed by the author except in post-modernist "deck of cards" novels; and normally, even when "story" (what happened) is not identical to "narration" (order of telling), there is a chain of events, which operates through causal relationships. This is true even if the narration — or, to use Gérard Genette's well-known term, *récit* — does not conform to the order established in the story or *histoire*. Positioned along this chain is a system of functions, or in A. J. Greimas's terms, actants, which include subjects (or "heroes"), objects of the action, helpers, *opposants* (adversaries), senders, and receivers (to which action is directed).[10] This nomenclature and the analysis it allows are critically convenient because they assist one in describing "lines of force" other than the rudimentary ones of hero and adversary, and thus are particularly advantageous in historical fiction, in which public and private matters, collectivities and individuals, and large-scale events and developments intersect variously. Receivers of a military action can, for instance, be or be perceived as the nation for which the men are fighting, or as ideas, their officers, their social class, or themselves. Senders can likewise be the nation or class (in civil warfare), or an idealized history, or God, or some other determining agent — even a hypostasized evil. (The motivation can thus be circular: the nation *sends* its soldiers to fight *for* the nation.) The more complex field of novelistic forces that characterizes much French fiction beginning with Romantic realism (Balzac and Stendhal) — incorporating variously, sometimes in the same work, two or three social classes, multiple social institutions, multiple political forces and ideologies, and events both in France and outside — marks off the genre from its seventeenth- and eighteenth-century precedessors by implying a different understanding of fictional causation and requiring a more complex analysis; in particular, the idea of nation, which from the Revolution onward was reinvented, assumed a fictional presence that the model I have proposed helps describe.

· 10. A. J. Greimas, *Sémantique structurale* (Paris: Larousse, 1966), trans. Daniele McDowell, Ronald Schleifer, and Alan Velie as *Structural Semantics* (Lincoln: University of Nebraska Press, 1983), chap. 10; Gérard Genette, *Figures III* (Paris: Editions du Seuil, 1972), part. trans. Jane E. Lewin as *Narrative Discourse: An Essay in Method* (Ithaca: Cornell University Press, 1980).

Whether these functions are abstract or concrete, whether or not they are symbolized or allegorized in the narrative—as they are in graphic works that personify France as the female figure of Marianne or "La Marseillaise," for instance—they exert their influence in any historical fiction by the very nature of historical action. Through their interplay, the functions provide the elements of plot progression toward an end, either furthering or opposing it. These functions may be collective or individual. In analyzing the taking of the Bastille, the principal and now prototypical crowd action of French history, Sartre argued that it was truly a collective act by what he calls a "fused group," expressing an embodied general will, not the action of a leader and followers.[11] But whereas painted crowd scenes were popular in the Revolutionary and Napoleonic period, and crowds remain today a favorite device of many cinematographers, practice has shown that the effective creation of collective subjects in fiction is difficult, although Zola's success in portraying crowds is noteworthy. Authors wishing to animate a collective force usually fall back upon a few representatives that occupy the foreground, while the collectivity remains in the background, suggested or abstract rather than fully portrayed.

To the basic structure are joined metaphors, tropes, patterns, and other decorative or compositional elements, articulated into the rest, which contribute to the whole and convey a personal vision—that of one or more characters, that (ordinarily) of the author. There may be ambiguity, because of the tensions between the different lines and modes of structuring; but there is a tendency toward closure, which points to the practical fact that events do have beginnings and ends and to the human desire to shape time, as well as toward totalization. These literary elements, which can be used only sparingly in an historical account but purport nevertheless to render reality, often tend, paradoxically, to underline their own inadequacies as historical representation, while helping to define historical experience.

While Greimas calls the relationship between subjects and objects *desire*, I prefer the term *will* or *purpose*; and because war, unlike random violence or the use of force in primitive societies, is carried out in the name of a state, for generalized political ends, in the war novel this will is directed, in part at least, toward assumption, resumption, extension, or redefinition of collective

11. Jean-Paul Sartre, *Critique de la raison dialectique* (Paris: Gallimard, 1960), 416.

power, by way of a military goal, which furnishes both narrative and historical teleology, about which I shall say more in a moment.

In a progression of will, the beginning leads by cause and effect into intermediate actions and reactions, such as false starts, confrontations, crises, trials, perhaps partial success, or reversals and failures, then new attempts,
thence to the end or closure. The articulated or interfering functions can include subsets of opposing forces, such as rivalries among men in the same
ranks (often on ethnic or social grounds), or between enlisted men and officers, or among large fighting groups, or political forces shaping the war; in
twentieth-century war fiction, the struggles are often psychological, and the
self, as I have suggested, becomes the ultimate battleground.

The goal or object of will or purpose—which justifies ostensibly the loss
of life—is defined by the ideological elements in an oppositional structure,
explicit or implicit, that runs parallel to the opposing functions. This structure
on the level of idea underlines the dualistic, binary essence of war fiction.
Both ideological thesis and goal are normally identifiable at the diegetic
level—that is, at least the ostensible purpose to the war is usually indicated—
but the goal may be qualified by authorial statement or implication. In addition, on the plot level, conflicting goals may exist, such as disagreement with
the war leading to desertion or sabotage; and there may be complicating subsets of purpose, including the desire simply to save one's skin and those numerous cases where combatants are indifferent to the collective ends of the
war but have their own aims that it can fulfill. An unequivocal ideology does
not necessarily produce a propagandistic fiction, although the risk is there.

Certain moments and actions on the plot axis characterize many examples
of war fiction and can be considered as structural tropes or clichés. (The fact
that they are not without parallels in epic battle passages underlines the generic connection between epic and novel.) Among them are: introduction into
a barracks or unit, and initiation (often painful) into its rules, habits, and esprit de corps; conflicts with fellow soldiers or officers; receiving of orders;
preparation for battle; and especially, the eve of the engagement—a moment
that focuses attention on war's essential function of taking life, and its moral,
national, sentimental, and physical implications for the participants. To conclude part 1 of *La Débâcle*, for instance, Zola has a superb "battle's eve" episode, situated before Sedan; one of his heroes falls asleep, but the other, despite his fatigue, watches and reflects on how the encounter will take place

and its inevitable consequences. (Whether Zola intended it thus or not, the passage is constructed on the model of the Garden of Gethsemane scene.) Communality versus conflict on the microlevel mirror their opposition on the macrolevel of international relations. The appearance on the plot line of non-military actions or considerations (erotic love, family, rivalries, other concerns or interferences from private life or behind the lines) is common. Meetings with civilians, especially women, and encounters with those taken to be spies characterize many plots through the Great War at least. (The fact that the supposed spies are often women reveals the cultural connection between attributed patriotic/political and erotic promiscuity.) Other such tropes include the stages of the engagement with the enemy—usually with a baptism of fire for one character at least—pursuit or withdrawal, wounding or death of some participants (often one's fellows and enemy both), mopping up, final success, failure, or ambiguous outcome. There may be, either during or after fighting, some sort of conversion. Since genuine heroism (not just thoughtless risking of life) is an elitist position, involving the concept of superiority (over nature, over others), it requires challenges on the plot level and usually appears only after a personal ordeal constituting a break with previous actions or with others' behavior.

Similar postbattle actions include writing to next-of-kin and gathering belongings of the dead, transfer to another theatre of action or unit, "moments of truth" marked by disabusement or elation. Variations on these patterns are innumerable, with mutations of the basic trajectory reappearing sometimes within the same novel. The plot then moves toward closure, which consists of transformation, reaffirmation, recognition, victory, apotheosis, or defeat, or some other form of the affirmation of either thesis or (if the subject has been converted to the opposing ideology) its antithesis, either of which is prolonged into a limitless future. In some cases there may be reconciliation or partial synthesis, a resolution of the collective or individual elements of conflict.

The ideology—which is above or beyond the facts of action—tends in war fiction to be transcendent, insofar as the idea of nation or other sender or receiver is a transcendent one, as it has been for millenia and continues to be in many quarters. When the transcendent aims of war are accepted by author and/or senders or receivers, the sacrifice of individuals is justified with respect to one-half of the binary opposition. The transcendent purpose does not necessarily conform to immediate, obvious goals of individuals; a higher syn-

thesis may preside over the antagonism of thesis and antithesis. The p ‗‗‗‗
for such divergence is found in the Old Testament, where Jehovah's way of
handling the Hebrews' military dilemmas is not what they ask for. Victor
Hugo revived this dialectic in his interpretation of Napoleon's defeat. Similarly, Zola, writing in 1892, twenty-one years after a defeat that had amputated and bled France, saw the Franco-Prussian War in a dialectical light, as
divine punishment for the sins of France; this did not mean, of course, that
he had adopted a Bismarckian vision of Europe with a subservient France,
but rather had a higher idea of his nation's destiny: having been cleansed by
such bloodletting, France would reassume its true colors and its rightful position on the European political and ideological landscape. (There is considerable resemblance between this understanding of the war and that displayed
by numerous essayists and journalists after the 1940 defeat of France.) Alternatively, a war work may reject both sides absolutely and opt for a higher
ideology such as internationalism or pacifism. Walt Whitman's lines from
"Reconciliation" suggest such synthesis:

> Word over all, beautiful as the sky,
> Beautiful that war and all its deeds of carnage
> must in time be utterly lost
>
> .   .   .   .
>
> For my enemy is dead, a man divine as myself is dead,
> I look where he lies white-faced and still in the coffin—I draw near,
> Bend down and touch lightly with my lips the white face in the coffin.[12]

Barbusse's *Le Feu* contains elements of this ideological leap beyond the struggle of French against German.

Prior to the modern period, in European accounts of war such as chronicles, histories, and poems, the teleology was furnished normally by an eschatological rationale or vision built on a theological foundation such as the establishment of a divine-right monarch, reassertion of feudal rights springing
from divine will, the imposition of Christianity, or protection of a nation-
state. When the belief system is explicitly theological, wars are declared as

---

12. Walt Whitman, *Leaves of Grass*, ed. Emory Holloway (Garden City, N.Y.: Doubleday,
1926), 269.

acts of God—the supreme subject—and human beings serve merely as agents of His greater power; this, it was observed, was the position of Joseph de Maistre, and it underlines, of course, the historical books of the Hebrews. The advantage to such a teleology is that it operates on both the individual and the collective scales: as each finite destiny moves out from its closure into the infinite destiny of the final end, of which it is a part, a universal purpose is being advanced.

With the creation of popular government and the rise of post-Revolutionary nationalism in Europe after 1789, the teleology became generally more narrowly political. Added to visions of nationalistic or pan-ethnic consolidation or aggrandizement were dreams of socialist states, or of the sheer defense of the nation against invaders, in the name of a collectivity but with individuals' concerns and destinies ("Liberté") often singled out as they were not in earlier periods. Although they underlie much thinking on war of the last two hundred years, such nationalist visions are not painted ordinarily in broad strokes in modern war fiction, since they normally go without saying—the purposes of defending France, for instance, needing no exposition. (To be sure, French novels inspired by socialist realism, such as *Les Communistes* and others by Louis Aragon, tend on the contrary to be heavy-handed in dealing with the ideal of nation.) Official propaganda, journalism, and popular art are more likely to display the blunt lines of teleology, in crude terms. It will be noted, however, that during World War I even serious work by artists and writers from the Allied side was marked by references to God and Christ versus Satan, which had the effect of painting a nationalistic conflict as a great moral and theological struggle. Romains ironized on this rhetoric: "Dieu était sommé d'exister . . . non certes pour juger entre les deux causes, mais pour les épouser l'une comme l'autre et s'en faire le champion" [God was commanded to exist . . . certainly not to judge between the two causes, but to espouse both of them and become their champion].[13]

———

With these observations in mind concerning structure and ideology in war narratives, I should like to consider the subgenre from another point of view,

13. Romains, *Prélude à Verdun*, 29.

the pragmatic one of classification of types, following (roughly) the definition of war fiction proposed earlier. No literary historian has yet, to my knowledge, proposed a thorough taxonomy of the French war novel and its subtypes. The following is an attempt to do so, using criteria other than structure. It is suitable especially to twentieth-century examples, which range widely—I draw in particular from the large corpus of novels concerning 1939–1945—but in some instances is applicable also to other periods. My point is not to force works into categories or to limit ways of analyzing them—still less, to restrict the corpus of war writing to works that fit a formula. But analytical classification serves to bring to readers' attention the features of individual works and trends in types, as well as emphasizing that characteristics and meaning are often a function of these criteria.

The quantity of material relating to war in a given work, the manner of presentation, the ways in which the events and experiences relating to war function in the text, the attitudes of the characters and, when visible, the author, and other factors not only warrant examination as part of the historical approach, which I set forth at the outset of this chapter, but can also be used as criteria for a typology. Of course, the typology itself is historically pertinent and can affect reading of the work in question. War novels and stories can be usefully classified by several external criteria, including: (1) *time of composition:* whether before or after the cessation of hostilities (or, in fantasy novels, a war that is future with respect to time of composition)—thus, whether the writing is sufficiently removed from the conflict for subsequent historical factors to influence its presentation (as with Martin du Gard's *L'Eté 1914*), or perhaps long after, when all witnesses are deceased; and, in the case of narratives published some time after, date of composition vs. publication date (as with Marguerite Duras's *La Douleur*, a diary-type text written, she says, at an undetermined date in the past, published only in 1985), and the age of the writer with respect to the events (those who had some experience of the war in question vs. those very young or not yet born); (2) *circumstances of publication and reception:* the author's status with respect to the conflict, the possibility of his reaching an appreciative audience, or, in the case of World War II fiction, whether the works were passed by the censor and appeared in censored form, were published abroad or by a clandestine press in France, and what the reception was; and, for later works, the mood in France at time of publication; (3) *acquaintance of the author with war:* whether the writer had combat experience of the particular conflict or another (as Stendhal, for instance, had *not* participated in the battle of Waterloo but was not unfamiliar with the Napoleonic armies—whereas Tolstoy, the author of one of the greatest fictional evocations of war, wrote well after the period); (4) *historical grounding:* whether the work was based on research as well as, or instead of, experience.

Readers of a war novel would normally wish to know something of such circumstances as well as have general knowledge of the events, to facilitate reading in general—including the coordination, within the plot, of history and invented matter. They also could utilize such knowledge to assess, for instance, the probable accuracy of certain depictions, the bias (explicit or otherwise) that the work might exhibit, the need for critical or ironic ("defensive") reading, and the significance the work may have had for its contemporaneous readers. A pertinent case is that of Antoine de Saint-Exupéry's *Pilote de guerre*, dealing with the battle for France in May–June 1940: it was composed in 1941 in New York, published in 1942 in both the French original and English translation in New York as well as clandestinely in French in Lyons, brought out contemporaneously in English in London that year (thus made available to be adopted as a statement of patriotism by French exiles), then passed by the censor and republished openly in Paris in French, only to be withdrawn from circulation after its contents attracted attention from German authorities less friendly toward the book's implications, and subsequently republished in an underground edition in Lille. As S. Beynon John has pointed out, the outlook of the book does not reflect accurately the changes that took place in France in the months right after the action of the book but, rather, later events, some contemporary with its composition—the founding of France Libre (the Free French movement) in England, the success of the British in the Battle of Britain, the increasing support in the United States for the Allied cause.[14] What some critics see as the ambiguity of the novel, praising the French people without taking a political position, honoring patriotism and sacrifice on the one hand while having a distinctly defeatist note on the other, is reflected in its reception and its destiny in France in 1942. What the book was intended to mean and for whom, and what it means now, depends on this publication history and one's reading of it.

14. S. Beynon John, "Saint-Exupéry's *Pilote de guerre*—Testimony, Art and Ideology," in Kedward and Austin, eds., *Vichy France and the Resistance*, 101.

The degree to which narratives parallel the author's own experience—that is, their greater or lesser autobiographical quality—is particularly significant for purposes of reading and of placing the work in a historical context. Many works in the twentieth-century corpus are personal narratives, based on the author's thinly-veiled or clearly transposed experience, or resembling a feature-journalism account or *reportage* (for instance, books by Henri Barbusse, Jean Cocteau, Louis-Ferdinand Céline, Jules Roy, Joseph Kessel, and others) or a diary (*La Douleur* by Duras). In these first-person narratives, usually limited in range of action and characters, there is a presumption of veracity and authenticity, hence of authority, especially when readers can establish the quasi-identity of main character and author, as in Roy's *La Vallée heureuse*, Saint-Exupéry's *Pilote de guerre*, and Duras's volume, in all of which the speaker is identified as the author. Along with the implied authority, however, is the risk of bias. Contrasted to this type is the impersonal novel, often a wide fresco with a considerable cast of characters and multiple plots, narrated in the third person; examples are Sartre's *Le Sursis* and *La Mort dans l'âme*, Zola's *La Débâcle*, and Victor Hugo's rendition of the Battle of Waterloo in *Les Misérables*. The form of the impersonal novel does not, however, rule out authority: in the last two examples, the pretense to authenticity is even greater than in some personal narratives, since the author adopts the anonymous third person and objective sources are cited (maps, eyewitness accounts); there is also a dimension of completeness not available through the narrative of a single witness or participant.

Other factors to consider, though they cannot alone create a distinct type of war novel, are stylistic ones: the dominance of plain style in contrast to elaborate writing with long complex sentences and parenthetical elements; standard syntax opposed to elaborate or disarticulated syntax as illustrated by modernist and postmodernist writers; popular language or slang as opposed to elevated speech (Henry de Montherlant's *Le Songe*, for instance). The audience for a work, the relationship between author and reader, and the role and success of a work's "message" or ideology depend considerably upon such stylistic choices. *Les Centurions*, Jean Lartéguy's straightforward novel of combat in Indochina, sold extremely well, as did works by Kessel and Romain Gary dealing with the Resistance; part of their success was due doubtless to the prestige of the respective authors and the actions recounted, but part almost surely was due to their plain style and linear composition. Barbusse's *Le Feu* was popular because of the positions it adopted; it also appealed, as did René Benjamin's *Gaspard*, by the use of military slang and popular speech, which suggested authenticity and concern for the common soldiers. (*Le Feu* deserves mention as one of the works that in the early twentieth century helped break down the canons of taste and high style in fictional language, which had persisted throughout the nineteenth century.) Claude Simon's *La Route des Flandres*, while incorporating some of the military slang of the 1939 war, embeds this in a stream-of-consciousness style, highly complex and with few markers such as punctuation and transition sentences, so that the work is accessible only to those readers well versed in modernist style; it creates its own sort of elitist reader, against a background of a war that eroded such differences.

Other compositional choices may be similarly significant, affording subcategories by which to analyze works. The choice of analeptic (retrospective) narration versus simultaneous narration and the place of war episodes on the chronological axis of a work may be significant. Whether or not there is quasi-identity between author and narrator or hero, and whatever the judgments implied, events of war narrated shortly after their occurrence—especially those *written* shortly after their occurrence—inevitably are seen in a light different from that shed, intentionally or otherwise, by retrospective narration and especially if the account is composed well after the event. Balzac's understanding of the civil wars in the Vendée, which took place at the time of his birth, was partly a function of the evolving politics in the following decades. Victor Hugo's and Zola's understanding of Waterloo and the Franco-Prussian War, respectively, was shaped by the decades that had intervened between the events and their writing, just as Martin du Gard's *L'Eté 1914* was—as the author made clear—colored greatly, first by the events that had taken place between 1914 and the end of the war and then by those between 1918 and the mid-1930s, when he composed it. Jules Roy's narratives about the air campaigns of World War II written in the mid-1940s vary considerably from those of the late 1960s and 1970s, when the development of Franco-German relationships in the context of NATO and the European Economic Community gave an entirely different coloring to the Franco-German question, and when his lengthy reflections on the morality of bombing dictated very different ways of handling plot and character.

The place of war episodes in any story that includes other types of experience is also significant. In novels of the fresco or picaresque type that include war episodes but deal with other topics and events also—for instance, Céline's *Voyage au bout de la nuit*, which has a lengthy section on World War I, and Simon's *La Route des Flandres*, which appears to be set in wartime, but whose action goes back to the prewar era and which in fact takes place afterwards—the position of the war episodes on the story axis of the work and the relationship of these episodes to the rest of the action are normally determinative of plot and character. The disabused attitudes of Céline's hero Bardamu and the maladjustment from which he suffers at each turn (a maladjustment that may be his or society's) are to be seen as a function of the absurdity of the war experience he has undergone, just as the quest of Simon's hero Georges for Corinne after the war is an outcome of what he learned and dreamt obsessively in the prisoner-of-war camp.

Works can usefully be classed also by historical and chronological parameters of the events treated and by the author's area of emphasis, which sometimes point to popularity of topics and controversial issues: for example, fiction dealing with the events leading up to a war (most of Erckmann-Chatrian's *Waterloo* fits this pattern, nearly all of Martin du Gard's *L'Eté 1914*, all of Sartre's *Le Sursis*) and, for World War II, novels dealing with the bizarre "phoney war," such as Julien Gracq's *Un Balcon en forêt*, in contradistinction to those that deal with combat proper; novels concerned with the early stages of World War I, such as Benjamin's *Gaspard*, contrasted with those of stalemated trench warfare or those of the major battles of 1916 and 1917; works treating occupation or the aftermath of war (to take two examples only, Guy de Maupassant's "Mademoiselle Fifi" and Simone de Beauvoir's *Les Mandarins*; the latter is scarcely a war novel, but since the early action is situated in 1944–1945, it is in part a work of *wartime*).

Another factor by which to classify war fiction of any period is its relationship to ideology. Some war fiction is, of course, only occasionally ideological, emphasizing rather the *action* of combat; although there is ultimately an underlying telos and outlook in such works, events and character, referring to nothing beyond themselves, dominate. Other works are more meditative than directly ideological. Yet the explicitly ideological novel, in which the sense of history, a political ideology, or a personal ideological message is drawn from and presides over the war narrative, is a common type from Zola on. At its most extreme, the ideological war novel becomes, as I suggested earlier, the *roman à thèse*, as in Aragon's *Les Communistes*. More nuanced examples are offered by André Malraux, Saint-Exupéry, and Céline. In all three, there is a tendency toward mythifying the historical experience, as in Malraux's *Les Noyers de l'Altenburg*, which is often criticized as being over-intellectual and ponderous, although the discerning Malraux critic Robert Thornberry has called its central section "magnificent."[15] This tendency became even clearer decades later in Malraux's *Lazare*, in which he rewrote World War I episodes of *Les Noyers* in the context of a meditation on history, death, and himself. Similarly, in Michel Tournier's *Le Roi des aulnes* and Simon's *La Route des Flandres*, myth and archetypes are integral, not merely ornamental.

The political or other ideological contents are commonly arranged on an axis of oppositions created by the characters' positions (usually, by extension, the author's). In fiction concerned with the Franco-Prussian War, one finds on the one hand chauvinism, as in Daudet's story "La Mort de Chauvin," whose character's name has become synonymous with exaggerated patriotism and the call for revenge; and on the other hand, explicit or implicit condemnation of war (as in numerous stories by Maupassant), whether or not in the name of patriotism. Novels dealing with the Great War include works that glorify the experience, even if for idiosyncratic reasons (Montherlant's *Le Songe*), or poeticize it (Cocteau's *Thomas l'imposteur*), in contradistinction to those expressing a dutiful patriotism or the condemnation of war (Barbusse's *Le Feu*). With respect to World War II, the political range reaches from the extreme right—Céline, notably, although his positions were idiosyncratic and he was not a Vichyite—to orthodox Communist positions, of which Aragon's sections on war in *Les Communistes* offer a striking example, with various shadings in between. For this last conflict, one could consider, similarly, positions taken on the Jewish question, from the aggressive anti-Semitism of Céline to the espousal of the Jewish experience by Elie Wiesel.

The historical and ideological typology for World War II novels is especially fragmented and complicated, given the political complexities of that conflict and the Occupation. Among the types are:

(1) Novels and novellas of combat in 1940, the exodus, and the defeat (Robert Merle's *Week-end à Zuydcoote*, Sartre's *La Mort dans l'âme*, and

15. Robert S. Thornberry, "André Malraux," in Brosman, *French Novelists, 1930–1960*, 262.

Simon's *La Route des Flandres*), and of the Occupation (Beauvoir's *Le Sang des autres* and Vercors's *Le Silence de la mer* and other stories);

(2) Novels and novellas of the Resistance and the *maquis*—that is, concerning what was in some ways a *civil* war under military occupation by a foreign power—whether entirely favorable to the movement (such as Gary's *Education européenne*, Kessel's *L'Armée des ombres* and *Le Bataillon du ciel*, Triolet's *Le Premier Accroc coûte deux cents francs*, and Roger Frison-Roche's *Les Montagnards de la nuit*), or somewhat critical (as in Roger Vailland's *Drôle de jeu* and Jean-Louis Curtis's *Les Forêts de la nuit*); Pierre-Henri Simon's *Histoire d'un bonheur* belongs to this general category;

(3) Air war novels (Saint-Exupéry's *Pilote de guerre* and Roy's *La Vallée heureuse*);

(4) Novels and novellas about prisoners of war (the two volumes by Sartre and Claude Simon just mentioned, Vercors's *Les Armes de la nuit*, André Lacaze's *Le Tunnel*, and Tournier's *Le Roi des aulnes*) and extermination camps;

(5) Combat novels concerning the campaigns of 1944–1945, when the French were again fighting (Roger Nimier's *Le Hussard bleu*);

(6) Novels concerning Vichy, collaboration, and the black market, sometimes indicating approval and tinged with Nazi ideology (Pierre Drieu La Rochelle's *Les Chiens de paille*, Maurice Sachs's semifictionalized memoir *La Chasse à courre*—an account of his activities under the Occupation—Marcel Aymé's *Le Chemin des écoliers*, *Les Fins dernières* by Pierre de Boisdeffre, Céline's *D'un château l'autre*, and Tournier's *Le Roi des aulnes*);

(7) Works concerned with the Liberation, *épuration*, and the immediate aftermath of the war (Beauvoir's *Les Mandarins*, Jean Cayrol's *On vous parle*, Aymé's *Uranus*).

There are, in addition, many works that involve more than one of these aspects. Some critics, adopting a stricter definition of the subgenre than mine, might wish to exclude one or more of these World War II types on chronological or substantive grounds—no real fighting is visible in many of them, and for some of their heroes the greater world conflict is without interest. Nevertheless, I generally wish to place them all under that rubric, a decision that

reflects their connection to *wartime* and my understanding of the national experience of 1939–1945. Novels of Jewish persecution in the 1940s belong to
the genre if their plot involves the war; but in numerous cases, the action does
not reflect or depend upon the conflict (Georges Perec's *W ou le souvenir d'enfance*, Elie Wiesel's *La Nuit*). Merle's *La Mort est mon métier* (1952), a fictionalized biographical and psychological portrait of a Nazi commander at Auschwitz, deals not directly with the war, but rather with those who launched it
and the internments and persecutions that took place within its context; the
light it sheds on the German mentality is, however, part of the larger war
picture.

Notable is the fact that the subcategory of aviation fiction (reconnaissance
and bombing raids) is nearly new: in French, there was little writing about
the air war in 1914–1918 or during the Spanish civil war. (Kessel's *L'Equipage*, concerning World War I, and Malraux's novel of the Spanish conflict,
L'Espoir, are exceptional.) The appearance of such works underlines one of
the features that distinguish the 1939 war from its predecessors. Similarly,
while earlier narratives often referred to prisoners on one's own side or the
enemy's, and there was some prison-camp literature written in French during
1914–1918 (such as Jacques Rivière's *L'Allemand: Souvenirs et réflexions d'un
prisonnier de guerre* [1918] and sketches of captives by Georges Duhamel), the
phenomenon of immense prison camps, either in France or to the east, for
civilians and deportees (such as Resistance activists and other political de-
tainees) was unknown to the French before the 1930s and 1940s. The number of French nationals interned in these camps, plus the huge numbers of
French soldiers who were imprisoned after June 1940, if only temporarily,
contributed to a considerable development of *la littérature concentrationnaire* —
works by Cayrol, Sartre, and others — constituting virtually a new subgenre.
One should note that the camps and prisons of World War II also led to a
flowering of prison poetry, including poems by Robert Desnos (d. 1945) and
Jean Cassou's brilliant *33 sonnets composés au secret*. The element of espionage
is, unlike concentration camp experiences, a more traditional feature of war
novels; it is present as a minor or major vein from Stendhal's Waterloo episode in *La Chartreuse de Parme* through Maupassant's stories of the Franco-
Prussian War and in fiction of both world wars, especially in the form of be-
hind-the-lines secret-agent activities during the Occupation.

The purpose of such classifications as those I have suggested is practical, not prescriptive. They serve to give a sense of the range of French fiction concerning war, help identify tendencies both of content and form, and facilitate analysis and commentary. The system of classification also facilitates the drawing of comparisons among accounts of the different wars, particularly between World War I and World War II narratives, when a wide variety of ideology, action, and chronological focus developed from the more complex political field and less homogeneous experience.

4

THE GRANDE ARMÉE AND WATERLOO
The Napoleonic Wars in Fiction

KEEPING IN MIND the iconographic background explored in chapter 2 and the characteristics of war fiction proposed in chapter 3, we can now turn to literary accounts of early nineteenth-century warfare and some other military writing of the period. I shall examine in particular accounts of the Battle of Waterloo to see how they relate and shape the events and what characteristics they have in common with each other or with later works.

The major French literary reflections of the Napoleonic Wars are either in verse or in fictional passages that come well after the event, such as Victor Hugo's *Les Misérables* (1862), which Holly Richardson calls "perhaps the most vivid evocation of the sublime aspects of war," and Erckmann-Chatrian's *Histoire d'un conscrit de 1813* (1864) and *Waterloo* (1865).[1] With some exceptions, such as early verses by Victor Hugo celebrating Napoleon and the pro-Bonapartist poetry of Pierre-Jean Béranger, the Romantic fascination with events of the Napoleonic period did not develop fully in literature until the 1830s and 1840s, whereas graphic artists turned to Napoleonic material almost immediately.

The reasons the emperor's campaigns and final defeat did not appear more in works nearly contemporaneous with them are multiple. The first, of course, is political: Bonaparte's regime was followed by the oppressive Bourbon restoration; sympathizers were dead or in exile or, at the least, obliged generally to be quiet. Following that regime was the July Monarchy, during which Napoleon's official reputation was rehabilitated only gradually. Other

1. *All the Banners Wave*, p. 9.

reasons are literary. The realistic novel had not been fully shaped in the first decades of the nineteenth century. By *realistic novel* I mean the novel freed sufficiently from the influences of end-of-the century melodrama, the Gothic novel, and the historical novel of Walter Scott to adopt at least some plausibility of plot and to concern itself with some broad segments of French society and ordinary heroes. The novel of the individual had already taken shape in its extremely Romantic form, with the romantic, idiosyncratic personages that populate most fictional or semifictional narratives of the first three decades of the century. But until Honoré de Balzac and Stendhal published their major works, the novelistic vision that placed an individual's drama in the midst of a shaping collective drama had not yet been formed. As for poetry, the Romantic poets used chiefly the personal lyric until later in the century, when Victor Hugo and Alfred de Vigny turned to epic and other narrative verse. In any case, some writers would surely have never made of Napoleon the hero of a literary work.

Another reason for delayed representations of the emperor's campaigns has to do with national consciousness: despite dazzling triumphs by Napoleon, the retreat from Russia and Waterloo three years later were such setbacks to the nation—political, not just military—that years were required for them to be assimilated into a mode, either heroic or realistic, such that they could be re-created in imaginative prose. Nevertheless, the image of the emperor arose from the ashes of Waterloo and proved astonishingly resilient throughout the century, as did the image of the battle itself. As Napoleon III's General Trochu said: "We have a special talent for explaining and justifying our defeats." Pierre Barrière wrote: "Nommé ou non, Napoléon est derrière les personnages de Balzac, de Stendhal, derrière tous ceux qui, au cours du siècle, en France et à l'étranger, seront les promoteurs de l'énergie individuelle" [Named or not, Napoleon is behind the characters of Balzac and Stendhal, behind all those who, in the course of the century, in France and elsewhere, will be the promoters of individual energy].[2]

The case that warrants attention first is that of Balzac, a writer who put Napoleon into a novel in the 1820s, then, by means of an embedded narrative, into his 1833 novel *Le Médecin de campagne*. Although Maurice Bardèche wrote

---

2. Gildea, *Past in French History*, 113; Saint-Paulien, *Napoléon Balzac et l'empire de "La Comédie humaine"* (Paris: Albin Michel, 1979), 11.

that the novelist idealized Napoleon, and at least one critic has spoken of Napoleon's "rôle primordial dans une vingtaine de romans et de nouvelles" [primary role in a score of novels and novellas], in *La Comédie humaine* the position the general-emperor and his battles occupy is, in fact, less important than the phrase suggests. The Battle of Jena is evoked in *Une Ténébreuse Affaire*, the retreat from Moscow in *Le Colonel Chabert*, and some other works have Napoleonic elements. Yet, fascinated though he was with society under the empire, and determined to be the novelist of his century's history, Balzac carried out very little of his projected series *Scènes de la vie militaire*. Well before putting together *La Comédie humaine*, he had, however, conceived a novel to be called "La Bataille" and centered on Napoleon. First it was to concern the Battle of Marengo; later, he chose Wagram as its center, then Essling, then Dresden; he even visited some Napoleonic battlefields. As late as 1845 he still planned to carry out the project under the title "La Bataille de Dresde." Nothing came of these intentions, however, except the title "La Bataille," a chapter title, and a fragmentary sentence.[3]

What is known of his intentions is revealing: it was to be entirely a military novel, with no love interest, and it was to convey the very feeling of war to the reader. "Faire un roman nommé *La Bataille*, où l'on entende à la première page gronder le canon et à la dernière le cri de la victoire, et pendant la lecture duquel le lecteur croie assister à une véritable bataille comme s'il la voyait du haut d'une montagne, avec tous ses accessoires, uniformes, blessés, détails" [To do a novel called *The Battle*, where on the first page one might hear the cannon roar, and on the last, the cry of victory, and during the reading of which the reader believes he is present at an actual battle as if he saw it from the height of a mountain, with all its props, uniforms, wounded men, details]. It would be panoramic, like wide-angle battle painting of the Romantic period, yet provide close-ups. "Napoléon dominant tout cela. La plus poétique à faire est Wagram, parce qu'elle implique Napoléon au sein de sa puissance" [Napoleon dominating all that. The most poetic one to do is Wagram, because it implies Napoleon at the heart of his power]. Later he expressed the wish that the reader "voie, sente" [see, feel] in every movement of the great armed body its center, the emperor.[4] Despite Balzac's change of politi-

3. Saint-Paulien, *Napoléon Balzac*, 77, 135; Honoré de Balzac, *La Comédie humaine*, vol. 12, ed. Pierre-Georges Castex (Paris: Gallimard/Bibliothèque de la Pléiade, 1981), 649–53.

4. Balzac, *La Comédie humaine*, 12:650.

cal position in the early 1830s, from liberal (or Jacobin) to legitimist, the emperor would have remained (although invisible) in all his prestige. This plan suggests a work both panoramic and encompassing—a sweeping historical view—yet directed toward eliciting readerly reactions as well. Balzac's inability to carry it out may reflect his general difficulties with the historical novel as well as his dominant interest in social units and mechanisms within civil society. It is known that he envied Stendhal's success in treating Waterloo in *La Chartreuse de Parme* (discussed below).

Les Chouans (1829, revised 1834), the only Balzacian work that might in any sense deserve the label *war novel* and the only volume written of his proposed "Scènes de la vie militaire," deals with the guerrilla warfare in the Vendée in 1799–1800 between "Blues" (regular republican forces) and "Whites" (irregular bands of royalists). The novelist gives the primary role to individual passion of the most implausible sort. The result is that, although ambushes, skirmishes, and massacres are recounted, amid appropriate settings evoked in the excessive Balzacian manner, and the politics of this irregular warfare are not overlooked—including the role played by the distant First Consul, who has proclaimed that pacification of the rebellious western provinces must be achieved—*Les Chouans* is principally a novel of violent love, acted out in a political setting. In narratological terms, the historical senders (Vendéen royalist sympathizers, the republican government and the First Consul) are subordinated to the hero and heroine as senders and receivers of their passion. To be noted also is the lurid manner of recounting the engagements. Given an implausible psychology, in which unitary passions—hatred, avarice, sexual love, jealousy—act as wholes, opposed to each other like pieces on a checkerboard, and given also the absence of regular military engagements, as well as an excessively romantic coloring of setting and action, this novel is less an illustration of war fiction as such—even civil warfare—than a counterexample. It shows the limits of Balzac's interest in the military life and sheds light perhaps on his inability to carry through to its conclusion a novel in which war furnished the only plot. One can note that his difficulty in dealing with scenes of collectivities, and his consequent decision to depict only segments of the action, offer a precedent to Stendhal's literary strategy in *La Chartreuse de Parme* some years later, and perhaps influenced it.

The Napoleonic element in *Le Médecin de campagne* is handled differently.

In this novel, the action of which takes place in 1829, the emperor's name comes up often, always in the most favorable light, as the veteran officer Genestas, who figures prominently in the story, recalls his campaigns. There are several Napoleonic anecdotes, reminiscences, and battle summaries, plus the long embedded narrative alluded to earlier, that of Goguelat, who served in the infantry. (This narrative, in which Balzac comes the closest to realizing the project of "La Bataille," was first published separately, put into the novel, and again appeared by itself more than once, and as late as 1904.[5]) The novelist sought out veterans of the campaigns in order to get information. Goguelat's account, before a rapt audience of country people in a barn, can be taken as representing the widely shared admiration for the deceased emperor as well as nostalgia for glories recently passed. It traces Bonaparte's career from his birth through his early battles, the imperial period, the Russian campaign, the events of 1814 and the farewell at Fontainebleau, the Hundred Days, and Waterloo.

Although the savory narrative style is that of a simple soldier, motifs of both classical epic and the medieval *chansons de geste* are echoed, with mentions of presages, wonders, divine protection, ill omens, and extraordinary accomplishments—all guaranteed as true by this eyewitness. The narration is linear, not panoramic, and consists mostly of summary, with a few scenes sketched very briefly. It is a paean, a memorial; there is no correction offered by any other voice, including the author's, no nuancing of the sort an historian or a critical novelist would bring to bear.

Illustrating the Messianic view of the emperor, as well as Balzac's fascination with powerful figures, Napoleon is represented as larger than life, his destiny partaking of the supernatural. "Aussi alors fut-il prouvé que Napoléon possédait dans son fourreau la véritable épée de Dieu" [Thus was it proven then that Napoleon possessed in his scabbard the true sword of God].[6] In dramatic, romantic terms, the soldier depicts him in his exile on St. Helena, dominating the island and the world from the (exaggerated) height of a promontory: a solitary, Promethean prisoner, "dieu du peuple" [god of

---

5. On the publication history, see Maurice Allem, introd. to Honoré de Balzac, *Le Médecin de campagne* (Paris: Garnier, 1956), xxviii.

6. Honoré de Balzac, *La Comédie humaine*, vol. 9, ed. Pierre-Georges Castex (Paris: Gallimard/Bibliothèque de la Pléiade, 1978), 529.

the people], who has given himself for the nation. There are suggestions of immortality; the fact of his death is denied. Everything he did was in the name of France; he is truly a popular hero. In his mouth, as quoted by the veteran, the word *soldats* has tremendous resonance: not mercenaries, but the true and the brave. Symbolism of various sorts is attached to him, especially the standards or *aigles* (the French resounding in a pun on *aigle* meaning eagle). At the Berezina, "les plus courageux gardaient les aigles; parce que les aigles, voyez-vous, c'était la France" [the most courageous guarded the standards; because the standards, you see, were France]. At his return from his first exile, "à la vue de l'aigle, une armée nationale se refait, et nous marchons tous à Waterloo" [at the sight of the standard, a national army is reconstituted, and we all march to Waterloo]. After the defeat, which in the veteran's retrospective account appears inevitable, Napoleon burns the colors to keep them from disgrace. The social as well as national implications are vast, since Napoleon's armies are identified with the very nation: "La France est écrasée, le soldat n'est plus rien, on le prive de son dû, on te le renvoie chez lui pour prendre à sa place des nobles qui ne pouvaient plus marcher" [France is crushed, the soldier is nothing, he is deprived of what he is owed, they send him back home to put in his place aristocrats no longer able to walk].[7]

Another nineteenth-century writer who included Napoleon in his fiction as a background figure—this time in a negative light—was Vigny, whose positions on the condition of the soldier and questions of honor and obedience were examined in chapter 1. An aristocrat by birth, breeding, and taste, he despised and feared the disorders of the Revolution. Even as he acknowledged and missed the grandeur of spirit and deed displayed in Napoleonic campaigns, he exposed the emperor through one of his characters, Captain Renaud, as a comedian (actor), playing with enormous stakes, including soldiers' lives and indeed the entire welfare of France, for the sake of an image of himself that is empty at the core, but as such all the more powerful.

Although Vigny was the major military writer of his time and displayed in other forms an epic imagination, he undertook no sweeping depiction, in either verse or prose, of the wars of his time, and is not properly speaking a war novelist. His choice was to create in *Servitude et grandeur militaires* a hybrid work, which John Cruickshank rightly calls "ideological fiction": part re-

7. Ibid., 515, 533, 536.

flection on the military condition, as chapter 1 has shown, part narrative, done in the first person but with three embedded novellas featuring other actors chiefly, and within which occur further digressions and interruptions. Vigny apparently did not wish to recount the great Napoleonic battles; he was interested in military *virtue*—honor, sacrifice, abnegation—virtues found in the shadows of campaigns, not at the luminous center where Napoleon presided. Perhaps, moreover, he could not imagine in his own time a conservative counterhero like those aristocrats he brought to life in his historical novel *Cinq-Mars*. Certainly it was not a period of grand military deeds among the nobility; one of his functions as a young officer in the Garde Royale (reflected in *Servitude et grandeur militaires*) was that of accompanying Louis XVIII into exile during the Hundred Days, surely a deplorable phase for monarchists. His own military career had been a disappointment to him: no campaigns, no glory, endless garrison assignments. "Nous lisions sans cesse la vie de ces généraux de la République si purement épris de la gloire . . . et . . . nous tombions dans une amère tristesse en mesurant notre destinée à la leur" [We would read ceaselessly the lives of those generals of the Republic, so purely in love with military glory, and we fell into bitter sadness upon comparing our fate to theirs].[8]

While it would be unsound to suggest a close causal relationship between the form of this work and Vigny's disabused view of the army and his time, it is not impossible to imagine the one as function of the other. The failure of all the regimes he witnessed, the decline of genuine patriotism in favor of self-aggrandizement, the breakdown of structures, the foreclosing of military grandeur after 1815 would not encourage a writer to undertake a full-spread, cohesive fictional reconstruction. Vigny's aesthetic choice foreshadows, roughly, the way certain writers of the Great War rejected inherited narrative structures in favor of forms they deemed more fitting to the event. The whole is a meditation on war and ethics, not unlike the meditative work of Saint-Exupéry a century later in *Pilote de guerre* and Jules Roy's *Le Métier des armes* [The war trade], a reflection on the implications of 1940 for the French military.

The discursive pages of Vigny's *Servitude et grandeur militaires* and three sto-

8. Vigny, *Servitude et grandeur militaires*, ed. Dorchain, 192. John Cruickshank's term comes from his edition of the same work (London: University of London Press, 1966), 9.

ries that constitute the remainder of the volume reflect war obliquely; there are only occasional glimpses of campaigns, such as that in Egypt and the 1814 battle for Rheims. Napoleon appears chiefly as emperor, in his dealings with the pope. Yet his campaigns cast their shadow over the entire work, the emperor standing for the sort of *arrivisme* and ethics of expediency that Vigny loathed, and the social and political consequences of the Napoleonic period reaching far into the moral and social fabric of France, as Vigny judged it in the 1830s. The three stories, as well as the reflections in the author's own voice, emphasize the servitude of those who have taken the military oath, against a background of institutionalized injustices and the moral problem of war. "Laurette ou le cachet rouge," I noted in chapter 2, deals with the Directory and its unconscionable demands on military authority, by which pointless injustices are perpetrated in the name of order, and for which no one takes responsibility. More generally, it raises the issue of obedience in conflict with conscience. "La Veillée de Vincennes" [The Vincennes vigil] pays tribute to an obscure adjutant who illustrates Vigny's ethic of duty and abnegation. "La Canne de jonc" includes more than one panel: it discusses the appeal of military glory; it presents the unmasking of the emperor by the pope as *commediante* and *tragediante*—whereby the scales fall from the eyes of the hero, the young Renaud; it portrays the spirit of sacrifice shown by a British officer and the essence of military honor; it condemns the distortion of the army's role when it is obliged to act as a police force; and it inquires into the difference between killing in war and murder. Stories and commentary alike deal, directly or indirectly, with the ethical and civic foundation of the army in terms of the period, and they conclude that the authentic *gloire* and grandeur available to those who risk their lives is almost invisible—a grandeur of the soul.

Stendhal was less concerned than his contemporaries de Maistre and Vigny with the justification of war and the ideological questions involved, and less influenced than Balzac by an overall historical design. Having learned to dissect the mind and heart from inside and, as he put it, *écrire sec* [to write dryly], he interests modern readers by his treatment of war from the subjective point of view, principally as a phenomenon that cannot be circumscribed. In this respect, as in numerous others, he shows himself to be astonishingly modern. I am referring of course to the conclusions one can draw from the Battle of Waterloo episode in *La Chartreuse de Parme* (1839), written especially for Eugenia de Montijo, who would become the empress Eugénie. It serves as a paean to the author's hero, Napoleon, who, despite his defeat that day, represented to Stendhal surpreme energy and vitality as well as political liberalism.

It seems clear that the author accepted *raison d'armée* as a matter of course, for the imprinting of Napoleonic heroism in him was very strong, and he never entirely denounced the Romantic militarism that characterized his youth and appears in his two greatest novels as well as *Lucien Leuwen*. It is true that in *Le Rouge et le noir* he mocks the hero's excessive admiration for Napoleon, which leads him to see daily human relationships in terms of battle. His close friend Prosper Mérimée wrote, "Il était difficile de savoir ce qu'il pensait de Napoléon. Presque toujours il était de l'opinion contraire à celle qu'on mettait en avant. Tantôt il en parlait comme d'un parvenu ébloui par les oripeaux. . . . D'autres fois, c'était une admiration presque idolâtre" [It was hard to know what he thought about Napoleon. Almost always he was of the opposite opinion to that put forward. Sometimes he would speak of him as a *parvenu* dazzled by tinsel and sham. . . . Other times, it was an almost idolatrous admiration]. This idolatrous admiration is seen repeatedly in his most cherished heroes, even when it is is treated ironically and ultimately corrected. Nor would his *beylisme* and his particular brand of logic (*lo-gique*, as Mérimée said he pronounced it, accentuating each syllable) have led him to the idealistic belief that conflict can be overcome or purified through honor and self-sacrifice, or ended through utopian schemes.[9]

Moreover, one discerns in him a Romantic attraction to conflict and opposition: the antithetical forces within the self, and those within society, which call forth human energy and lead to self-surpassing. War is, of course, an illustration of these forces, which serve as a point of contact between Stendhal and Nietzsche, who admired the French novelist greatly. There is also parallelism between Stendhal and Hegel, for whom conflict was essential for the development of the human spirit. But at the same time Stendhal saw how the dynamics of experience escape from rational categories; and if what was meant by "war" posed no problem to him, the *experience* of battle, hence its meaning, was a different matter, which bears examination.

9. Prosper Mérimée, *Portraits historiques et littéraires*, ed. Pierre Jourda (Paris: Honoré Champion, 1928), 155, 157.

The episode stands out as one of the first pieces of modern military fiction in France; between it and a text such as Voltaire's poem on Fontenoy—and even Balzac's *Les Chouans*, composed barely fourteen years before—there is a literary and epistemological gulf. It is an early instance of combat recounted from the subjective point of view as an initiation experience. It is true that in the sixteenth century, Monluc, one of the principal military writers in France before 1800, recorded war in his *Commentaires* as a personal experience, but he was concerned with—or at least used only the rhetoric of—the *outer* experience: how the campaigns and individual battles developed, the tactics employed, the outcome, and the political background. The same holds true for the comte de Guibert's treatises on war in the eighteenth century. While Balzac was concerned in *Les Chouans* with an affective element, the latter is only enhanced by military action, not dependent upon it; and the psychological pulsions—conveyed from the outside, as wholes—preclude all probing in depth of what war feels like. This is why Stendhal's work constitutes a major step beyond Balzac's *Les Chouans*. While the latter likewise has an early battle episode that can be seen as a prelude, and at least one critic has claimed that the connection between it and what follows is both atmospheric and psychological, in my view the motivations and actions of this episode are so capricious and implausible that it must be judged a failure. In contrast, for Stendhal's hero, the battle is part of a personal apprenticeship experience; and thus the work belongs to the Romantic genre of the *Bildungsroman* and can be connected to the war-as-initiation novels of the following century.

Initiation—which is considered by critics concerned with archetypes as a mythic pattern—is almost universally found in the war novel of the nineteenth and twentieth centuries, one of the most pervasive patterns discernible in texts that otherwise eschew mythic elements. As chapter 3 mentions, scarcely a war novel exists that does not include a baptism by fire, usually for the principal character, often under the tutelage of a buddy or seasoned sergeant, perhaps complicated by the presence of a sadistic officer or rivals of his own rank. Placed early in the plot, it tests the subject's will, under the pressures of war, which are both enabling and interfering. From this experience, which may include fear, temptation, and error, the initiate emerges perhaps shaken, a momentary failure, but inwardly strengthened for the next test. Occasionally, the novice is disappointed by his first contacts with the war, which does not seem as grand as he had supposed. Alternatively, the rite of passage is contrasted with failed or negative initiations, including the early death of buddies, wash-outs, and even treachery. It may also include the coarsening of the hero or the transformation of his notion of war from a romantic, idealistic one into one where only survival counts and valor is meaningless, or it may be the occasion for a pessimism that outweighs the desire to survive.

For Stendhal's hero, Fabrice, the battle is an experience in knowing. His approach is almost existential, if by that one means personal experience as the source of truth. There is no overview furnished by the author comparable to the summaries and panoramas found in the classical poets and, later, in Victor Hugo's *Les Misérables*, no neat evaluation of the political or military consequences of the battle, no totalization. Although the narrative is done in the third person, Stendhal limits the point of view to that of the hero. Fabrice's initial purpose, as he arrives from Italy, entirely unofficially and anonymously, to join the emperor's armies, is to ally himself with the leader who is for him the model of personal achievement and the liberator of the Piedmont. But when he reaches Belgium, on the eve of the engagement, he is less concerned with its military importance for Napoleon and France than with himself: the encounter is to offer him the chance to know himself — specifically, to see how he will measure up to the standards of his ancestors, whose exploits are chronicled in the family archives. His phrase "Enfin je vais me battre" [Finally I'm going to be in combat] conveys the desire to prove himself under fire.[10] But this "proof" demands some sort of historical verification: he needs to be absolutely sure that he is indeed participating in the central action, not just some peripheral skirmish.

The problem is that, from the experiential viewpoint, there is no center, or at least not for him, a foreign volunteer participating incognito; at first he cannot even find a unit to join. He is the model of the outsider: the individual whose action cannot be subsumed into that of the collectivity. Although troops are aligned in squares, in the traditional manner — this is classic Napoleonic warfare — and order is supposed to prevail, the battle cannot be grasped as a whole as it is being fought, in part simply because, for a participant, it is as yet incomplete as an event, and in part because, as Stendhal depicts it, the military operation is utterly fragmented and disorganized: strate-

---

10. Stendhal, *La Chartreuse de Parme*, ed. Henri Martineau (Paris: Garnier, 1961), 52.

gic planning cannot impose itself or succeed in defining and regulating the maneuvers, which escape from images in the mind. Add to this the multiplicity of troops, the psychological and physical factors—men are not inert, but rather are mentally and physically affected by their experience—and the topological ones—folds in terrain, trees, ditches—and the reader senses the impossibility of grasping the event as a whole. The result is Fabrice's difficulty in relating his own participation to a general rationale. As Keegan has observed, others had written of Waterloo in the same manner; battle has been a confusing thing from time immemorial. But the records to which he refers are personal texts—letters and diaries. Stendhal is, to my knowledge, the first French author to write modern subjectivity into war literature.[11]

More broadly, Stendhal demonstrates that reality does not conform to the mind and its categories—that is, either to the ideal battlefield as conceived in military theory up to that time, or to an individual's conceptual ability. (Despite the author's rationalism, there is an anti-Cartesian suggestion here that announces modern thought.) Fabrice repeatedly is struck by the confusion of the whole affair. It can be objected that he is intoxicated during some of the action, after having drunk numerous shots of brandy, and thereby is not aware until it is too late that the emperor is passing by. But, recognizing this, he shakes off his drunkenness and remains sober throughout the rest of the episode. Some commentators believe, in addition, that Stendhal exaggerated the difficulty of grasping Waterloo. Maurice Rieuneau writes: "Une bataille de Napoléon pouvait être suivie, comprise et décrite dans son ensemble, par un observateur judicieusement placé" [A Napoleonic battle could be followed, understood, and described as a whole, by a judiciously placed observer]. (Napoleon was, presumably, placed in just such a position, to direct the campaign.) If this is so—though such is by no means sure—it just reinforces the thesis that Stendhal deliberately distorted reality (as Rieuneau puts it, he had to "fausser les données") in order to create the psychological and epistemological dilemma, or he simply refused to put his hero in the position of "judiciously placed observer," being more concerned with the experience, which, after all, would be that of most other participants likewise.[12]

11. Keegan, *The Face of Battle*, 129–30.

12. Stendhal, *La Chartreuse de Parme*, 46, 50; Maurice Rieuneau, *Guerre et révolution dans le roman français* (Paris: Klincksieck, 1974), 23.

Afterward, Fabrice's chief preoccupation is determining whether the experience was genuine. He had already inquired earlier: "Ceci est-il une véritable bataille?" [Is this a genuine battle?]. Afterwards, the question is still unanswered. "Ce qu'il avait vu, était-ce une bataille, et en second lieu, cette bataille était-elle Waterloo?" [Was what he had seen a battle, and in the second place, was this battle Waterloo?].[13] The sought-after recognition is a type of initiation rite, leading to adulthood; only if he has really fought in the battle, under the presiding figure of Napoleon, can he identify with his actions and achieve selfhood.

Throughout the novel, Fabrice's historical space is clearly identified, the narrative real corresponding to the historical real; but imposed upon it always is a powerful psychological one. The tension between the hero's inner reality and that around him provides a principal source of the novel's dynamics, as he seeks to reconcile his own values with those around him. The moving center of his world is himself, but for this center to hold, it requires ratification in historical space by *its* center: Napoleon, who displaces the king of earlier texts. That this is so shows that Stendhal was still in touch with the heroic mode in which earlier war accounts were usually written, although the replacement of the hereditary monarch by a powerful *arriviste* personality is a crucial change. What happens when the heroic contract is broken, and the sense of historical space is transformed or disintegrates under the pressures of war, is for later writers to discover.

What Stendhal offered, in short, is an eccentric vision of war in which personal experience is primary and meaning is relative to the individual participant and the myth he chooses. The deeds of heroes and the prestige of history do not disappear entirely, since they can legitimize the individual experience after having inspired it; but they are pushed to the edge, and at the middle is the feeling subject who seizes war experientially and by fragments, and whose concern is to totalize these fragments to find meaning that is not already in the events but must be seized in relation to himself. Stendhal's text should be seen as a crucial one in modern war literature in France, more significant than Victor Hugo's famous lines on the battle from "L'Expiation" and his rendition of it in *Les Misérables*, because it poses the problem of the self in relation to history. It also poses the larger problem of whether one can

13. Stendhal, *La Chartreuse de Parme*, 44, 72.

give an account of war, in the narrative sense and perhaps the moral one as well.

As a contrast to the Stendhalian account, one can turn to the second part, first book, of Victor Hugo's great novel, published in 1862. Titled simply "Waterloo," the account of the battle constitutes a flashback or analepsis, said by the narrator to be crucial for understanding the action of the novel and thus making it part of the diegesis. "Une des scènes génératrices du drame que nous racontons se rattache à cette bataille" [One of the generative scenes of the drama that we recount is connected to that battle]. It is, however, non-fictionalized, and is preceded by a description of the site both as it was at the time of the novel's composition and as it appeared, reportedly, in 1815. Although Hugo asserts that he does not pretend to "faire l'histoire de Waterloo" [write the history of Waterloo], his summary presents the battle as a whole and offers reasons for its development. The analepsis is in both the plot and, obviously, the history. The account would seem to have objectivity as its chief aim — the sort that the realists wished to practice, here based explicitly on research. The author does not claim originality in the account; he himself cites in the text the historians whom he consulted, and there appears to be no significant departure in his summary from the standard views on the battle.[14]

Cast in the third person, the account nevertheless is closely identified with the author who speaks in the book: "L'an dernier (1861) [i.e., one year before publication], par une belle matinée de mai, un passant, celui qui raconte cette histoire, arrivait de Nivelles et se dirigeait vers La Hulpe" [Last year (1861), on a lovely May morning, a passer-by, the person who is telling this story, was coming from Nivelles, going toward La Hulpe]. It is the pseudo-author's voice and gaze that are heard and followed by the reader, and, beyond them, that of Victor Hugo himself, who does not take pains to dissimulate his personal judgments. One notes in particular his assessment of the contributing factors in Napoleon's defeat: the rain, which caused postponement of the hour at which combat was engaged, and thus gave Blücher time to arrive; the emperor's failure to send in the infantry at a crucial moment; two or three significant but hidden features of the terrain, including a deep ditch. Yet although he presents these circumstances as causal factors, Victor Hugo the

14. Victor Hugo, *Les Misérables*, ed. Maurice Allem (Paris: Gallimard/Bibliothèque de la Pléiade, 1951), 325.

idealist and epic poet judges that it was God who was ultimately responsible for the French disaster: the victory of Napoleon, "ce grand bûcheron de l'Europe" [this great logger of Europe], was not part of the "loi du dix-neuvième siècle" [the nineteenth-century law].[15] The summary of the battle thus serves as an occasion for interpreting it, in unstated accordance with the moral and historical vision that governs the rest of Victor Hugo's long novel.

The approach is clearly different from Stendhal's, since the battle is recounted not as if contemporaneously and from the point of view of a fictional participant, but comprehensively, as replayed retrospectively by an authorial intelligence having historians' accounts at his disposal and able to totalize his information. Hugo moves logically, both through geography and chronology, in his description of terrain and summary of the battle, totalizing initially, then going through the day's events episode by episode, field and hedge by field and hedge, to arrive finally back at his point of departure—the battle as a whole, which he assesses in its general lines and its historical importance. He relies frequently on eyewitness accounts gathered by others but also on his personal examination of the site, where he spent more than two months, speaking to inhabitants who were children at the time of the battle, inspecting buildings and trees that had been damaged, and studying the terrain. The voice of the novelist, writing as historian, is thus one of authority, based on personal study and recognized accounts in contradistinction to personal experience.

Yet despite the fact that Victor Hugo's clear purpose is to present an overview, between his account and Stendhal's fictional presentation done from Fabrice's vantage point there are some common elements. Hugo paints the battle as a series of tableaux, as an artist might have done, and with an eye toward their color, seeing there "ce qu'il faut à Salvator Rosa" (a painter) [what Salvator Rosa needs] and suggesting that Rembrandt would have been the ideal artist for reproducing the mêlée. "La guerre a d'affreuses beautés" [War has frightful beauties], he contends. This aesthetic dimension might, of course, be remarked upon by any historian, but Hugo's descriptive passages are vibrant and subjective. He likes symbolic elements in the tableaux. "Les nuages de l'horizon s'écartèrent et laissèrent passer à travers les ormes . . . la grande rougeur sinistre du soleil qui se couchait. On l'avait vu se lever à

15. Ibid., 315, 317, 344.

Austerlitz" [The clouds at the horizon parted and let through the elms . . . the great ominous crimson of the setting sun. It had been seen rising at Austerlitz].[16]

Victor Hugo likewise stresses the confusion, as an observer would experience it if he were there (and as Fabrice saw it): that is, he creates an implicit fictional observer, whose perceptions appear in the present tense. The battle is, as it were, going on now: "Le milieu de cette bataille est presque indistincte et participe du sombre de la mêlée. . . . On aperçoit de vastes fluctuations dans cette brume, un mirage vertigineux" [The center of this battle is almost indistinct and shares in the obscurity of the fray. . . . One sees great fluctuations in the mist, a dizzying mirage]. The confusion results in part from the very nature of the event, which consists in actions, reactions, and counteractions. "Le choc des masses armées a d'incalculables reflux. . . . [Les] deux plans des deux chefs entrent l'un dans l'autre et se déforment l'un par l'autre" [The shock of the armed masses has innumerable ebbing effects. . . . [The] two planes of the two leaders invade each other and are deformed by each other]. As the squares—ideal elements from both visual and tactical points of view—are broken and crushed in what he calls his "hallucination de la catastrophe" [hallucination of catastrophe], military and mental confusion reign. "Tout fléchit, se fêle, craque, flotte, roule, tombe, se heurte, se hâte, se précipite. Désagrégation inouïe. . . . [Ney] est débordé . . . [Les] amis s'entre-tuent pour fuir" [Everything gives way, cracks, rips, drifts, swirls, falls, collides, hurries, rushes. Unheard-of disintegration. . . . Ney is overwhelmed. . . . Friends kill each other in order to flee]. Even the generals do not understand the battle. "Elle est aussi obscure pour ceux qui l'ont gagnée que pour celui qui l'a perdue. Pour Napoléon, c'est une panique; Blücher n'y voit que du feu; Wellington n'y comprend rien. . . . Les bulletins sont confus, les commentaires embrouillés. Ceux-ci balbutient, ceux-là bégayent" [It is as obscure for those who have won it as for the one who lost it. For Napoleon, it's panic; Blücher is taken in; Wellington doesn't understand anything about it. The reports are muddled, the commentaries confused. The latter stammer, the former stutter].[17]

Victor Hugo then resumes the Archimedean point from which historians

16. Ibid., 329–30, 351, 368.
17. Ibid., 329, 352–53, 358, 362.

recount but which is nevertheless imperfect, totalization of the event being impossible: "Chaque historien trace un peu le linéament qui lui plaît dans ces pêle-mêle. . . . L'historien . . . a le droit évident de résumer. Il ne peut que saisir les contours principaux de la lutte, et il n'est donné à aucun narrateur, si consciencieux qu'il soit, de fixer absolument la forme de ce nuage horrible qu'on appelle une bataille" [Each historian draws a bit the lines that he wishes in those jumbles. The historian obviously has the right to summarize. He can only seize the main outlines of the struggle, and it is given to no narrator, however conscientious he may be, to determine absolutely the form of that horrible cloud that is called a battle].[18] In short, the subjective sensations that an observer would have—and which Victor Hugo's prose re-creates for others and himself (an author being always his first reader) in an almost visionary manner—are embraced within a quasiobjective, realistic overview that makes him less modern (because less subjective, less fragmented) than Stendhal.

In one respect, however, Victor Hugo is forward looking. In the battle that his nation lost, he sees a gain: "Souvent bataille perdue, progrès conquis. Moins de gloire, plus de liberté. Le tambour se tait, la raison prend la parole. C'est le jeu à qui perd gagne" [Often a battle lost means progress won. Less glory, more freedom. The drum is quiet, reason speaks. It's the game of loser wins]. This is so despite the fact that the victors at Waterloo were monarchists and reactionaries, attempting to crush the liberal principles that had been enunciated with the French Revolution. The Bourbon Restoration notwithstanding, "un ordre constitutionnel à contre-coeur est sorti de Waterloo, au grand regret des vainqueurs. C'est que la révolution ne peut être vraiment vaincue" [a reluctant constitutional order came out of Waterloo, to the great regret of the victors. It's because the revolution cannot really be vanquished]. With his characteristic use of antitheses, which marks the entire Waterloo book ("Dieu se plaît aux antithèses" [God enjoys antitheses]), joined to his vision of a "vaste lever d'idées qui est propre à notre siècle" [a vast rise of ideas which belongs to our century], Hugo applies to nineteenth-century history a dialectic of inevitability that appears naive and yet prophetic. The Revolution (that is, progress, or "tomorrow"), "étant providentielle et absolument fatale" [being providential and absolutely fated], reappears at each

18. Ibid., 329–30.

stage. Hugo does not yet denounce nations and nationalism—France, England, and Germany are all seen as grand actors on the stage of history—but in other respects he prefigures those novelists such as Barbusse and similar commentators who in the midst of the Great War and after would challenge and deconstruct the idea of victory. Their position would be borne out, first by the failure of the "victory" of 1918, then by the "loser wins" effect after World War II and, in Hugo's term, finally Reason itself speaking.[19]

A not entirely dissimilar view of Waterloo is found in the work of Alphonse Esquiros, one of the "Petits Romantiques," that is, the relatively minor Romantics of the second generation. Esquiros, like numerous other Romantic figures such as Pierre Simon Ballanche, Edgar Quinet, and A.-L. Constant, had an idealistic vision of a new society of justice and peace that can be called "messianic nationalism." According to this view, the people (that is, the lower classes) would finally occupy the position due them—and promised them by the Christian Gospel, to which he refers constantly. This vision was not, however, an international one, but rather very French. The bloodletting of the Revolution and the struggle against European tyrants were seen as stages in the progress of humanity toward this new society; France, at the expense of her own blood, had begun to show the way. Thus, in Esquiros's poem "L'Aigle" [The eagle] (1834), Napoleon describes himself as the new Christ, sacrificed for his people upon the cross of Waterloo. Similarly, in his long work *L'Evangile du peuple* [The people's gospel] (1840), Esquiros writes: "Voici bientôt trente ans qu'à Waterloo les rois / Après l'avoir frappée ont mis la France en croix" [It's been almost thirty years since, at Waterloo, kings, / after having struck France, crucified it]. In the same vein, [?] Ganneau, known as "Le Mapah," wrote in his *Retour des cendres de Napoléon en France* [Return of Napoleon's ashes to France] (1840): "WATERLOO EST LE GOLGOTHA-PEUPLE / WATERLOO EST LE VENDREDI-SAINT DU GRAND CHRIST-PEUPLE" [Waterloo is the human Golgotha / Waterloo is the Good Friday of the great Christ-People].[20]

Erckmann-Chatrian's *Waterloo*, part of their *Contes et romans nationaux et populaires*, offers another version of Napoleon and his final battle. This series,

19. Ibid., 363–64.

20. These quotations come from Anthony Zielonka, *Alphonse Esquiros (1812–1876): A Study of His Works* (Paris and Geneva: Champion/Slatkine, 1985), 170, 188, 190.

which is essentially a collection of chronicles and includes other volumes set during the Napoleonic Wars, has, to modern judgment, little literary value. While the style is not brilliant, neither is it awkward or dull; but there is considerable sentimentalism. Moreover, the authors are unsuccessful in dramatizing their material, and the conflicting forces that constitute historical action—not to mention the personal conflicts that compose a destiny—are, for the most part, simply described, in linear fashion, by a single voice whose vision colors the whole, and without the sort of oppositional elements that I have identified as fundamental in the plots of much war writing and political fiction. Erckmann-Chatrian's works have, in short, a very simple structure, both narrative and ideological. Yet it is significant that these novels, which have been reprinted in a modern illustrated edition, sold widely and were especially popular as school prize books; they were a didactic tool and certainly contributed to forming the view on the Napoleonic Wars that prevailed in the late Second Empire and early Third Republic. The words of the overall title—*nationaux et populaires*—are to be taken literally: these are national works, assuming and illustrating a national identity and ethos.

Related in the first person, ostensibly a half-century later, by a participant—a simple soldier, Joseph Bertha—the account of Waterloo, which closes the volume *Waterloo* and to which all the rest leads, comes with a sort of guarantee: "I was there, and I saw it and fought it." The narrator avoids synthetic, panoramic reconstitutions of the type provided by Victor Hugo, limiting himself instead to what he witnessed and to reports of other action as told to him contemporaneously by participants (soldiers met during the retreat). He corrects certain false reports and even rejects broad accounts from other participants of what took place, objecting that they seem to speak of things he did *not* see: the distance between narration and experience is too great. In contrast with Stendhal, however, he does not interrogate the battle as such phenomenologically. In fact, the battle as a great historical event is a given of the volume and Bertha's narration; it has already been reified, historicized, and elevated above incidental history by the decades between the act and the telling and the countless means by which Napoleon became rehabilitated and glorified. Thus, although the eyewitness report guarantees the battle, in one sense, the battle also gives authority and justification to its participant and reporter: Joseph is important for that reason and that reason only. Despite numerous allusions to the difficulty of seeing, the dispersion of troops, the multiplicity of components, and the dreadful confusion during the engagement with the English and Prussians and then the retreat—all of which, he says, have to be explained—the narrator thus neither questions the battle as a whole—its coherence, its knowability, his presence in the essential thing—nor attempts to recount the entire event. He makes what purports to be a modest contribution to his pseudonarratees' understanding of one corner of the battle, including the dreadful disorder and confusion of the retreat, in which many were left to die of wounds or be massacred. Personal experience circumscribes the account but also implies authenticity. "Les choses qu'on a vues soi-même sont le principal" [Things that one has seen oneself are the main part].[21]

This corner of the battle is not so obscure, however, that he does not participate in some crucial episodes. And there is more than one glimpse of Marshal Ney and of the emperor himself, in addition to countless allusions to major figures. The account is thus to be taken as synecdochal, the part standing for the whole, just as he, along with a few friends and family members, stands for the whole of France. This is because France is seen homogeneously (with the exception, noted below, of Bourbon supporters, who belong to a different caste and whose loyalties, as the émigrés make clear, go to the monarchy as an institution and not to the nation). National character is not a "myth," to quote the title of J.-C. Baroja's 1975 book.

This point is made clear by *Waterloo*'s very explicit discussions of politics: the implications of the Revolution and the republic (and its wars), the early empire and Napoleon's achievements on the battlefield, the emperor's errors, the Restoration, the Hundred Days, and finally defeat and the second return of the Bourbons. Clearly concerned with forming readers' views while recounting the heroic Napoleonic past—creating in effect a sort of popular epic—Erckmann-Chatrian distributed political views among their characters and then had them argue for and against them in a kind of political survey of the early nineteenth century. On the one hand, Joseph, despite enthusiasm for the return of Bonaparte, is more inclined to passivity: he would prefer to stay home and not risk his life for what he views as dynastic quarrels ("des choses qui ne me regardaient pas" [things that did not concern me]). On the other, his adoptive father, M. Goulden, who served under the republic, is

21. Erckmann-Chatrian, *Le Conscrit de 1813*; *Waterloo*, 429.

charged with enunciating wiser views, which amount to reasonable (not fa-
natical) support of Revolutionary and republican values as set forth in the
Declaration of the Rights of Man and defended in the pre-empire years with
the blood of citizens.[22]

Goulden's judgments are made always in reference to the general good;
greed, ambition, and other self-serving motives, as well as injustice and fanaticism, are out of the question for true sons of France. (It is the Bourbons and
their legions—including an oppressive church—and particularly returning
émigrés, who embody such vices.) *La gloire* is revealed to be a false value,
cultivated in the past by social parasites, at the expense of the nation. Although in the preceding volume, *Histoire d'un conscrit de 1813*, Erckmann-
Chatrian portrayed the emperor as a tyrant and a usurper who had established a new aristocracy after French blood had flowed to abolish the old and
abusive one, the return of Napoleon during the Hundred Days appears as a
welcome end to émigré rule and a reinstatement of republican virtues, which
the emperor had betrayed but now, repentant, has come to defend and illustrate. "Les Droits de l'homme et le bonheur de la patrie seront reconquis"
[The rights of man and the happiness of the fatherland will be won again],
says Bonaparte on the eve of the battle.[23] Thus the defeat at Waterloo is not
that of an aggrandizing, megalomaniac emperor but of the republic, once
again, in the person of a savior and its principles of justice. Unlike Esquiros
and other contemporaries, Erckmann and Chatrian neither invested these republican principles with any sort of religious symbolism nor suggested an eschatological vision of ever-expanding popular welfare and of a new society;
no socialist element is visible at all. But the Bourbons are viewed as retrogressive, and Napoleon's defeat by the monarchies of Europe in league against
France implies, according to the book's politics, the need for a new revolution
and republican restoration.

However the attitudes illustrated above and accounts given by Victor
Hugo and Erckmann-Chatrian may vary from each other, they show how *la
gloire* as understood under the ancien régime was replaced as a motivation for
armed struggles by *la patrie*, the nation, and its values. Authorities exist to
encourage commerce, spread instruction and freedom, multiply good exam-

22. Ibid., 361.
23. Ibid., 364.

ples—not to oppress the people; and "les peuples sont bien bêtes de glorifier" [are certainly stupid to glorify] warfare for those who do not protect the interests of their nation.[24] Apart from *La Chartreuse de Parme*, there is in these works little exaltation, little of that heightened sense of being and fulfillment that soldiers know, paradoxically, as they risk their lives in battle. The end (defense of the nation) is primary, the means secondary; and the predominant psychological dimension whereby later war novels become nuanced personal trials is not yet present. War has become problematized; but the problem is not yet generally represented within the individual soul. It would remain for later generations of writers, chiefly those of the Great War, to place the crux of war within individuals, even as they were overwhelmed by the scope of battle and power of machines.

24. Ibid., 424.

5

THE FRANCO-PRUSSIAN WAR
AND EARLY THIRD REPUBLIC
War Fiction and Nationalism

IF ONE IS to judge by their aftermath, the Franco-Prussian War and the ensuing Commune (1870–1871) had a far worse effect on the French mind than Waterloo. The latter defeat, after all, was due to the combined forces of several European powers, and was seen by admirers of the emperor against the backdrop of stunning military successes and political achievements that, for the most part, endured through or resurfaced after the reactionary post-Napoleonic governments. Previous chapters of this study that followed the vicissitudes of Napoleon's image and reputation and the uses to which they were put in his century, as well as the treatment of the emperor and his wars in fiction, showed the resistance and richness of his legend. Despite the compromises Bonaparte had made with Church and other social forces, many post-Napoleonic liberals (excluding the uncompromising Jacobin republicans) associated the emperor with the Revolutionary aspirations from which his rule had sprung and saw him as still the hero of the new Europe.

The defeat in 1870 in an absurd dynastic war (with nationalistic overtones and consequences), wherein approximately 150,000 Frenchmen died at the hands of the distinctly superior Prussian army only weeks after the fighting began, was much more ignoble. The capitulation at Sedan of a disorganized army and an incapacitated emperor far inferior to his uncle, followed by the declaration of a republic, the formation of new armies, and the unsuccessful attempts to defend the national territory and drive back the Germans, then the siege of Paris, in which thousands starved, finally the loss of Alsace and most of Lorraine and the imposition of heavy indemnities: this costly series of events brought to a tragic end the period of the Second Empire. Civil disorders and political differences led thousands of French to take arms against their fellow citizens, especially during the 1871 Commune, an experiment in popular government put down by a bloody military intervention. Order was finally restored — at the price of banishment for many radicals — by what became the Third Republic, which, although it endured until 1940, was plagued by scandals, dissensions, and national trauma.

The Franco-Prussian War also created a national inferiority complex and, for the conservatives, a lasting fear that any war would be followed by new popular uprisings, anarchy, or even a successful socialist revolution. The motif of the lost provinces and its corollary, *revanchisme*, weighed heavily upon the French imagination, as reflected in literature and the political arena. At age fourteen, the youth who would become General de Gaulle wrote an essay in which he envisaged himself as commander of a French army defeating the Germans after their 1930 invasion of France. The burden of defeat and call for revenge and retribution assumed great importance throughout pre-1914 politics and even after, influencing the terms of the Treaty of Versailles. In the decades after the war and especially following the turn of the century, a new nationalism arose, which Eugen Weber takes pains to distinguish from the liberal nationalism of the previous decades. He characterizes its adherents thus: "This group stood for *revanche*, for national unity and power based on traditional institutions (Church and army first among them), for clearing out Jews and other foreigners. . . . It radiated an acute and often exclusive patriotism that blended well with the *revanchard* aspirations and with the exaltation of the army."[1]

Although the French weaponry ultimately failed the army, the war of 1870–1871, as one of the few French campaigns against a European opponent since Waterloo, was also a technological experiment. A highly mechanized warfare had been introduced in the previous decades, especially in the United States, using technology whose effects, when carried to still a higher level, would dictate the conditions and awful effects of the Great War. True, the modified armaments and techniques in the post-Napoleonic period did not change strategy and tactics entirely. Indeed, in *The Art of War in the Western World*, Anson Jones argues that, despite changes in weaponry and compo-

---

1. Eugen Weber, *The Nationalist Revival in France, 1905–1914* (Berkeley and Los Angeles: University of California Press, 1959, 1968), 2–3.

sition of armies, with consequent modifications in tactics and strategy, the *re-lationships* among weapons systems and types of combatants had altered little, and in some cases not at all, from earlier practice. "In spite of significant technological progress that changed missile weapons and logistics, nineteenth-century warfare retained the essential character of the French Revolution and Napoleon." Using examples from twentieth-century engagements, Jones shows how—despite their new technology—units of tanks, antiaircraft artillery, submarines, and aircraft usually functioned with respect to enemy forces the way earlier types of armed foot and mounted soldiers had: for instance, as light cavalry (for reconnaissance) in the case of planes, and as heavy cavalry, in the case of tanks.[2]

In contradistinction to this point of view, however, one must recognize that after Waterloo technological changes and increases in numbers meant that what had often been rather rapid engagements between well-balanced and similar armies—engagements that, by themselves, had decided international quarrels—were increasingly replaced by long and more destructive wars: "Industrialization enormously enhanced material power to wage long wars. . . . And technological revolution threatened armies which did not buy weapons wisely—and extravagantly—with defeat at the hands of a better equipped foe. . . . Modern weapons . . . had a potentiality for the infliction of death far greater than those of any previous age." While the most extensive illustrations of this development came for France in the twentieth century, some sense of it is reflected in the literature of the Franco-Prussian War.[3]

That conflict is the first war in France to be recorded widely in contemporaneous fiction. There were also many near-contemporaneous drawings, engravings, and lithographs of the major battles and the civilian disruptions—including some done from life—as well as photographs of camps, battlefields, and ceremonies. The scathing political caricature of the time turned on such figures as Achille Bazaine, viewed as a traitor for his failure at Metz. The artist Edouard Détaille, who produced numerous individual and group scenes in the 1870s and 1880s, was one of the principal recorders of the campaigns and the military; another was A. Darlet. Not only military successes

2. Anson Jones, *The Art of War in the Western World* (Urbana: University of Illinois Press, 1987), 387, 495.

3. Keegan and Holmes, *Soldiers*, 31.

were recorded; scenes of carnage, disaster, and civilian flight also were drawn, and all were distributed in the popular media of newspapers and *images d'Epinal.*

By 1870 writers had at their disposal two genres that had not been fully developed in the very first decades of the century: first, the short story (and the novella), as developed by Romantic, then realistic and naturalistic fiction writers; second, the panoramic social novel, which had similarly evolved into an instrument for depicting the encounter between individuals and groups, on the one hand, and historical events and situations on the other. Although after 1900, especially after 1918, some critics and authors came to view these forms as ossified and inadequate to the complex material and psychic realities of their modern world, and sought other modes of fictional representation, at the end of the Second Empire and during the following years these realistic genres, based on mimetic principles, were widely considered (*pace* their enemies, who objected to the sordid realities described) as the supreme literary expressions of their time. These genres combined analysis with description, the inner world with the outer. The short story, to be sure, favors the outer world, that of behavior and events illustrating character; it was preferred by contemporary writers over longer forms. Quickly and presumably more easily produced than novels, the short story lent itself to conveying brief impressions and snapshots of war. Under the pens of Guy de Maupassant and Alphonse Daudet, this genre approaches the vignette. For purposes of comparison, one can note that during the Occupation of 1940–1944, a time not entirely unlike the period 1870–1871, the short, episodic novella and group of loosely connected short stories were the preferred fictional forms: under the press of contemporary events and especially the enemy's proximity, a writer preoccupied with the historical circumstances, perhaps playing an active role, could not easily make use of longer forms, and perhaps had no desire to employ panoramic fictional creations. Albert Camus noted that "Tolstoï a pu écrire, lui, sur une guerre qu'il n'avait pas faite, le plus grand roman de toutes les littératures. Nos guerres à nous ne nous laissent le temps d'écrire sur rien d'autre que sur elles-mêmes" [Tolstoy was able to write, concerning a war in which he had not participated, the greatest novel in all literature. Our wars do not allow us to write about anything except them].[4]

4. Albert Camus, *Essais* (Paris: Gallimard/Bibliothèque de la Pléiade, 1965), 405.

Writers also had wide audiences, increased by the developing literacy of the French, which had led, among the middle classes, to the habit of devouring huge quantities of fiction, whether in newspaper and magazine *feuilleton* (serial) form or in cheap volumes. Major figures, chiefly Maupassant, Daudet, Emile Zola, and some less well-known authors devoted fiction to the Franco-Prussian War, starting quite early: Théodore de Banville's *Idylles prussiennes* appeared in 1871, and Daudet's *Contes du lundi*, including some stories contemporaneous with the war (the first originally appeared 28 December 1870 in *Le Figaro*, many others in *Le Soir*), was published two years later.

Much fiction concerning the Franco-Prussian War and the following occupation of the eastern provinces resembles *images d'Epinal*. The political and ideological lines are often drawn uncritically: it is assumed that the German alliance had no justification for invading and occupying France. (The facts that Lorraine had been joined to France only in the eighteenth century and that the Rhenish area was, in some ways, Germanic in history and culture, even in language, were not considered.) Such clear-cut ideological positions tend to create similarly simple fields in fiction, marked by sentimentalism such as that in Daudet's "Alsace! Alsace!" or his popular story "La Dernière Classe" [The last class], in which a schoolmaster bids adieu to his pupils as the school passes from French to German authority.

These stories, like Daudet's "Le Siège de Berlin" and others, were read with enormous interest and even reverence. Daudet was the first chronicler of the war among major fiction writers; his *Contes du lundi* and *Robert Helmont* (1874) remain repositories of valuable glimpses of the fighting of late summer and fall, and especially the occupation, the siege of Paris, and the Commune. Comprised mostly of vignettes, sketches, and purportedly personal impressions (in truth, arranged quite after the fact), Daudet's pages are marked by apparent authenticity and immediacy. Because of a broken leg, he did not participate in the fighting of the summer, but did become a member of the Garde Nationale, 96th Battalion, and served during the siege; he was thus "aux avant-postes" [at the forward posts], as the title of one story puts it, and in a position to observe many of the incidents that reappear in his stories. While most of the characters he sketches are modest foot soldiers, guards, peasants fleeing the invasion, or Parisians caught up in the events, he also portrays some officers, notably Bazaine, whose surrender in October made him infamous. "La Partie de billard" shows him playing billards, obsessively and aggressively, concerned only to beat his younger opponent at the game, as an engagement takes place within sight of the château that serves as his headquarters. "Des bataillons entiers sont écrasés, pendant que d'autres restent inutiles, l'arme au bras. . . . Rien à faire. On attend des ordres. . . . Comme on n'a pas besoin d'ordres pour mourir, les hommes tombent par centaines derrière les buissons, dans les fossés, en face du grand château silencieux" [Entire battalions are crushed, while others remain useless, their arms at hand. . . . Nothing can be done. One waits for orders. As there is no need of orders to die, men fall by the hundreds behind bushes, in ditches, facing the large, silent château].[5] The author's style draws his reader into the experience: present tense narration, second-person address, exclamations, rhetorical questions, personal commentary all contribute to the evocative power of his prose.

Daudet's ideological views are in some places obvious, elsewhere less so. His attachment to Alsace, noted above, is grounded in personal experience and a rather conservative and sentimental patriotism, though not in ancestral ties. His national feeling is displayed in another vein when he mocks, in "La Défense de Tarascon," citizens in Provence who vaunt their patriotism and play at defending their territory, while in fact doing nothing; meanwhile Strasbourg has been bombed and Paris occupied. His concern for the peasants, who constitute the heart of France but are displaced as the invasion proceeds, is visible in a number of vignettes, including "Les Paysans à Paris" [The peasants in Paris]. In "Le Bac" [The ferry], he criticizes obliquely the esprit d'argent [money-grubbing mentality] so characteristic of the Second Empire and Third Republic, which leads to the devaluation of patriotism because it does not produce revenue. "La Mort de Chauvin" [Chauvin's death], in which Daudet reintroduces a patriotic type that first appeared at the beginning of the July Monarchy, presents, in the first person, a range of reactions to excessive patriotism: initially, recoil from Chauvin's exaggerated and bellicose sentiments; then pleasure at hearing his patriotic declarations, though they are perceived as illusory; finally, pity for him, as he is caught in the cross-fire between the Versailles troops entering Paris and the defending insurgents, "pris entre ces deux haines qui le tuèrent en se visant" [caught be-

5. Daudet, Œuvres 1:589.

tween those two hatreds which killed him while aiming at each other]—an image of destructive internecine warfare.[6]

One of the earliest novels of the war and ensuing occupation is Erckmann-Chatrian's *Le Brigadier Frédéric* (1874), subtitled *Histoire d'un Français chassé par les Allemands* [Story of a Frenchman run off by the Germans]. Unlike their earlier novels concerning the Napoleonic campaigns, this novella-like work is based in part on personal observation. The ideological field is simple: good French Alsatians, bad Germans, the injustice of fate, feelings of indignation and resentment, the obligation to be courageous and faithful to the fatherland. The charm of the work comes from its directness and unnuanced sentiments; the substance and the form correspond and support each other.

Narrated by an autodiegetic narrator (a principal character in the plot), to borrow Gérard Genette's term, some four years after the events, to the named but silent narratee Georges, the novel furnishes the model of occupation fiction—a genre that would flourish in the early years of the next century, as *revanchisme* increased, and during the 1940s.[7] Although it does not recount combat directly, the eponymous hero, Frédéric, a civilian *garde forestier* (forest ranger) in Alsace, follows the reports of the fighting, hears the canons from the siege of Phalsbourg, which lasted until December, and sees the German occupants gradually take over his area, driving him finally from his home when he becomes known as uncooperative.

The novel contains—and may have helped, along with Maupassant's fiction, to establish—what became clichés of French fiction dealing with Germans. They generally appear as brutes (not, to be sure, to the degree illustrated in literature of the French underground and concentration camps during World War II): they are gluttonous; coarse in manner, speech, and appearance; stupidly obedient to their leaders, completely lacking in subtlety. The authors represent them driving out the helpless, believing denunciations, levying assessments, requisitioning (that is, stealing) property without compunction—including cows, essential to rural families—spreading anti-French propaganda, and threatening with punishment those who protest. Some of these fictional Germans appear well behaved—a view that reappears in post-

---

6. Ibid., 668.

7. Gérard Genette, *Figures III* (Paris: Editions du Seuil, 1972), part. trans. Jane E. Lewin as *Narrative Discourse: An Essay in Method* (Ithaca: Cornell University Press, 1980), 244–45 (trans.).

1900 occupation novels such as Maurice Barrès's *Colette Baudoche* and again after 1940 — but the majority turn on the populace brutally, and they keep "le talon sur la nuque" [their heel on the back of its neck], their boot crushing the nerve-center of the French citizens. The narrator recognizes that France was not prepared for the war, and feels humiliation at the defeat: but it is the fault of the generals and of the fact that the French were outnumbered: no superiority of the Germans is recognized. What Barrès would call "la terre et les morts" [the earth and the dead] are evoked in the determination of the young to defend their ancestral territory, the place where their dead are buried, when they cannot prevent occupation, they think only of revenge. The moral suffering of the inhabitants is said to be indescribable — except for those few "collaborators," who foreshadow only too well those of seventy-five years later.

The well-known collective publication *Les Soirées de Médan* (1880), to which some of the Médan group owed their first success, was an anthology of stories about the war that had taken place ten years earlier, far enough removed in time for the authors to wish, initially, to call it "L'Invasion comique." The aim was generally to attack and undermine conventional, that is, idealized, attitudes toward the conflict. The collection is marked by farce (as in Maupassant's "L'Aventure de Walter Schnaffs"), and grotesque turns of plot as well as burlesque characters figure alongside examples of frank, ingenuous patriotism. Although denying any antipatriotic intention, Maupassant wrote to Gustave Flaubert concerning the enterprise: "Nous avons voulu seulement tâcher de donner à nos récits une note juste sur la guerre, de la dépouiller du chauvinisme à la Déroulède, de l'enthousiasme faux jugé jusqu'ici nécessaire dans toute narration où se trouvent une culotte rouge et un fusil" [We attempted only to give to our accounts the correct tone concerning war, to rid it of Déroulède's chauvinism, of the false enthusiasm deemed necessary, until now, in any narrative where red trousers and a rifle are found].[8] This is in contradistinction to the *revanchiste* current, which by 1880 was powerful and growing.

Maupassant's fiction in general contains numerous reflections of the war of 1870–1871 and the sufferings of the occupied areas. He did not relate major encounters on the field or full-scale operations. A painter of human be-

---

8. Maupassant, *Contes et nouvelles*, 1:1295.

havior, both individual and collective, he was less interested in the phenomenon of war, its political or other causes, its history, than in individual behavior during fighting and occupation; yet the implications of war for the understanding of human nature and its relation to the France of his day did not escape him. He had served in the "army of the north" as it moved westward and was nearly captured. "Boule de suif" (1880), "Mademoiselle Fifi" (1882), and "Deux amis" [Two friends] (1882) are among the best-known of stories referring to the war. These were the very years when Déroulède was publishing more of his chauvinistic verse (the famous poem "Le Clairon" appeared in *Marches et sonneries*, 1881) and when the Ligue des Patriotes, forerunner of the Action Française, was founded (1882). Maupassant's short stories, some based on real happenings and tending toward the anecdotic, contain elements of patriotic feeling, speech, and action on the part of the characters, and considerable heroism as well as foolhardiness (the latter serving constantly as a correction to the concept of the former). But their dominant tone is disabused, and war appears not only brutal but senseless and unjustified, in contradistinction to the rationalizing positions of a developing chauvinism.

"Mademoiselle Fifi," which can serve as an example of a well-made war story, includes both patriotism and what would become war clichés. In a requisitioned château, the Prussian occupying officers amuse themselves by crude destruction: one shoots a painting and destroys whole rooms, as a pastime, by means of impromptu explosive devices. Prostitutes who are assigned to them suffer from their brutal manners and boorishness. The Germans, Maupassant implies, care less about culture and others' property rights than the prostitutes do. When an officer nicknamed "Mademoiselle Fifi" attacks the reputation of French women and slaps Rachel, one of the women, she stabs him, then escapes; the local curate hides her. Here are combined the coarse, boorish Germans, patriotic prostitutes, and *esprit revanchard* visible in so much fiction of this war and the two world wars. An ironic touch is the friendly fire to which five Germans succumb during the attempt to find Rachel. As Louis Forestier remarks, Maupassant, while perhaps unaware of it, "ne s'en accorde pas moins à la représentation mythique que les principaux écrivains du temps se font de l'Allemagne et de l'Allemand: froid, cruel, lourd, sans-gêne et destructeur. On voit où et comment les doctrines nationalistes, qui conduiront à 'l'été 1914,' prennent leur forme littéraire" [nevertheless is in agreement with the mythic view of Germany and Germans held by the principal writers of the time: cold, cruel, clumsy, ill-mannered, and destructive. One sees where and how nationalistic doctrines, which will lead to "summer 1914," assume their literary form].[9]

Several other stories by Maupassant and the unfinished novel "L'Angélus" concern the period after the Prussian invasion. In all these works he makes the Prussian soldiers speak with a thick accent ("Je fous prie Matame") and sport the spiked helmet, a sign of their brutality known throughout the countryside. One Prussian is described as a "géant velu" [hairy giant]; others have a "mouvement de pantins" [a puppet motion] when they march; some are so insensitive that they fry and eat the fish caught by the two innocent fishermen whom they have shot and thrown in the river. The Germans in "Les Prisonniers" (1884) are typically slow-witted: they allow themselves to be lured into a cellar by a young Frenchwoman, who locks them in, and subsequently are captured by the local militia in a farcical scene. Such farce does not cancel out the powerful patriotic feeling of the heroine, although the militia come off badly, both vainglorious and cowardly. Courageous patriotism and German gullibility are displayed likewise in "La Mère sauvage" [The primitive or fierce mother], where a widow, in whose house some Prussians have been billeted, takes revenge on them after learning that her son Victor has been killed elsewhere in the fighting: she persuades them to pad their loft with hay as insulation against the cold, then sets fire to them.

In "Saint-Antoine" (1883), a German of the occupying army in Normandy is first associated with the word *cochon* [pig], then literally overstuffed with food, finally killed and buried under some manure; another peasant is charged with the crime. The burlesque side to the plot does not obscure the stupidity of the soldier, still less the horror and injustice of war, to which Maupassant revealed himself as fully sensitive. "Mon esprit resta hanté par les horreurs que la guerre avait amenées dans notre pays, par toutes les misères" [My mind remained haunted by the horrors that war had brought into our country, by all the misery]. One can speak even of the *absurdity* of war as he depicts it—a view that foreshadows the challenge of war's rationale after 1914. Without any revolutionary intent, he recognized that war was inspired from the top of society, not from the lower rungs: "Les paysans n'ont guère

9. Ibid., 1410.

les haines patriotiques; cela n'appartient qu'aux classes supérieures" [Rural people scarcely have patriotic hatred; that belongs only to the upper classes]. He showed himself particularly cognizant of the suffering of the lower classes, who furnish the *chair à canon* (cannon fodder, an expression used by Daudet and others also), are the weakest and least resistant, and stand to gain little from these "ardeurs belliqueuses, ce point d'honneur excitable et ces prétendues combinaisons politiques qui épuisent en six mois deux nations, la victorieuse comme la vaincue" [bellicose passions, excitable sense of honor and would-be political arrangements which, in six months, exhaust two nations, the winner as well as the loser].[10] While the superior classes in his stories proclaim their patriotism, the marginalized pay: the most striking instance is "Boule de suif," the prostitute who must pay with her body so that the group of anxious middle- and upper-class travelers can proceed on their way to escape the occupation, and who then is scorned as a whore by these sanctimonious patriots.

Indeed, Maupassant was aware of the brutality in human nature—not just Prussian—which war seemed to bring out and from which perhaps it derived. In "Les Idées du colonel" [The colonel's ideas] (1884), a French captain and his small band of retreating soldiers give up their cloaks to warm a young woman, similarly caught in the exodus, and carry her after her strength fails; yet they take pleasure in killing some Prussians and their horses and boast of making widows. Similarly, the hero in "Le Père Milon" [Old Man Milon] (1883), a civilian, kills sixteen Prussians before being arrested—although fellow French are shot as reprisals; his act is less a patriotic one than personal revenge for the theft of his cow, the death of his son, and his father's death under Napoleon I. Thus is violence perpetrated from one generation to another.

The outstanding literary depiction of the Franco-Prussian War is Zola's novel *La Débâcle* (1892), from the series *Les Rougon-Macquart*, of which the subtitle is *Histoire naturelle et sociale d'une famille sous le Second Empire*. This is a true war novel, a model of the genre, as chapter 3 presents it. Not coincidentally, perhaps, it dates from the same decade as Stephen Crane's *The Red Badge of Courage* (1895), sometimes considered the first genuine illustration of the genre by an American. Zola's approach is quasiobjective and sweeping, and

10. Ibid., 1219–20, 1638.

in some ways appears retrogressive, compared to Stendhal's; whether the war experience is knowable and in what manner are never at issue, any more than is human behavior, according to his deterministic and positivistic view of history. The omniscient narrator assumes a panoramic view, switching locations and actions. Because, even in such a substantial work, he cannot recount in the dramatic, or scenic, mode every aspect of the war, Zola makes considerable use of the *tirade*, or long report by a witness. In addition to ample background on the causes of war, there are detailed accounts of the battles of August and September 1870, in which the narrator furnishes technical information on weaponry and analyzes military strengths and weaknesses.

Like Victor Hugo in his reconstruction of Waterloo, Zola visited battle sites and used contemporary sources, including published accounts, dispatches, maps, and interviews with participants in the fighting of summer and autumn 1870 as well as the subsequent events; however, unlike Hugo, he embedded all the historical material in a fictionalized narrative, rarely quitting its diegesis. Scholars studying Zola's battle scenes and descriptions of military equipment, emplacement, and tactics have found few technical errors; Henri Mitterand, in his edition, identifies only an occasional, minor mistake in geography or dating. Critical editions furnish maps, which corroborate Zola's descriptions of the distances, lay of the land, natural barriers, villages, and disposition of troops by unit. In the background is the extensive historical space of all of France, which the battlegrounds indicate by metonymy. What matters ultimately is the movement of history, the collectivity, and not the individual: the moral and mental space of the fictional characters is articulated with that of the historical actors and intended to fit perfectly into, and be representative of, the real historical and geographic space.

The battle scenes tend to be very posed initially, like the graphic work of the war I discussed in chapter 2; Zola turns his camera on the action, so to speak, only after having set up carefully his actors and props and disposed the walk-ons at the edge. The scene then becomes animated, giving the action a high epic tone. Initially the vantage point—a road or woods, a village house—is peripheral to the central point of the pending encounter between Germans and French. Indeed, part of the drama is that French troops repeatedly avoided engagement when it would have been to their advantage; but eventually the characters are placed centrally at the height of the fighting.

The two principal characters are a peasant, Jean Macquart—a retired corporal who has joined up again at the threat of war, after having seen the Battle of Solférino; and a soldier in his company, Maurice Levasseur—an "intellectual" who has studied law. They are heroes, or "subjects" in narratological terms, although, as soldiers, they can exercise no influence whatsoever on the main events of the war and very little at even the microlevel. Zola also provides characters from other ranks: a lieutenant, a captain, a major and medical doctor, a colonel, various generals (historical figures), and finally the emperor himself, glimpsed numerous times as he moves from one village to another along the Meuse. Other types—the totally unlettered peasant, the pious Catholic, the socialist from Paris, the avaricious peasant—and women, generally of striking courage and endurance, add to the cast of characters intended surely as representative.

The sender as well as receiver is, obviously, France; the idea of the nation is omnipresent. But France functions in the form of its political apparatus, in this case the emperor and especially the empress Eugénie, who is machinating in Paris to place her son on the throne. Precisely because they, as well as others responsible for France, are (in Zola's eyes) incompetent, unreliable, they also function as opponents, interfering with French interests, or at least her immediate interests. Opposition is thus at the heart of France as well as between France and the German belligerents—a fact brought out in the last part of the novel, dealing with the Commune.

This opposition consists not only in practice—a bungling emperor and other state apparatus, inept generals, who fail the nation rather than protecting it—but in structures; and of course the two are related, Bonapartism being not just political but also class-based and dynastic. The class opposition between the heroes, which foreshadows that delineated in countless war novels of the following century, is complemented by a political one: the peasant Jean tends to support the emperor and what he sees as the established order, involving social and economic structures, whereas Maurice, it gradually appears, is a republican and ultimately becomes a radical one. Yet the two quickly become friends despite dissimilar backgrounds, and the personal opposition appears resolved, thanks to the overriding national concern as well as to personal sympathy. Since, however, they later adopt different positions on the radicalization of France through the Commune—an opposition dramatized when Jean, incensed by the social anarchy and the destruction of Paris by the Communards, shoots one of them, who turns out to be Maurice—it is clear that the different strains in France they represent, which assume the features of order and revolution, have not yet been reconciled.

It is evident both from his theoretical work *Le Roman expérimental* and from his novels that Zola intended his characters to be specimens of social laws, including those of hereditary and social determinism and generalized conflict. Yet in *La Débâcle*, as in certain other novels, he also displays a strong idealistic vein, for he sees these laws operating in the context of a French historical destiny, which is the great receiver of the action. Conceiving the book as a patriotic act, intended to help France rise from the very debacle portrayed, Zola attempted to show the moral and political weaknesses of the Second Empire, which made the war possible, and to indicate those moral standards by which the nation could reassert its grandeur, through the raw material of the French people. A telling fact is the narrative voice: he used the grammatical third person generally but switched at times into a first-person plural *nous* whereby he identified himself and his enterprise with the defeat recounted and the epic renewal imagined.

Throughout, characters reflect on the tragic disparity between the leadership offered by the ailing Louis-Napoleon—"Badinguet"—and his generals, on the one hand, and the first emperor and *his* generals, on the other. Whereas Napoleon III is pitiable, and the rumors that generals have been bribed by Bismarck are grotesque, the gross propaganda, the inefficiency of the entire military operation, and the incompetence of high officers are underlined repeatedly, often in an authorial voice that escapes the diegetic plane; Zola similarly brings out the political maneuvering in Paris intended to advance Eugénie's interests. In contrast to these failings of France lie its real strengths, connected to the soil. In this connection, it is significant that the educated Maurice comes from a village near Sedan.

A pseudoscientific element creeps into the metaphoric language of the novel. Significant is the use of the terms *race* and *sang* in reference to the French and Germans, and of the medical metaphor of the "dégénérescence de la race, qui expliquait comment la France victorieuse des grands-pères avait pu être battue dans les petits-fils . . . telle une maladie de famille, lentement aggravée" [racial degeneration, which explained how the victorious France of the grandfathers could have been beaten in the grandsons . . . like a family illness, slowly aggravated].[11] The medical metaphor then assumes a

---

11. Zola, *Œuvres complètes*, 6:954.

moral and political sense: a "sang nouveau" [new blood] can revive the blood, "membres gâtés" [rotten limbs] can be amputated, and a good thrashing is always salubrious, making one reflect and mend one's ways.

This scientific metaphor, connected to Zola's understanding of historical and social process in terms of natural laws, underlies the book's vision. It re-appears in different form at the end, as an organic image: "C'était le rajeunis-sement certain de l'éternelle nature . . . l'arbre qui jette une nouvelle tige puis-sante, quand on en a coupé la branche pourrie, dont la sève empoisonnée jaunissait les feuilles" [It was the sure rejuvenation of eternal nature . . . the tree that puts out a strong new shoot, when the rotten branch has been cut off, the poisoned sap of which was yellowing the leaves]. While as narrator Zola shows distress at the great massacre of men in the battles he recounts (Zola did not subscribe to Flaubert's standard of impersonality and impassiv-ity), the passion of the war must be accomplished. "Ne maudis pas la guerre. . . . Elle est bonne, elle fait son oeuvre" [Do not curse war. It is good, it does its work], says the dying Maurice. Addressing Louis-Napoleon in a narrator-ial apostrophe, Zola writes: "Marche! Marche sans regarder en arrière, sous la pluie, dans la boue, à l'extermination, afin que cette partie suprême de l'Empire soit jouée jusqu'à la dernière carte. Marche! Marche! Meurs en héros sur les cadavres entassés de ton peuple" [March! March without look-ing backward, in the rain, in the mud, to the point of extermination, so that this supreme game of the empire may be played to the last card. March! March! Die like a hero on the piled-up corpses of your people].[12]

Only then would there be a renewal such as that prefigured by the authen-tic French grandeur of former times. Significantly, the following volume of the *Rougon-Macquart*, the action of which is posterior to the war, identifies this potential for renewal: "La France a la vie dure, et je trouve qu'elle est en train d'étonner le monde par la rapidité de sa convalescence. . . . Certes, il y a bien des éléments pourris. . . . Mais vous ne m'entendez guère, si vous vous ima-ginez que je crois à l'effondrement final, parce que je montre les plaies et les lézardes. Je crois à la vie qui élimine sans cesse les corps nuisibles, qui mar-che quand même à la santé, au renouvellement continué" [France is tough, and I find that she is astonishing the world by the rapidity of her convales-cence. Certainly, there are many rotten elements. But you understand me

12. Ibid., 770, 1114, 1121–22.

very ill if you imagine that I believe in the final collapse because I point out the wounds and the cracks. I believe in life that eliminates ceaselessly harmful bodies, that progresses toward health and toward continued renewal].[13]

In the background of the desired renewal, which projects the book's teleology indefinitely into the future, hovers the shadow of the great Napoleon. It is not surprising that the call to grandeur is placed under his sign, not so much that of his military victories as that of grandeur of soul and vision—as Zola saw them. After all, this grandeur allowed for, and justified morally, the victories of the Empire, and even, by extension, those of midcentury, in Africa, Italy, and Russia. The narrator summarizes some of the great Napoleonic victories, concluding: "En fin de compte, tous étaient battus, inévitablement battus à l'avance, dans une poussée d'héroïsme et de génie qui balayait les armées comme de la paille" [Ultimately, everyone was beaten, inevitably beaten beforehand, in a burst of heroism and genius which swept away armies like straw].[14] The novelist is thus not totally out of touch with the heroic tradition, although it is represented by an absence, and points to a national ideal more than a personal or chivalric one.

Zola's dialectical understanding of the war as an expiation for French decadence in the post-Napoleonic period, especially the Second Empire, foreshadows similar arguments made after the fall of France in 1940 by spokesmen for the Vichy government and by such writers as Paul Morand, Henri de Montherlant, and Pierre Drieu La Rochelle. These conservative thinkers considered governmental and personal corruption in France in the between-the-wars period a cause and indeed a sufficient justification for French defeat by the Nazis. Yet his strong dislike of the Germans—to judge by his portraits—sets Zola apart from the later generation: the dialectical process does not absolve the enemy. The depiction of a Prussian, rejoicing at the burning of Paris—"la monstrueuse fête que lui donnait le spectacle de la Babylone en flammes" [the monstrous celebration which the spectacle of Babylon in flames afforded him]—shows that the avenging hand, this "froid et dur protestantisme militaire" [cold and hard military Protestantism], serves historical purposes despite profound flaws: "Il avait dit sa haine de race, sa conviction d'être en France le justicier, envoyé par le Dieu des armées pour châtier

13. Ibid., 1227.
14. Ibid., 725.

un peuple pervers. Paris brûlait en punition de ses siècles de vie mauvaise, du long amas de ses crimes et de ses débauches. De nouveau, les Germains sauveraient le monde, balaieraient les dernières poussières de la corruption latine" [He had expressed his racial hatred, his conviction of being the righter of wrongs in France, sent by the God of armies to chastize a perverse people. Paris was burning as a punishment for its centuries of wicked life, for its long accumulation of crimes and debauchery. Once again, the Germanic peoples would save the world, sweep away the last dust of Latin corruption]. The Christian model, by which salvation comes through expiatory suffering at the hands of the evil and culpable, is visible: "Désormais, le calvaire était monté jusqu'à la plus terrifiante des agonies, la nation crucifiée expiait ses fautes et allait renaître" [Henceforth, Calvary had been climbed to the most terrifying of agonies, the crucified nation was atoning for its sins and was going to be reborn].[15]

A totally different treatment of the Franco-Prussian War, by the twentieth-century novelist Jules Roy, shows a characteristically modern subjective relationship between events and characters. *Les Cerises d'Icherridène* [The cherries of Icherridène] (1969) constitutes part of a six-volume series of historical novels concerning Algeria, and is one of the few late twentieth-century novels to deal with the war of 1870. Roy concentrates, like Stendhal, on the experiential aspects of the war, but instead of showing his hero, Griès, involved in the fighting, he places him in the position of the thinker meditating on the surrender that has just taken place at Sedan. The entire episode is recounted not just from the subject's viewpoint, but in the retrospective and almost oneiric mode, as Griès relives his experience in France as the waking sequence to a dream. That is, the actual war is in the past and at the periphery; at the center is the subject reacting to it, in an experience of recognition.

In the analeptic recounting of the experience, Griès, an officer of the *tirailleurs algériens* (Algerian riflemen) who is in France traveling on a military mission, must deal with the recent defeat as it relates to his military vocation and his sense of himself. The identity of his nation, from which he draws his identity as an officer, seems precarious; this is partly because popular resentment against what is perceived as treason and incompetence in high places leaves a vacuum, as it deprives France of needed outward manifestations of unity.

15. Ibid., 1100, 1118.

Griès experiences the defeat in shame and confusion, which are associated thematically with actual death when he finds himself standing over the body of his former commanding officer, a much-respected figure who has died, not coincidentally surely, shortly after the French capitulation. Griès also lives the defeat in the mode of love, through a passionate night with the officer's young widow. The dual experience, with its stress on both military honor and love, leads to a significant change when, back in North Africa, he is charged with putting down native uprisings that have expanded precisely because French authority has been undermined in Europe. He now views the ongoing colonial conflict between indigenous peoples and French occupants in terms of the defeat and occupation of France by Prussia, seeing himself in the role of the Prussian oppressor and the natives in the role of the French. In a dramatic reversal of his previous conduct, the thinking self assumes solidarity with the enemy, affirming itself as allied to justice as defined by the Revolutionary triad "Liberty, Equality, Fraternity," that is, to a generalized principle of justice, not to a particular government. Like Stendhal's hero, Griès experiences war subjectively; the defeat is, paradoxically, the locus of an experience of self-knowledge, followed by a moral victory.

After the *Soirées de Médan* group had treated the events of autumn 1870 and Zola had published his superb fictional reconstruction of the battles and subsequent events, novelists toward the turn of the century and the period before 1914 shifted their attention away from the conflict as such to the political question of the post-war German occupation of Alsace and part of Lorraine. Barrès's *Les Déracinés* (1897), which, in the name of fidelity to the local soil and its dead, condemns the uprooting of Alsatians to Paris, served as a nationalist manifesto by upholding the particular values of the region, seen as French, not German. His *Colette Baudoche* (1909), another novel of occupation, explicitly calls for resistance to German hegemony, cultural, political, and genetic. A number of other novelists, now mostly obscure—Paul Acker, Georges Ducrocq, Emile Moselly, Frédéric and Jeanne Régamy, and others—published works stressing the unfortunate consequences of the 1870 war for the region's citizens and the need for resisting and ultimately overthrowing the German yoke.[16]

16. For information on these novelists, see Frank A. Anselmo, "Alsace-Lorraine and the Patriotic Novels of the French Nationalist Revival from 1905 to 1914," Ph.D. diss., Tulane University, 1995.

These early twentieth-century novels tend toward the simplistically binary. The senders are Alsace, Lorraine, and the dead who cry out from their
tombs for their land to be returned to them; the subjects are those who resist
their oppression, in any way they can, including those who simply look for a
better time; the opponents are the occupying Germans and, secondarily,
those who too willingly cooperate with them—*collaborate* would be the word
in another war; the receivers of the action are the same Alsace and Lorraine,
present and future, and, more distantly, France, to whom they belong (although many French had by then lost interest in retaking the provinces). The
binary opposition is reduced frequently to a racial matter, the French and
Germans being viewed as *essentially* different and the word *race* used to indicate this distinction—notwithstanding the trope, appearing in *La Débâcle*, for
instance, of cousinage across the Rhine. Germans appear generally as brutish
and selfish, lacking in subtlety, exploiting the lost provinces for themselves;
any counterexample, such as *Colette Baudoche*, where the Alsatian heroine refuses to marry a German despite his genuine personal integrity and distinction, merely underlines the strength of the opposition (which reappears in
Vercors's *Le Silence de la mer*). The enmity of Napoleonic days is absent, however: it is modern imperial Germany alone that is at fault.

While, except for that of Barrès, the name of almost none of these writers
is often recognized in France today, their works sold widely and surely must
have contributed to the *revanche* mentality that developed increasingly in the
early years of the century. Unlike the period after 1918, when the League of
Nations was charged with preserving national identity and furthering national interests within a framework of enduring peace, pacifism and nationalism were not allied in the post-1870 period; rather, antimilitarism was pro-
fessed by those supporting anarchism and international socialism, and
nationalism grew increasingly militant. That war should come to an end was
not the call of Zola, Barrès, Charles Péguy, and their fellows. Zola had
wished for *La Débâcle* to offer "la vision vraie de la guerre, abominable, la nécessité de la lutte vitale, toute l'idée haute et navrante de Darwin dominant
le pauvre petit, un insecte écrasé dans la nécessité de l'énorme et sombre nature" [the true vision of war, abominable, the need for vital struggle, the
whole lofty and distressing Darwinian idea dominating what is pathetic and
small, an insect crushed in the necessity of enormous and somber nature]. His
hero Maurice "était pour la guerre, la croyait inévitable, nécessaire à l'e-

xistence même des nations. Cela s'imposait à lui, depuis qu'il se donnait . . . à toute cette théorie de l'évolution" [was for war, believed it inevitable, necessary to the very existence of nations. That was obvious to him, ever since he had devoted himself . . . to all that theory of evolution].[17]

The Darwinian model for individual life and nation is not the only one visible here; de Maistre's views are echoed when Zola speaks of "la guerre qui est la vie même, la loi du monde. . . . L'impassible nature n'est qu'un continuel champ de massacre. . . . Si tous les peuples ne formaient plus qu'un peuple, on pourrait concevoir à la rigueur l'avènement de cet âge d'or; et encore la fin de la guerre ne serait-elle pas la fin de l'humanité?" [war that is life itself, the law of the world   Impassive nature is but a continual killing field. . . . If all peoples formed but a single one, we might, conceivably, imagine the advent of that golden age; and yet would the end of warfare not be the end of humanity?][18]

The parallelism between such views and the economic and colonial competition between France and the German empire in the last years of the nineteenth century and first years of the twentieth is obvious. By their demand that the lost provinces be retaken and Germany punished for its territorial and economic brutality, the novels of occupation mentioned above provided a continuous line between the militant nationalism of a hundred years before—going back to battles of the Revolution and Napoleon's great victories, and passing through the humiliating defeat of 1870–1871—and the call for war in 1914, whether idealistic or crassly chauvinistic. War narratives of 1914–1918 must be seen in this light, as well as in that shed by the war itself, in all its horror, and the denunciations both contemporaneous and subsequent.

17. Zola, *Œuvres complètes*, 6:691, 1136.
18. Ibid., 824.

Antoine-Jean Gros, *Murat Defeating the Turkish Army at Aboukir,* oil on canvas, ca. 1805.

Horace Vernet, *Soldier on the Field at Waterloo*, ca. 1818, oil on canvas.

Courtesy Norton Simon Art Foundation.

François Rude, *The Departure of the Volunteers in 1792*, 1835–1836, high-relief sculpture. Popular title: La Marseillaise.

G. Guillaume, *Turks: Return from Sedan*. Drawing from *L'Illustration: Journal universel*, no. 1439, 24 September 1870.

Smeeton, *Our Conquerors!* Lithograph from
L'Illustration: Journal universel, no. 1486, 9 August 1871.

Honoré Daumier, *Promethean France and the Eagle-Vulture,* 1871, drawing.
Courtesy Harvard University Art Museums.

Maximilien Luce, *Patrie*. From the *Almanach du Père Peinard*, 1894. Originals collected at the Institut français d'histoire sociale, Paris.

Gino Severini, *Cannon in Action*, 1915, oil on canvas.
Courtesy Volker W. Feierabend.

Eugène Chaperon, *O Braves!* ca. 1880. Drawing reproduced in *Chants du soldat* by Paul Déroulède (Paris:
Modern-Bibliothèque / Arthème Fayard, 1909).

Patriotic postcard, *On the Way to Victory*, 1916.
Courtesy Centre Jeanne d'Arc, Orléans, France.

Théophile-Alexandre Steinlen, *Sale Exhibition of Paintings by Artists for the Benefit of the Relief Department for the War Blind*, 1917, color lithographic poster.
Courtesy the David and Alfred Smart Museum of Art, 1993.9.

6

WHERE ARE THE WARS OF YESTERYEAR?
The Great War and French Modernism

THE FIFTY-ONE MONTHS of the Great War, whose literary expressions in French and their implications and effects are the concerns of this chapter, surpassed anything that those then alive had known. That trench warfare on an extended and prolonged scale was new in both military and experiential terms is rarely debated, despite basic features and strategies shared with earlier campaigns. "It is virtually impossible," writes John Cruickshank, "to find exceptions to the claim that this . . . war . . . far exceeded the anticipations of its participants in terms of its scale, its duration, and its savage horror." Stanley Cooperman called it "a collective trauma such as the world had never known. . . . [Its] impact . . . on writers and thinkers . . . literally defies description." This war exceeded both historical and aesthetic bounds, as Jules Roy notes: "L'on parlait bien jusqu'aux antipodes des horreurs de cette guerre; mais personne n'en avait l'expérience ni l'image" [People talked about the horrors of this war as far away as the antipodes; but no one had either the experience nor the picture of it]. René Benjamin said of his title character in *Gaspard*, "Décidément il ne comprenait rien à cette bataille cruelle, où on ne voyait toujours aucun ennemi, et où son régiment fondait sous un feu d'enfer" [He really didn't understand anything about this cruel battle, where you still couldn't see any enemies, and where his regiment was melting away under a hellish fire]. Another character puts it very simply, "Je m' figurais pas la guerre comme ça" [I didn't imagine war like this]. In the disorder of the front, wrote Jean Paulhan, "le sens [of words] leur échappe et il semble qu'ils se peuvent appliquer à n'importe quoi, ou peu s'en faut" [the meaning (of words) escapes them and it seems that they can be applied to anything, or almost]. Observers and thinkers of the era were led to imagine total destruction, expressed through powerful Biblical prefigurations: the flood, the destruction of Babylon, of Sodom and Gomorrha, and chiefly the Apocalypse, with its elaborate rhetoric and images and its dramatic clashes between good and evil.[1]

Militarily speaking, there was a radical break between this conflict and the Franco-Prussian War. Jules Romains explained the break this way: "Depuis des siècles, toutes les guerres, au moins en Europe, ont eu une décision conventionnelle. Les gens se reconnaissaient battus, parce qu'ils avaient accepté la partie et les règles du jeu. . . . Il a suffi que les peuples n'acceptent plus cette convention pour que tout soit changé" [For centuries, at least in Europe, all wars had a conventional outcome. People acknowledged themselves to be beaten, because they had accepted the match and the rules of the game. All it took was for nations to accept that convention no longer for everything to be changed]. In France, conscription produced huge armies composed almost wholly of untested soldiers, usually led by only slightly more experienced officers. Although Romains quoted the dictum, "C'est une guerre faite par les sous-lieutenants de 14 et conduite par les sous-lieutenants de 70" [It's a war carried out by the second lieutenants of 1914 and led by the second lieutenants of 1870], the latter were few in number and, moreover, contributed to the disaster by thinking the war in terms of the earlier conflict.[2] From the first month of the war, armies found themselves facing off against the enemy over a line stretching from the North Sea to Switzerland. The initial expectations by each side of an early, and favorable, conclusion to the fighting gave way to predictions of an end in three months, then six, and so on, as mobile warfare turned into entrenchment, that is, siege warfare; evidence suggests that, once entrenchment was accomplished, the war seemed to the participants endless. From the absence of hygiene came the nickname *poilus* —at first used pejoratively but shortly turning into a pious cant phrase. The mud and water—which Stendhal's and Erckmann-Chatrian's heroes had already

---

1. John Cruickshank, *Variations on Catastrophe* (Oxford: Clarendon Press, 1982), 4; Cooperman, *World War I and the American Novel*, 7–8; Romains, *Prélude à Verdun*, 28–29; René Benjamin, *Gaspard* (Paris: Arthème Fayard, 1915), 118–19; Jean Paulhan, *Le Guerrier appliqué* (1930; reprint, Paris: Gallimard, 1982), 71.

2. Romains, *Prélude à Verdun*, 101, 133.

noted at Waterloo and Zola had his soldiers suffer through in 1870 — became, if one is to believe a number of novels and numerous eyewitness records, enemies worse than the Germans because they threatened to paralyze activity. Human and animal forms disintegrated, when the mud literally swallowed some who fell.

The terrible loss of life — more than one million killed and wounded per year just for the French and some 1,335,000 French military dead for the entire war — can be attributed in part to three technical inventions: barbed wire entanglements; the magazine-fed rifle; and the huge howitzers, which destroyed the landscape as well as men and fortifications. Added to these was the misguided policy of repeatedly launching frontal attacks, with misapplication of tactics, such as having men carry sixty-pound packs while "going up over the top" (over breastworks) in front of machine-gun fire — attacks that were countered by heavy artillery intended for use against fortifications but turned against waves of soldiers. Mass infantry charges, writes Frederick Forsyth, were "suicidal. And yet that was exactly the tactic of the generals on both sides for four long years . . . so that Flanders became the scene of the most horrific battlefield slaughter. It was an exercise in obscurantism and blindness to make the mind numb."[3]

There was also huge magnification of means on both sides. In *Prélude à Verdun*, Romains describes an attack of 1915 on a small sector, in which 100,000 shells were fired in twenty-four hours, followed by a heavy artillery storm and an assault that failed. When one reflects that the total territory gained or lost by either side in such bloody offensives as the Somme (July 1916) was often just a few square miles, at the most two hundred, and that the soldiers were often aware of the insignificant gains, sometimes measuring the ground covered by repossessing trenches they had occupied previously; when one then compares such figures to the loss of life — in the hundreds of thousands for individual offensives — it is little wonder that the sense of purpose to the war was eroded for many. Men were driven near madness by losing large numbers of their squads, seeing friends blown up before their eyes, living for days next to corpses and rotting blown-off limbs, existing in conditions of cold and filth and deprivation. "The war's violence was total," writes Gabriel

---

3. Quoted in Keegan and Holmes, *Soldiers*, 9. For war statistics, see Romains, *Prélude à Verdun*, 46; Jones, *The Art of War*, 441, 463; Keegan and Holmes, *Soldiers*, 72, 97, 141.

Kolko, "involving every aspect of social systems down to their very roots, and their leaders' initial assumption that the relentless conflict could be fought without considering the implications of such trauma on the men in the trenches was one of their greatest miscalculations."[4]

In extreme cases, self-coherence and moral judgment almost disappeared with the sense of purpose. As Michael Walzer puts it, "The slaughter of modern warfare overwhelm[ed] [men's] capacity for moral understanding." The increasing sense that the war was going nowhere, that each belligerent was suffering losses such that the destruction would devour even the victor, and that civilization itself, that is, the West, was somehow threatened, undercut the nationalist rhetoric that had presided over the beginning of the war and increased as it endured. D. H. Lawrence's *Lady Chatterley's Lover* begins: "Ours is essentially a tragic age. . . . The cataclysm has happened, we are among the ruins." "Nous autres civilisations, nous savons maintenant que nous sommes mortelles" [We civilizations now know that we are mortal], asserted Paul Valéry in 1919, and Georges Duhamel antiphrastically entitled his fictional sketches of the war, published in 1918, *Civilisation, 1914–1917*.[5]

In the background as well as the foreground of the Great War was technology, the servant that turns on its master. This technology, and its uses, were in turn founded on an erosive and deluding doctrine of progress. In Valéry's words, "Il y a l'illusion perdue d'une culture européenne et la démonstration de l'impuissance de la connaissance à sauver quoi que ce soit; il y a la science, atteinte mortellement dans ses ambitions morales" [There is the lost illusion of a European culture and the demonstration of the powerlessness of knowledge to save anything whatsoever; there is science, mortally wounded in its moral ambitions]. Winston Churchill, seeking to identify what made this war so terrible, wrote of the role of science, which "unfolded her treasures and secrets to desperate demands of men, and placed in their hands agencies and apparatus almost decisive in their character. In consequence, many novel features presented themselves. Instead of merely starving fortified towns, whole nations were methodically subjected to the process of re-

4. Gabriel Kolko, *Century of War* (New York: The New Press, 1994), 125.

5. Michael Walzer, *Just and Unjust Wars* (New York: Basic Books, 1977), 109; D. H. Lawrence, *Lady Chatterley's Lover* (1928; reprint, New York: Grove Press, 1959), 1; Paul Valéry, *Œuvres*, vol. 1, ed. Jean Hytier (Paris: Gallimard/Bibliothèque de la Pléiade, 1957), 988.

duction by famine. The entire population in one capacity or another took part in the War, all were equally object of attack." Michael Adas summarizes what he calls "the theme of humanity betrayed and consumed by the technology that Europeans had long considered the surest proof of their civilization's superiority," and, like numerous other commentators, he notes the disappearance, amid advanced technological destruction, of the notions and vocabulary of chivalry.[6]

The break with the past that I emphasize here may appear to contradict the historical perspective of synthesis for which I argued in the second chapter, concerning symbols and their cultural role. But synthesis is, of course, a reconciliation, a subsuming or surpassing of opposites, a jump across historical time, painted space, or other contraries. Despite the persistence of many cultural codes and forms and a patriotic rhetoric designed to recuperate the past unchanged, *tel quel*, the First World War provided, unhappily, a new way of reading French history and culture, as an unstable confluence of destructive impulses, whose fulfillment would be Verdun, the Somme, and surrealism. Jay Winter denies that the cultural history of the Great War is "a phase in the onward ascent of modernism," the rupture of 1914–1918 being "much less complete" than believed. While he is right to point out that the cultural break constituted by the war years was far from entire, and it is obvious that the seeds of modernism and even its first harvest antedated the conflict, it would be a mistake to subsume all posterior developments in France under the label of continuity and to ignore the role of the war in subsequent aesthetic and cultural changes. As Roger Martin du Gard wrote in 1911, with reference to the Agadir crisis and the threat of war, "C'est l'effroi désespéré de la feuille dans un vent de tempête. . . . Cette crise démolit tous mes espoirs intellectuels, toutes mes convictions, toute ma foi dans le progrès. . . . Je pense que rien de tout cela n'en sortira indemne" [It is the desperate terror of the leaf in a storm wind. This crisis demolishes all my intellectual hopes, all my convictions, all my faith in progress. I believe that nothing will come out of this unscathed].[7]

6. Valéry, *Œuvres*, 1:990; Winston Churchill, *Thoughts and Adventures* (New York: Norton, 1991), 175–76; Michael Adas, *Machines as the Measure of Men: Science, Technology, and Ideologies of Western Dominance* (Ithaca: Cornell University Press, 1989), 371.

7. Roger Martin du Gard, *Journal*, vol. 1, ed. Claude Sicard (Paris: Gallimard, 1992), 352.

World War I also provided the cultural and political framework for the next decades, including the economic crises of the 1920s and 1930s, the re-armament of Germany, the next world conflict, and the artistic revolution of surrealism. "It was a peculiarity of the First World War that it remained contemporary ever after in the imaginations of men who . . . had fought it when they were young," writes Francis Spufford, adding that "it has the permanent function in the culture of reducing military glory to the equivalent of an invitation to walk into the blades of a combine harvester."[8] The burden of the war is still with Europeans at the end of the twentieth century, as is demonstrated in its continuing presence in fiction and drama and the not-inconsiderable recent scholarly research.

The moral dislocation and cultural catastrophe produced by the conflict were both foreshadowed and paralleled by literary and graphic modernism: in my definition, a willful departure from previous aesthetic norms and their rationality in order to create a uniquely twentieth-century art. A striking example is Roger de la Fresnaye's cubist canvas "L'Artillerie," dated 1911. In hindsight, the prophetic, or at least foreshadowing, insights of pre-1914 modernism appear remarkable. The disintegration that Katharine Kuh and others have called "break-up" in modern art fits well the fractured mental space of Europe after the war. In German art, the expressionists' singularly innovative canvases seem to prefigure the disaster to come, whatever their immediate context may have been. In music and dance, such phenomena as the scores of Arnold Schoenberg, perceived as cacophonous and "nerve-jangling," and of Igor Stravinsky and the Russian Ballet, notably *The Rite of Spring* (1913), constituted not only a rebellion against previous forms of developmental music and classical techniques but, as Modris Eksteins argues, a foreshadowing of cultural disintegration.[9]

In French painting, first the impressionists and neoimpressionists, then Cézanne, the Fauves, and the cubists progressively eroded and then shattered line, color, and perspective, and redefined space. The overlapping planes,

8. Francis Spufford, "The War That Never Stopped," *TLS*, 22 March 1996, pp. 11–12.

9. Katharine Kuh, *Break-Up: The Core of Modern Art* (Greenwich, Conn.: New York Graphic Society, 1965), 11; Winter, *Sites of Memory, Sites of Mourning*, 3. The term "nerve-jangling" comes from Cruickshank, *Variations on Catastrophe*, 4. See also Daniel R. Schwarz, *Reconfiguring Modernism: Explorations in the Relationships Between Modern Art and Modern Literature* (New York: St. Martin's Press, 1997).

fractured and superimposed forms, and disappearing perspective of the cubists are especially vigorous spatial parallels to the fleeting, confused, somnolent psyches of modernist heroes. As what Kenneth Silver calls "a system for the breaking down of forms and a method for organizing pictorial decomposition"—that is, a paradoxical order within disorder—cubism could portray a war that broke all rules. Its "lack of association with the past was the analogue of the *poilu*'s general sense of dissociation." It was cubism that made dissociation and discontinuity an aesthetic principle and, among other things, taught observers to "read" or interpret history as a juxtaposition of elements both disparate and similar, rather than as coherent meaning progressively developed. As Guillaume Apollinaire wrote, "Les rapports qu'il y a entre les figures juxtaposées de mes poèmes sont tout autant expressifs que les mots qui les composent" [The relationships between the juxtaposed elements of my poems are just as expressive as the words that constitute them].[10] After 1914, against the background of a flourishing nationalistic iconography, which built on the icons and tropes that developed throughout the nineteenth century and especially around the Franco-Prussian War, some artists recognized immediately the correlation between the war experience and cubism. There were even patriotic cubist works, such as Jean Metzinger's "L'Infirmière," 1916. Yet, ironically, many patriotic writers and cartoonists between the wars attacked this movement as being German, which it was not.

In the great modernist works of fiction, the traditional idea of story was abandoned, discredited on the grounds of being inadequate, simplistic, and psychologically or culturally indefensible. Plot was disarticulated, contradicted, or otherwise assailed; characters lost their stable selves; language was stretched by loosening of syntax; thematic centers were undermined; most important, the narrative lost its authority through erosion of the narrator's identity, duplication of plot, lack of closure, and so forth. In poetry, flexible forms replaced strict ones, coherence gave way to incoherence, and rationality to irrationality, especially in 1916 among the dadaists, as a deliberate reaction against the war. Although a number of the major French avant-garde works appeared after 1918, and surrealism dates only from the 1920s, the signs of literary break-up were already visible earlier, in André Gide's ironic

---

10. Silver, *Esprit de corps*, 84; Claude Debon, *Guillaume Apollinaire après "Alcools"* (Paris: Lettres Modernes/Minard, 1981), 63–64.

texts such as *Paludes* (1895), in Marcel Proust's *Du côté de chez Swann* (1913), and in Apollinaire's *Alcools* (1913). In these developments, related to (though not generally influenced by) the schema of Freudian psychology in so far as it is antirational, the central consciousness, or perceiving I/eye, seems to have lost its organizing ability, which the Cartesian *cogito* had explained and represented.

These developments took place against a background of national militancy that proved, in 1914, far more powerful than the countercurrents of socialist internationalism. The Moroccan crises of 1905 and 1911, which involved clashes with Germany at Tangiers and Agadir, had ended favorably for those who supported French interests in Morocco, but contributed to mounting tensions between France and Germany and a developing war mentality. The calls for revenge against the Germanic empire for the perceived rape of Alsace-Lorraine became more and more frequent in the period 1905–1914. As chapter 2 has shown, the image of Joan of Arc was evoked frequently, with major publications on her by Anatole France (an objective study) and others. When war broke out in 1914, the *union sacrée*, by which the socialists were sacrificed to the rightists, represented supposedly a national consensus — and the vindication and fulfillment of nationalist doctrines of all shades. In official pronouncements, journalism, and some literature appeared the theme of a holy war or crusade, expressed in rhetoric borrowed from the Revolution and its sequels and the old rhetoric of chivalry, joined often to a crude and bellicose slang. What Eksteins writes about Germany applied to some degree in France: "In August 1914, most Germans regarded the armed conflict they were entering in spiritual terms. The war was above all an idea. . . . The government and military had no concrete war aims, only a strategy and vision. . . . War was regarded . . . as the supreme test of spirit . . . a test of vitality, and culture, and life."[11]

Shortly before the outbreak of the conflict, a number of literary figures expressed particularly well the strain of militant nationalism. One was Ernest Psichari, author of *L'Appel des armes* [The call to arms] (1913). The grandson of the historian and defrocked priest Ernest Renan, Psichari reacted against the positivism and materialism of many of his elders, became an officer, converted to Roman Catholicism, and adopted an idealistic militarism based

11. Eksteins, *Rites of Spring*, 90.

partly on Vigny's notion of passive obedience. He understood war as a means for both an individual and a nation to achieve the moral and political grandeur to which they are called by divine will. Psichari's death in September 1914 may have constituted the ultimate realization of his ideas on the individual plane, but his heroic discipline would seem to have attracted few followers.

Another spokesman for militant nationalism was the poet and journalist Charles Péguy, who, before he was killed (again, in September 1914), borrowed alike from French socialism, republicanism, Roman Catholicism, and militant nationalism to forge his personal vision of a renewed French society, faithful to its medieval principles. He had supported Dreyfus through his journalism, but in the name of a *mystique* founded on the idea of nation. To protect this traditional France he sounded, in his poetry, drama, and journalism, a call to arms. In his view, the soldier was neither a common hireling nor a dispensable raw material, but rather a superior figure, a national model as well as a servant of the nation, inspired by patriotic altruism and ready to risk all. Echoing the Horatian "Dulce et decorum est pro patria mori," he spoke of a just war for the carnal earth—the war, of course, that would restore to France Alsace and Lorraine, the very homeland of Joan of Arc, reestablishing the territorial integrity necessary to moral rebuilding. Péguy's genius was to present the patriotic ideal as embodied and expressed in the very tongue of France. The spiraling repetitions that characterize his style in both poetry and prose mirror his vision: the past is an image of the future; France's destiny is a movement of historical return. (His influence on Mussolini has been noted.[12])

Unlike Stendhal and Zola, Péguy took as his patriotic idol and standard-bearer not Napoleon—associated with the breakdown of tradition and evils of imperialism—but Joan, who, it will be recalled, while serving as the monarchists' icon throughout much of the nineteenth century, had gradually been appropriated by republicans and even freethinkers. His first historical-polemical work on Joan of Arc was his drama of 1897, *Jeanne d'Arc*, consisting of twenty-four acts divided into three parts: *A Domrémy, Les Batailles, Rouen*. The drama was dedicated to all those "qui seront morts . . . pour l'établissement

12. Reed Way Dasenbrock, "Paul de Man: The Modernist as Fascist," *South Central Review* 6 (Summer 1989), 14.

de la République socialiste universelle" [all those who will die for the establishment of the universal socialist republic].[13] The emphasis is on Joan as *soldier and saint*—a rare combination, he shows, in modern times; she was a soldier for God, possessing the virtues of the warrior. She is associated with the
true France: anti-industrial, antimodern, peasant, royalist but not abusively
so, since land, nation, people, and king are understood as one. Péguy's idiosyncratic social thought allows him to see Joan as the true socialist type, as
well as a revolutionary who cared nothing for established authority. In his
later *Mystère de la charité de Jeanne d'Arc*, in which there is increased emphasis
on the collectivity, the saint is used less as a character than as a figurehead, a
symbol of the regenerative power of war. The historical and moral space of
medieval France, organized around throne and altar, reemerges in his vision
and assumes an atemporal (but very political) status.

A third figure whose militant nationalism helped shape attitudes in the first
years of the century was the anti-Dreyfusard Charles Maurras, a man of letters who was also founder and principal force in the Action Française movement; with Léon Daudet, he edited its newspaper. A monarchist, unlike
Péguy, and a supporter of "classical" (that is, ancient) artistic values, he ex-
alted in his journalism authoritarian and hierarchical principles and an aggressive, xenophobic nationalism, of which the soldier was seen as the defender.

The nationalism of Maurice Barrès, one of the major literary figures of the
period as well as a member of the Chambre des Députés for more than
twenty years, was centered around Lorraine, his birthplace. While he can be
considered one of the major conservative voices of France both before and
after World War I, he was also a severe critic of his nation in its radical and
modernist incarnations; he was staunchly anti-Dreyfus and criticized harshly
all forms of decadence as he saw them, including the presence of foreigners,
the movement of population toward Paris, and social instability. For him, *revanche* and recovery of Alsace and Lorraine—"the land and the dead," with
the claims of the past on the present—constituted a moral as well as a political
crusade. His *Colette Baudoche*, the last volume of a triology called *Les Bastions
de l'Est*, concerns the Prussian occupation of Metz. As the previous chapter
noted, the heroine rejects the suit of a German, in this case a boarder in her

13. Charles Péguy, *Jeanne d'Arc* (1897; reprint, Paris: Gallimard, 1948), dedication.

mother's house; the powerful image of French soldiers sacrificed in the Franco-Prussian War, standing for the timeless community of Lorraine and France, makes compromise in the present impossible. Such other titles as *L'Appel au soldat* (1900) and *Scènes et doctrines du nationalisme* (1902) suggest the militant element in Barrès's writing and politics.

At the same time that Psichari, Péguy, Maurras, Barrès, and others were promoting their nationalist, usually militant views, nationalism and the idea of nation were assailed in more than one quarter. The Dreyfus Affair, while mobilizing the right and much of the center around the army, the defender of the nation, had also given impetus to strains of internationalism developing through anarchist and socialist circles. It was only through a last-hour consensus that the *union sacrée* was achieved, in the face of what had been strong socialist opposition to any national war. And while the idea of nation may have seemed triumphant in 1914, it was constructed on ground that had been undermined already and would be so additionally in the months to come.

—

The following discussion of French war literature assumes the importance of the role of previous wars in mediating the Great War, and, subsequently, its function as a historical mediation for the following great European conflict. That such mediation on both sides of the 1914–1918 watershed took place is beyond doubt. From the outbreak of hostilities onward, an immense propaganda effort was visible in the form of words and pictures of the awful 1870–1871 defeat, which had to be avenged, and of past glories, which had to be revived. Henri Focillon wrote, "Il faut donc que l'art entre à son tour dans la bataille" [Art in turn must join the battle]; he saw it as "le programme d'une race" [the program of a race].[14] The indisputable fact of such mediation of the past offers one counterargument to the theses of some cultural critics on the irretrievability of the past. In 1914 statesmen, generals, other commentators and participants, and the general French public supposed that the conflict was to be a successful replaying of the Franco-Prussian War; similarly, in 1939, whatever the politics of the observer, it could not but be agreed that

14. Quoted in Silver, *Esprit de corps*, 418n66.

the new war was a continuation of the one that had ended twenty years before.

Quotation and juxtaposition of inherited images can, however, be ironic and self-critical. In Pierre Drieu La Rochelle's *La Comédie de Charleroi* (1934), a devastating critique of World War I, the hero, reflecting on the Waterloo episode of Stendhal's *La Chartreuse de Parme*, Zola's *La Débâcle*, and other fictional and painted depictions of nineteenth-century wars, reaches an ironic view of the new conflict, asking himself, "Où sont les guerres d'antan?" As David Carroll has put it, "The French soldier who for Péguy and Barrès went to war to save the homeland and the spiritual values of France and Western civilization returned from war in Drieu La Rochelle's work only to find that he had saved nothing, that all of the nationalist myths for which he had fought were empty. Everything in fact was reversed."[15] Montherlant's idiosyncratic treatment of the war in *Le Songe* (1922), even as it calls on models of military grandeur as old as the *Iliad* and Caesar's *Gallic Wars*, undercuts them with scattered irony toward the hero and its disabused view of the war. Moreover, contrasted with general iconographic recall of the past through quotation in this work is the opposite phenomenon: total rejection of the tradition, iconographically speaking.

These views of the past and its enduring imperatives do not in the least depend upon literary acknowledgment, of course; but it is important to note that they *were* expressed in fiction a great deal, as if it were particularly suited for meditation on the recurring patterns of history and their meaning or meaninglessness. To what degree subsequent events were really affected by such reflections—novel acting as event itself—is difficult to assess, as are the effects of changed tactics and weaponry, especially as mechanized warfare reduced the close contacts between adversaries and rendered battle distant and anonymous. The use of long-range artillery in World War I and the consequent invisibility of the enemy, whose situation, however, was felt to resemble very much one's own, seem to have created at once a sense of impersonality and the ability to imagine oneself in the place of the adversary. Certainly the effects of these changes on individual combatants and on their subjective

15. Drieu La Rochelle, *La Comédie de Charleroi*, 65; David Carroll, *French Literary Fascism: Nationalism, Anti-Semitism, and the Ideology of Culture* (Princeton: Princeton University Press, 1995), 128.

reactions are central to much twentieth-century war fiction. The thesis proposed in chapter 3 is supported by the Great War: that the definitive breakdown of nineteenth-century modes of European fighting, in which squares established a sense of collectivity, and the transformation of battle into trench warfare, air warfare, and, by midcentury, foxhole-type combat affected the way war was perceived and felt during the two great conflicts of the century, and hence affected its recording in imaginative work. The war novel built around irony, dissociation, and fragmentation, whether found in plot, thematics, syntax, characterization, or a combination of these modes, is the principal literary response to this development.

War fiction of this era reflects other cultural dilemmas also, of course, in particular the issue of heroism. Numerous works of the Great War, while emphasizing the slaughter of millions, of whom many made the willing and conscious sacrifice of their lives, adumbrate a radical departure from the earlier understanding of heroism, to which they necessarily look back. Heroism, as Barry Targan has written, is normally the prerogative of the victor—that is, it is *remembered* heroism. In its most visible form, at least, it is composed of those deeds that allow men to endure, then prevail—but actively, not merely by waiting things out, and sometimes dramatically. I would add that the context usually is that of a coherent polis, or at least important sectors of one, in which the public espouses their undertaking. There must be a moral component also: for instance, the application of the term *heroic* to even dangerous deeds and personal sacrifice of an SS officer is now deemed unacceptable. The heroic actions, even if numerous, must stand out against others—as dramatic, exceptional—and the hero must act willingly, with consciousness of his duty, his function, his contribution. By definition, such a man proves to be more courageous, more magnanimous, more skilled than others. His acts constitute, as Henry Phillips has observed, a triumph of culture over nature.[16]

In France, the models of heroism were ancient and numerous, going back to the Greeks and Romans, the medieval figures, historical and literary, such as Roland (whose presence in nineteenth-century French literature was noted in chapter 2) and Bayard ("chevalier sans peur et sans reproche"), and continuing through Renaissance figures, especially royal, and the great mili-

---

16. Barry Targan, "True Grit," *Sewanee Review* 103 (Fall 1995), 587; Henry Phillips, "Theatricality in the Tragedies of Corneille" (Paper delivered at the University of Sheffield, May 1996).

tary commanders of the seventeenth century, then peaking—for some admirers—with Revolutionary figures and Napoleon. The dramas of Corneille were responsible, it would seem, for one model of heroism, picked up in a different mode by Stendhal, who was nevertheless aware that the ideals he admired in Corneille's plays and Spanish drama, and any work tending toward an imperial *geste*, were no longer possible in post-Napoleonic France under Charles X and Louis-Philippe, the *roi bourgeois*. Heroism appeared unrenewable. Thus the character break between hero and others, which must characterize all assumption of the heroic status, became also a chronological break, and a problematics of heroism appeared in French fiction. It is chiefly with the first world conflict, however, that this questioning of heroism became widespread in war writing, as a consequence surely of the enormous scale of fruitless engagement on the western front and skepticism about meaningful action. Yet, counterbalancing this cynicism, a new understanding of heroics could be seen. In Georges Duhamel's war volumes (discussed below), the less self-aware the soldier and the less useful his sacrifice, the more heroic he appears: the new ethics of nationalistic war makes a martyr and a hero of the little man, lost in a meaningless battle. While fitting the ostensibly democratic form of twentieth-century society and the huge human scale of the war, involving millions of "little men," this understanding of the heroic, noble as it appears, would seem to be connected to the atomizing of fictional form, including the difficulty of constructing coherent plots around outstanding deeds.

Furthermore, there was the current perception—which has increased since—that "culture" had gone wild, devouring nature, figuratively and literally, or rather, breaking down into a new, degraded nature, of which the impassable mud fields of Flanders offer the best example. French victory was called into question, not only because, the first euphoria of autumn 1914 once past, it seemed by no means assured, but also by the character of the conflict, in which, as so many observers pointed out, the stalemated fighting tended toward mutual destruction. As the idea of victory was undermined, courage, skill, generosity of spirit, and sacrifice, while amply attested, tended to lose their direction and their meaning. This tendency would seem to have had an effect on war fiction, where valiant gestures are often undercut by authorial treatment (direct commentary, juxtaposition, or ironies of plot): often neither the agents themselves, nor their witnesses, nor the recording writers or novelists seem to believe in the possibility of heroism. The use of language to re-store the ideal is futile: the old words cannot create what is not there.

One of the consequences of these developments is that the narrative field, like the historical one, became more problematic for twentieth-century novel-ists than it had been for earlier writers. The fundamental difficulty was, how could one possibly know and recount the huge, prolonged, and complex con-flicts of this century? Victor Hugo could revisit Waterloo, have it explained to him by a few survivors and by historians, and recount it in a coherent fash-ion. After 1914 all an individual combatant, or writer, could hope for was to know *part* of the event and the historical space and present it as typical or metonymous. Problems of representation were felt alike by soldiers writing from the trenches and by those artists who, years later, attempted to re-create the feeling or meaning of the war. Drieu La Rochelle had his hero reflect, "Je ne croyais plus à la possibilité de réussir la représentation de la journée. . . . Ni pour les Allemands ni pour les Français. On se bat pour exprimer quelque chose, pour représenter quelque chose. . . . Mais cette représentation était ratée" [I no longer believed it possible for the representation of the day to succeed. . . . Neither for the Germans nor for the French. One fights to ex-press something, to represent something. . . . But this representation was a failure]. Drieu's statement suggests that how war appears and how it is inter-preted may be connected to its causes as well as its results.[17]

Romains is one of the best analysts of the phenomenon. First there is the problem of vision, which becomes that of perspective and comprehension. "Il n'y avait nulle part en Artois ni en Champagne une butte assez haute pour que le champ de bataille pût être embrassé du regard par le chef. . . . A plus forte raison n'y avait-il nulle part une tête pour penser cette guerre" [There was nowhere in Artois or Champagne a rise high enough for the commander to see the entire battlefield. . . . A fortiori there was nowhere a mind to think it]. Knowledge, even proximate, could be generalized only abstractly: in prac-tice, "la connaissance qu'ils [witnesses] en prenaient s'amortissait à vingt pas comme un feu de lanterne dans le brouillard" [their command of it dissipated twenty steps away like the light of a lantern in the fog]. The difficulty, as ana-lyzed by Romains, is not unrelated to problems in amalgamating a series of one-sided perspectives, problems addressed by Edmund Husserl's phenome-

---

17. Drieu La Rochelle, *La Comédie de Charleroi*, 69.

nology. Romains observes: "Les jointures entre ces vues partielles . . . ne pouvaient se faire que dans un lieu étranger à l'homme, comme l'indifférente pensée divine" [The connections among these partial views could be established
only in some spot alien to man, such as indifferent divine thought]. This disconnection can be expressed in narratological terms, the will and the sender
both being eroded and plot thus undermined. Romains, who had been for
decades interested in the mind of collectivities, saw that human will had become inadequate to history and in particular to the participants in its daily
development: "Pas une volonté non plus qui fût d'assez grandes dimensions
pour peser vraiment de son propre poids sur l'ensemble de la guerre, ni qui
sût se faire assez ferme et perçante pour parvenir telle quelle jusqu'à l'homme
de la tranchée" [Nor was there any will great enough to weigh with its own
weight on the whole of the war, nor that could become sufficiently steady and
sharp to reach men in the trenches].[18]

Another alteration in the narrative field, visible in much twentieth-century
war writing and devolving from the modern developments of warfare, concerned the psychological dimension, indeed the ontological sphere. Once the
old moral centers and *raison d'être* of chivalry, king, faith, hero, and finally
nation—the last incarnation of authority—had been called into question, how
could one account for the war, locate the moral center or meaning of such
conflicts, except by a vision imposed from without, a new myth, or by making
oneself the moral as well as the experiential center? But if neither the event
nor its meaning could be identified, where was the coherence to be found,
and what was the significance of the self that reflected upon it? Throughout
the century there developed an increasing tendency for both the historical
event and the feeling subject to explode, in a dispersal or denial of purpose
and meaning, giving the lie to what had been the teleology of fiction and history alike. Thus, whereas Zola saw the challenge to the military novelist as
that of establishing fact, hence credibility, by documentation, and problematized only the reasons for the French defeat and nothing about the experience
of war nor how it should be rendered, a number of French war authors from
1914 on tended to wrestle with, sometimes even to put at the center of their
texts, the related problems of knowing and telling the war and knowing and
telling the self. It would be erroneous, however, to overlook the literary pres-

18. Romains, *Prélude à Verdun*, 29, 31.

ence of those whose undertaking was to affirm, precisely, the military values
and the principles of national unity and legitimacy discussed earlier, which
were to be called into question by the phenomena I have just reviewed.

In any case, for writers who questioned the war, whether initially or later,
and rejected nationalistic rhetoric, the challenge was that of finding a language in which to deal with their war experience or that of others. If the linguistic and narrative forms of the past refuse to adhere to the new experience,
it becomes inexpressible—one is only trying to "say the unsayable." Romains
averred, "Aucune lettre, aucune conversation, encore bien moins aucune description de mauvaise littérature . . . n'en donnera une idée" [No letter, no
conversation, still less some bad literary description will give any idea of it].[19]
This term *unsayable*, or *indicible*—a trope formerly featured chiefly in love
poetry (unique among the main genres in recognizing the inability to convey
reality)—from 1914 on appears in countless documents and fictional pieces
about the Great War, underlining the relationship between rhetoric and narrative, on the one hand, and history on the other.

In a development that contrasts with the persistent mode of naturalism,
which I examine shortly, but that also interpenetrates it, fiction about the war
began to show a tendency toward the amorphous. Despite the mimetic intentions and unselfconscious narration of most accounts, including most contemporaneous ones, there arose a distrust of traditional aesthetic structures that
aimed at intelligibility and of the representative capacities of writing. Conse-
quently, the narrative model sketched in chapter 3, based on clear oppositions and teleology, tended to disappear in twentieth-century war fiction. If
historical *order*—a coherent movement toward fulfillment—is not possible,
then the novel loses its authority, its *plot*—that is, its former means of cognition—and the temporal undertakings it traditionally recounted begin to be
seen ironically, through self-qualification and self-subversion of the text, including juxtaposition of meaninglessness with desire for meaning. The function of subject is subverted, as identity between individual soldiers and the
collective subject—the army—and the nation—a sender—breaks down, and
the relationship of will between subject and ostensible object weakens. This
is a function of ideological breakdown, and of the order that ideology sup-
poses, as identification between the subjects and the thesis presiding over the

19. Ibid., 107.

war is qualified, even wholly rejected, as in certain later works that came out of the colonial wars.

Likewise, in some novels, the multiple subject—a squad or other small group—seems to be the reluctant and ineffective helper of a distant political force, with which the relationship erodes. Or the war itself becomes the subject, a power using human pawns for its own ends: a mechanical monster, a hostile historical force. In Cooperman's words, "No longer one subordinate element among many contributing to a total aesthetic structure . . . the war itself became the chief protagonist." Whence a weak underlying structure, by which the will of the ostensible subjects is directed not toward the nominal collective goal but either against the war itself (seen as negative object, opponent, or hostile subject) or simply toward survival; in this way, plot progression becomes merely negative. The plot can also include officers—again, with the power of life and death—whose decisions are perceived by the soldiers as hostile. Thus, from one perspective, subject, object, and opponent become identical—the war itself—giving rise to moral confusion, as illustrated by fraternization with the enemy, who is similarly crushed by a system of forces that instrumentalize the soldiers for ends they cannot identify. The outcome of all these developments is fatalism, which works against the earlier war narrative, based on a vector of will. This is true doubtless because narrative will depends upon a sense of human freedom. Sartre argued that literature itself can arise only in and from freedom, just as it appeals to the freedom of readers.[20]

Despite the correlation of disintegrated forms and the singular experience of the war, the naturalistic novel, as it had been shaped by Zola and others, was the dominant form for World War I novels in France, suiting well the sordidness of the trench experience and the sense of the collective drama (as Zola conveyed it in *Germinal*, for instance). This persistence of nineteenth-century forms may be what led one critic to assert that "major fiction" dealing with the war arrived later in France than in America or Germany—this despite numerous widely read novels that antedate her reference point (1929, with Ernest Hemingway's *A Farewell to Arms* and Erich Maria Remarque's *Im*

---

20. Cooperman, *World War I and the American Novel*, 194; Jean-Paul Sartre, *Qu'est-ce que la littérature?* (1948; reprint, Paris: Gallimard, 1985), 65, 79–82.

Westen nichts Neues).[21] Benjamin, for instance, used in *Gaspard* (1915) techniques of narration familiar to writers of the previous generation, as did Roland Dorgelès in his postwar novel *Les Croix de bois* [Wooden crosses] (1919) and, later, Romains in *Prélude à Verdun* (1938). Henri Barbusse, known sometimes as the Zola of the trenches, echoed in *Le Feu: Journal d'une escouade* (1916) his great predecessor's descriptions of the mines in *Germinal*. The naturalistic novel, I have noted, was particularly appropriate for dealing with crowds and groups of protagonists; and one of the phenomena to be noted in much writing of the Great War is the replacement of the early nineteenth-century hero (particularly the strong central personality that characterizes Stendhal's fiction) by groups of actors, often barely individualized or anonymous, passing quickly and replaced by others.

The subtitle of Barbusse's novel, the most famous French war book, points both to the collective character of the central presence—a squad—and the iterative quality of the plot (the word *journal* suggesting normally the routine of the quotidian), both departures from the Romantic model of extraordinary events for exceptional characters. Despite certain naturalistic features, it illustrates a new mode of composition, suitable to the ideological breakdown. It consists mostly of clusters of scenes, or vignettes, in which the setting and circumstances count as much as the characters, and whose order could generally be changed without disruption of the text; only those vignettes that complete the decimation of the squad, and those in which a moral awareness, based on extensive war experience, comes about must occupy their present position on the rudimentary plot line. The novel's questioning of not only modes but aims of war, in dramatic contrast to the nationalistic thinking that prevailed, though not unchallenged, in the nineteenth century, is facilitated by the first-person narration, a noteworthy departure from the naturalistic model.

The shockingly graphic depiction of the front and use of vulgar speech are intended to demystify the war experience and its rationale. (Barbusse was, reportedly, the first French writer to use the term *bourrage de crâne*, or brainwashing.) He emphasizes the social gulf between officers and men, in order to stress the fraternity of working-class soldiers on both sides. Likewise, he

---

21. Rima Drell Reck, *Drieu La Rochelle and the Picture Gallery Novel* (Baton Rouge: Louisiana State University Press, 1990), 71.

attacks the aggressive nationalistic propaganda by depicting front-line truces of 1914–1915, in which combatants of both sides gathered in No-Man's Land several times, including at Christmas, to talk sing, and exchange gifts. Praising the German socialist Karl Liebknecht, who had been imprisoned for protesting against the war, Barbusse has his autobiographical character look ahead to a future in which there will be total social revolution and no more war. "Honte à la gloire militaire! Honte aux armées!" [Shame on military glory! Shame on armies!].[22] Barbusse finds the war's meaning only by depriving it of meaning: nothing about the experience in the trenches makes any sense; and the war seems justified only by the hope that the war's very horror will make future conflicts unthinkable, a hope informed by the eschatological perspective which anticipates the fulfillment of the French Revolution—the elimination of the ruling classes.

In fact, the book was banned by the German authorities as being subversive to their war effort; the French authorities did not, however, dare censor or ban it, because of its immediate and wide popularity. After the mutinies among the French troops in 1917 and the Russian Revolution, Barbusse even dared to hope that his book would convince armies on both sides to cease fighting. Among its readers were Wilfred Owen, Siegfried Sassoon, and Nikolai Lenin. Copies of it were passed around at the front so that soldiers could get a more accurate picture of the war, which they experienced in small fragments. Le Feu appealed to those who believed that journalistic accounts were not to be trusted, since journalists came from the rear, wrote for the rear, and were in the service, officially or unofficially, of a belligerent government dominated by "hawks."

Romains's Prélude à Verdun and Verdun (1938) derive from the naturalistic model—including their status as part of a series, Les Hommes de bonne volonté [Men of good will]. The series bears strong resemblance to the multivolume novel as practiced by Zola, although Romains departed from the model in significant ways. Unlike Barbusse's book, these Verdun volumes date from twenty years after the conflict and incorporate what had become the commonplaces from both wartime reports and those of the après-guerre, the author calling on his administrative experience in the army as well as contemporaries' accounts and historians' treatments.

22. Henri Barbusse, Le Feu: Journal d'une escouade (Paris: Flammarion, 1916), 280.

Romains's two volumes on Verdun are preceded, in the series, by *Le Drapeau noir* (1937), whose title is symbolic: "Ce navire . . . [Europe] voyage avec le drapeau noir" [This ship (Europe) sails with the black flag]. Like Martin du Gard's *L'Eté 1914*, although much less lengthily, it deals with the approach of war, including the assassination of Franz-Ferdinand. Numerous historical figures, such as Lenin and Jean Jaurès, appear among the fictional characters, most of whom recur in the Verdun volumes. To the pessimism of Europe on the precipice, the conflict itself is supposed to offer a solution: as *Prélude à Verdun* puts it, officially this war will be the last of all: "C'est expressément pour cela qu'on la fait" [It is precisely for that that it is being waged].[23]

War thus justifies itself at the final moment of all known history. Militarily speaking, it means that all efforts, no matter how appalling the conditions and the losses, how apparently insignificant the results, are justified: by definition they help pay the price of historical redemption. The anonymous author/narrator, speaking as if from the high command, exhorts the troops: "Courage! C'est le suprême effort. Il s'agit cette fois-ci de libérer le territoire. L'heure de la victoire est arrivée" [Courage! This is the supreme effort. This time it's a matter of liberating our territory. The hour of victory has come]. Afterwards, victors and vanquished alike will construct world peace. Yet each time victory appears more remote: a few kilometers of territory gained merely push back the historical horizon. In the meantime, discrete actions, which the narrator recounts often in detail, lose their *raison d'être* and acquire an absurdist character. The narratives of pre-Verdun fighting and then of the great confrontation of 1916 move between lofty strategic considerations and sordid reality, vast plans and petty achievements. One of the characters predicts (in a ghastly foreshadowing, precisely, of Nazi Germany) not that an eschatological peace will follow but rather that an anticivilization will arise from the ruins: "Nous savons maintenant qu'on peut faire faire aux hommes exactement n'importe quoi—et aussi bien après qu'avant cent ans de démocratie et dix-huit siècles de christianisme. Le tout est d'employer le procédé convenable. On obtiendra quand on voudra . . . qu'ils abattent leurs père et mère âgés et les mangent en pot-au-feu" [We know now that men can be made to do anything at all—just as much after a hundred years of democracy and

---

23. Jules Romains, *Le Drapeau noir*, vol. 14 of *Les Hommes de bonne volonté* (Paris: Flammarion, 1937), 201; Romains, *Prélude à Verdun*, 16.

eighteen centuries of Christianity as before. The whole point is to use the right technique. At will, one will get them . . . to slaughter their old mothers and fathers and eat them in a stew].[24]

Romains's technique bears out the difficulties I have emphasized of grasping war, even of "saisir le détail . . . vécu par l'homme" [grasping the details . . . as experienced by men]. The scale is unknown and the stalemate nearly complete: "On vit alors un spectacle qui n'avait jamais encore été vu: deux immenses armées entièrement affrontées l'une à l'autre, très impatientes d'en finir et incapables de faire un mouvement" [A spectacle was seen then that had never before been seen: two immense armies facing each other from one end to the other, very impatient to get it over with and incapable of making a movement]. Romains used authorial omniscience and a panoramic presentation, showing how the politics of several European governments were involved (and there are scenes situated behind the German lines, as well as many in the rear, particularly Paris); yet, it has been noted, the connections among all these events escape comprehension. Despite this epistemological difficulty, the novelist found ways of conveying impressions of war. One solution is a microscopic focus, by which episodes appear in nearly as great detail as certain pages by Proust and, later, the New Novelists. These close-ups, like impressionist painting, combine precise observation with a sense of subjectivism, since they can be conveyed only through an observing consciousness. "On avait surtout l'impression de quelque chose qui était devenu profondément habituel" [Especially one had the impression of something that had become deeply habitual].[25] By rhetorical devices such as antithesis, parallelism, metaphors, irony (almost Swiftian); by drawing the narratee into the narration with the second-person-plural pronoun; by change of focus between micro- and macrolevels and deft use of summary, Romains lit up the abstractions and obscurities of the war experience.

Similarly episodic are Georges Duhamel's two works contemporaneous with the war, *Vie des martyrs, 1914–1916* [Lives of the martyrs] (1917) and its companion volume (1918), *Civilisation, 1914–1917*, mentioned earlier for its antiphrastic and sarcastic title. (Duhamel was appalled to learn that the latter volume, awarded the Goncourt Prize, was considered by authorities as useful

24. Romains, *Prélude à Verdun*, 22, 116.
25. Ibid., 12, 29, 30, 41.

propaganda for the war effort.[26]) These two chronicles of the war—in the form of sketches and stories—were followed by two others, even less novelistic, both published in 1919, which consisted of reminiscences, sketches, and reflections: *Entretiens dans le tumulte* [Conversations in the tumult], subtitled *Chronique contemporaine, 1918–1919*, and *La Possession du monde* [Possession of the world]. This second pair of works was intended again to attack modern war, but also to offer viewpoints on human happiness and values—above all, intangible, spiritual ones—in the aftermath of the conflict and to identify some crucial weaknesses of French social structure and attitudes. Like Barbusse's novel, the first two volumes in particular denounce war in the course of sketching it, not by means of panoramas or even scenes of combat, but by vignettes of its perpetrators and its victims, most of them wounded men seen at close range after they have been evacuated. Duhamel's own experience is clearly the source of his knowledge: a physician, he served for fifty-one months in a mobile surgical unit not far from the front, performing two thousand operations and caring for more than four thousand wounded.

The narration in most of the nine chapters in *Vie des martyrs* and in each of the sixteen discretely constituted sections of *Civilisation* is done in the first person by a homodiegetic narrator (bystander or minor player). But the narrative voice should not be taken generally as that of the author; names and details prevent such identification, and, moreover, the voice changes from one sketch to another. None of the voices is an omniscient narrator-*chroniqueur* bringing his judgments and comprehensive vision to bear on the war, but rather they are collectively the reported voices of those who have fought it in the trenches and who observed others fighting it. Each one is individualized: several section titles bear the names of those sketched, and the narrators provide concrete details by which each figure becomes singular. The general effect is like that produced by *Le Feu*: the sense of a collectivity, in this case mostly of wounded, whose particular destinies stand for and compose that of France. However, unlike World War I books by Benjamin, Barbusse, and Céline, Duhamel's accounts do not make extensive use of popular, uneducated speech; his narrators are mostly educated men.

In short, these books present character, not plot. Since Duhamel generally

26. L. Clark Keating, *Critic of Civilization: Georges Duhamel and His Writings* (Lexington: University of Kentucky Press, 1965), 28.

created coherent, organizing, and fully developed plots in his other fiction, one is led to inquire about the absence of a similar structure here. The change may reflect their composition in wartime, when it would have been difficult, perhaps, to conceive and write a fully developed novel. Then, too, the emphasis on character over plot may have been a choice: the war, which was the underlying plot, was formless, directionless, repetitious, apparently without purpose; atomistic, random, dissociated, and meaningless actions were its rule, so that an episodic structure, with emphasis on the psychology of typical participants, chosen nearly at random, may have seemed fitting. The technique may also have been Duhamel's way of denying rationality and closure in the war. Its effect fits the subject: as an American critic has asserted, "The pathos, anger, and frustration he made his readers feel as he described the agony of the wounded are unsurpassed in war literature."[27]

While clearly the suffering men are the subject of the author's pity—there is no sadism in his description—the world that has brought France to this pass is judged severely. For instance, the official view of the Battle of the Somme is juxtaposed to the reality behind the reports. "Quelle explosion de haine et de destruction! On eût dit qu'avec des millions d'étincelles une troupe de géants forgeaient l'horizon de la terre en frappant dessus à coups redoublés. . . . Des gerbes irisées fusaient en plein ciel, comme le marteau-pilon en exprime de la fonte incandescente. . . . Chacun de ces instants terribles n'était qu'un paroxysme dans une infinité de paroxysmes" [What an explosion of hatred and destruction! It was as if, with millions of sparks, a troop of giants were forging the earth's horizon by beating on it with intensified blows. Iridescent sheaves rose up to the sky, just as a hammer makes them fly from incandescent molten iron. Each of those terrible moments was only one paroxysm in an infinity of paroxysms]. Those whom war has not touched, ostentatiously enjoying themselves and refusing to participate even by their thoughts in the universal distress, are likewise condemned. The old notion of *la gloire* is evoked only to be denounced by what surrounds it: "L'ardeur enthousiaste du combat! L'angoisse exquise de bondir en avant, baïonnette luisante au soleil; la volupté de plonger un fer vengeur dans le flanc saignant de l'ennemi, et puis la souffrance, divine d'être endurée pour tous; la blessure sainte, qui, du héros, fait un Dieu!" [The enthusiastic ardor of

27. Ibid., 28.

combat! The exquisite anxiety of leaping forward, with one's bayonet shining in the sun; the delight at plunging an avenging iron into the bleeding side of the enemy, and then pain, divine from being endured for all; the holy wound, which, of a hero, makes a god!].[28]

Undermining this rhetoric is the entire book—the numbers of mutilated men, the dreadful conditions in which they have suffered on the front, the absence otherwise of redeeming value to the war, and the explicit denunciation of industrial civilization and the "mal immense engendré par l'âge des machines" [immense evil engendered by the machine age] that concludes the chronicle. Nowhere does Duhamel state or imply that any legitimate political aims are being advanced by the conflict, which he calls a "Moloch" with boundless appetites. Genuine civilization—if it exists—is in the heart of human beings, not in their mechanical products. "Je hais le XX* siècle," says a character, "comme je hais l'Europe pourrie et le monde entier sur lequel cette malheureuse Europe s'est étalée" [I hate the twentieth century as I hate rotten Europe and the entire world over which this unfortunate Europe has spread].[29]

The speech about glory is made by an upper-class woman who comes to visit the wounded. While her elegance and attention bring smiles to the miserable, for today's readers there is an implied condemnation of the class differences that make it possible for her to *choose* her participation in the war effort, whereas the dead, wounded, widows, and grieving mothers cannot choose. Yet no socialist vision comes to redeem the evils of industrial civilization; even the idea of a natural paradise is seen in a critical light, since Europeans have destroyed African culture, for instance, by colonizing the continent. Yet France itself remains (according to what appears to be the author's voice) "un peuple admirable" [an admirable people]—"mes frères . . . dont le monde connaît trop mal et la grandeur d'âme, et l'indomptable intelligence et la touchante naïveté" [my brothers . . . whose spiritual greatness, indomitable intelligence, and touching naiveté the world undervalues]—suffering with fortitude and grandeur a long martyrdom, but without a vision of "l'ordre et le salut" [order and salvation].[30]

28. Georges Duhamel, *Civilisation, 1914–1917* (Paris: Mercure de France, 1918), 25, 40–41, 50, 113.

29. Ibid., 257–58, 261, 269.

30. Ibid., 9.

Another volume on the Great War that borrows nineteenth-century techniques for a similar antiwar message is the novel *Le Grand Troupeau* (1931), by Jean Giono, who fought in the trenches for two years and then during World War II was imprisoned for his pacifism. The "herd" of the title (by definition a collectivity) is, of course, metaphorically, the millions of men who are sent off to battle as to slaughter. This slaughter stands in implicit contradistinction to the Biblical and other pastoral models of flock and shepherd. The metaphor of the herd is far from unique to Giono; one finds it in Benjamin's 1915 novel and in countless subsequent works, where it is associated usually with the theme of sacrifice, an enduring theme in war writing from the earliest texts of Western civilization and central in much French war rhetoric from the Franco-Prussian War on. (In World War II novels animal metaphors are particularly prevalent because of the shipment of prisoners and deportees in cattle cars.) But no one makes greater use of the metaphor than Giono, for whom it had particular resonance because of his pastoral vision of the world; and few subvert the theme of sacrifice quite as he does. The Germans themselves are seen as "that other flock of men." The reference is also literal, for the novel deals in part with a mountain village in which the principal livelihood is sheep tending.

The setting is alternately the front lines and the rural home of the characters. Such a rhythm has the advantage of offering a positive image of human beings as well as a negative one. The real villain is war: in Giono's view, where political considerations are singularly lacking, warfare goes totally against nature. The hero is a collective one, like that of Barbusse: not just the herd, but the village—seen as a timeless unit of French life—and behind it, the natural way of life to which men are called. When the shepherds are conscripted, the flocks must descend unseasonably from their high pastures to the plains in a brutal midsummer march; their decimation mirrors that of a pastoral way of life and of France itself. Walter Redfern has spoken in this connection of Giono's "distopia," by which "the modern age, in the amorphous and terrible shape of the 1914–18 war, burst into a private world that until then had seemed intemporal."[31]

One of the most virulent denunciations of war, perhaps the most existential and visceral by any French novelist, is Louis-Ferdinand Céline's *Voyage*

---

31. Walter Redfern, "Jean Giono," in Brosman, *French Novelists, 1930–1960*, 194.

au bout de la nuit (1932). Although the war years occupy less than one-fifth of the novel, and even less is devoted to action scenes, the unmasking of the war is a principal concern. It can be argued, moreover, that everything the hero, or antihero, does subsequently is colored by this experience; certainly, for the author himself the war cast a very long shadow. Following upon the surrealist revolution of the 1920s, this indictment of twentieth-century industrial society was symptomatic of the deep divisions revealed and heightened by the previous war and of its lasting presence — visible likewise in the fiction of Drieu La Rochelle and Martin du Gard (discussed below).

The war passages in Céline's great novel constitute two achievements, not unrelated. The first, which warrants extended examination, is the explicit and angry denunciation of French national idols, no matter how sacred, including what the narrator sarcastically calls "l'innocente petite Alsace" [innocent little Alsace].[32] Heroism, honor, society, fatherland, womanhood, sacrifice, poor ravished Belgium: all the causes and values for which France is ostensibly fighting, and the emblems and slogans that express them, are attacked, not on rival ideological grounds but on the grounds of ideology denied in favor of the one, supreme value: a fellow's skin. This value is discovered when the protagonist, Bardamu, peels away the layers of jingoistic rhetoric and convention that govern the behavior of the French, individually and collectively, during the war — even, or especially, the behavior of those citizens at the rear, since their sole contribution consists in patriotic piety. Bardamu, who in some ways is ingenuous, does not set out to denounce ideological fraud; in fact, at the outset of the novel he enlists, naively, through a patriotic caprice. Experience leads him, however — somewhat like Voltaire's Candide — to discover what war is really like, including the wry truth that generals eat well and sleep in warm beds while the riffraff suffer and die. He uncovers the counterpart of all the traditional verities: officers' uniforms and decorations cover naked bodies who have no authority, cowardice is preferable to bravery, the adversaries on the other side are poor fellows like himself, not moral monsters, and war, whatever the claims of those who direct it, can bear no existential relationship to him and therefore must be avoided.

Bardamu's indictment goes back to the sacred foundations of the French

---

32. Louis-Ferdinand Céline, *Romans*, 2 vols., ed. Henri Godard (Paris: Gallimard/Bibliothèque de la Pléiade, 1974, 1981), 1:84.

Republic, that is, eighteenth-century Enlightenment ideals, the Revolution, and the Revolutionary wars. The wars of the early nineteenth century, in his view, replaced the mercenary soldier—fighting for a king involved in mere dynastic quarrels and whose position precluded him from ambition and vicious scorn for his people—by "le soldat gratuit" [the unpaid soldier] sent in "cohortes loqueteuses" [tattered cohorts] by a few of his fellow citizens "pour la défense de l'inédite fiction patriotique. . . . La religion drapeautique remplaça promptement la céleste" [for the defense of the new patriotic fiction. . . . Flag-waving religion promptly replaced the heavenly one].[33] It is this development that led to nineteenth-century nationalist wars and finally the slaughter of millions. Rather than representing popular will, the war is a vast dupery. Céline used an age-old metaphor, widespread throughout writing about the Great War: that war is madness. Under his pen, however, it breaks out of its metaphorical status to become what is virtually a literal truth in Bardamu's eyes: the world having gone mad, he alone, along with a few other "lunatics" who protest against the war, is sane. In narratological terms, this means that both the sender—popular government—and the receiver—the nation—have lost their authority and ontological status; only one "plot" is rational, and that is the plot of individual interest.

Céline's other achievement in *Voyage au bout de la nuit* is to undercut the French literary tradition: both the enlightened humanism visible in the two previous centuries, and classic French prose and the rationality on which it is founded. This, too, is a denial of the values that France supposedly represents. Casting aside the aesthetic ideals of balance, beauty, and craftsmanship, which, in their various forms according to the period and its literary practices, have characterized some of the greatest French literature, and cynically denouncing the human values that such writing expressed and served, Céline has recourse instead to a narrative style incorporating vulgar speech, bad grammar, and colloquialisms—that is, an extreme naturalism—and favoring subjective impressions over objective observation (although there is a great deal of the latter). He had models, of course, including Rabelais and Zola: writers whose achievement was to emphasize the natural over the artificial, including, in Zola's case, the sordid truths of late nineteenth-century French society. But unlike that of the naturalists, Céline's writing verges on

33. Céline, *Romans*, 1:69–70.

the hallucinatory as the world of war and other experience tends toward the phantasmagorical, although it is not yet the apocalyptic night of his World War II books. The structure of the novel is not irrational; indeed, though episodic, it has coherence, thanks to Bardamu's first-person narration and the somewhat picaresque linear plot line consisting of his experiences and directed toward himself as end. But Céline did not have Bardamu shape his experience into meaning; sequence and consequence are aleatory, not significant, and rhetoric (for instance, in the form of a discourse his cell-mate in an asylum prepares to recite at a hearing) does not convey or construct reality. Only the narrator's identity, which remains approximately constant (although the presence of a doppelgänger, Robinson, complicates and perhaps undermines this identity), furnishes the affective and ontological center from which the narrative can flow. Paradoxically, of course, Céline's prose *does* give a sense of what someone could feel in the war and of its total lack of meaning to him.

Martin du Gard's *L'Eté 1914* (1936) is in many ways a naturalistic work, concerned with group and individual behavior in crisis and, like Zola's works, aspiring to be exhaustive. It recounts with underlying pacifism the crucial events from the assassination of the archduke Franz-Ferdinand in late June until early August. Indeed, its pacifism may have appealed to the Swedish Academy, which awarded Martin du Gard the Nobel Prize for Literature the year after the work appeared. The irony is that while the book's ideological tendencies, embodied in the dominant figure of the young socialist Jacques Thibault, incline toward pacifism, the tendency of the plot is to show the outbreak of war as inevitable. This orientation sounds like nineteenth-century determinism with a very pessimistic slant. But it has a peculiarly modern and antipositivistic quality (despite Martin du Gard's thorough positivistic training as a paleographer and the solid documentation visible as the book's foundation), for the novelist wrestles with the task of telling the event. Insinuated into the text is a sense that the historical process cannot be located in space, cannot ultimately be known, and hence is uncontrollable.[34]

Martin du Gard rendered this view of the historical process through a

34. Gyorgy Lukàcs's Marxist commentaries on the novel argue the opposite: that Martin du Gard's social analysis reveals, despite itself and despite his own conservative bourgeois outlook, the truths of modern history, especially the march of the bourgeoisie toward destruction.

double narrative focus, with multiple plots. The central intelligence alternates between the energetic and positivistic physician Antoine and his idealistic brother, whose opposing views on politics provide repeated correctives to each other. Some of Antoine's friends move in the nationalistic political circles of Paris, including official ones; Jacques resides in the garrets of Geneva, with other socialists who are attempting to forestall war. These loci of the plot compete with each other as sources of political meaning. The incapacity to control events, a parallel to the decentralization of the space of action, is illustrated repeatedly; the assassination of the socialist leader Jaurès—one of the most important events in France in the weeks leading up to the war—is a dramatic example of the way in which history seems to escape from those living it. Ultimately, the possibility of comprehending the war is called into question, since there is no verification either by a dominant hero or an editorial voice (the anonymous narrator remains as distant, as invisible, as objective as possible, according to the Flaubertian model). This diffusion of authority is precisely the opposite effect from that obtained by Zola, whose text claims comprehensiveness and scientific validity.

This effect is paralleled on the individual plane by the difficulty Jacques experiences in centering and taking cognizance of his own selfhood, for which he has rejected all the images and principles proposed by his social milieu and family. His answer is an act that will at once give unity to the self and establish, if only briefly, a totalizing perspective on the war. Escaping after war is declared from France, where he had been sent by his socialist colleagues on a last-minute mission, and now classed as a deserter, he arranges to fly what is a suicide mission (based on historic examples) over both German and French lines to distribute antiwar pamphlets, urging the workingmen of both nations to refuse to bear arms against their class brothers.

What World War I was like behind the lines, for those who remained there as civilians, invalided out, or went home on furlough, is a major strain in memoirs and fiction of the period. Many evocations of the rear by those who had been at the front are marked by cliché and built on facile contrasts between peril and safety, discomfort and ease, the virile friendships of war and the treacherous love of women. For instance, in Joseph Kessel's *L'Equipage* [The crew] (1923), the front line episodes, which concern reconnaissance aviators, are paralleled by contrasting chapters dealing with life behind them, especially their women, often engaged in infidelities with civilians or other soldiers, and incapable of comprehending either the rewards or the strains of flying over the lines. Montherlant's *La Relève du matin* [Morning changeover] (1920), a self-indulgent early work (his first published) concerned with relationships among boys and masters at a Catholic school, reflects the war in its sketches of pupils who are marked by destiny for an early departure and, presumably, an early death at the front, and in its glimpses of alumni who return in uniform. There is also considerable meditation on war, and the particular circumstances of 1914 and their relation to the end of the nineteenth century and the Franco-Prussian War ("Les conséquences de 1870 sont apparues quinze ans après") [The consequences of 1870 appeared fifteen years later].[35]

Other works emphasize the profiteers and *embusqués*—those who manage to stay out of combat or even the army, and who rationalize their role as being just as essential as that of "nos chers poilus." Drieu La Rochelle, in *La Comédie de Charleroi*, depicted the contrast between the front and Paris as one between authenticity and decadence. In combat, his autobiographical hero experiences an epiphany of the self in an explosion of will, which no peacetime experience allows, especially not in the corrupt social world of Paris. A similar motivation is visible in Montherlant's hero in *Le Songe*, discussed below. It is striking that these two authors were among the most severe critics of France in the 1930s and had collaborationist tendencies.

In the novels just examined, there is little treatment of World War I that deserves the term *poetic*, whether intended in the linguistic sense or in the wider, moral sense; the authors are concerned generally with the dreadful conditions of the war, the dismay caused by its prolongation and apparent pointlessness. It would seem, moreover, that the French, whatever their feelings and convictions, tended less than their British counterparts to write about the conflict in terms of self-development and lofty feelings; and the sporting metaphor, which, as Paul Fussell has shown, is recurrent throughout British literature of the Great War and harks back to earlier conflicts, is much less widespread. Yet, just a few months before the conflict broke out, Péguy, Psichari, and others had written lyrically of patriotism, and nearly the whole of France apart from socialists and other internationalists had thought of revenge against Germany as a satisfaction devoutly to be wished. One cannot

35. Henry de Montherlant, *La Relève du matin* (1920; reprint, Paris: Grasset, 1933), 141.

do more than speculate how Péguy and Psichari, had they not died in 1914, might have written about the war—whether their treatments would have accented self-development and lofty feelings had they survived its atrocities. It is true that Drieu La Rochelle expected war, initially, to be a virile, uplifting game, but he revised his attitude after his experience at the front.

Perhaps only in Montherlant—one of few French writers of the first half of the twentieth century to give sport a place in his work—does the theme of initiation in warfare develop in a positive light. Indeed, it leads logically to the postwar theme of athletic challenges, itself connected to aestheticism through the development of physical beauty. This emphasis on sport in the context of warfare may help to explain why, although he was a superb stylist, the eminently misogynistic and aristocratic Montherlant is one of the century's literary figures most disliked by readers past and especially present. In *Les Olympiques* (1924), the resemblances between war and sport—two contests, the latter without horror—are especially striking. Even more problematic is *Le Songe*, a novel of initiation that must be viewed also as war fiction, since roughly two-thirds of it takes place on the front, involving individual encounters (and Alban, the young hero, kills a German in one of these), shelling, air strikes, some trench scenes, and not infrequent passages concerning the wounded, dying, and dead. Yet the point throughout is the hero's soul or spirit; he is the only subject. There is, in addition, neither sender nor receiver, nor opponent, except in brief encounters with the enemy and the associated love plot—a very problematic one. Even the role of helpers is minimal, incidental. It is not that Alban views the war as pointless—a truism of trench novels; such a conclusion would require recognition, within at least a rudimentary political context, of what is ostensibly the war's aim, hence of a sender (France). *Le Songe* is almost entirely devoid of a sense of nation (only once does Alban reflect, "Pauvre patrie! [Poor country!]") and even of an historical and political sense (he discards the argument of invaders vs. defenders). Except for the fact that Montherlant respects the basic historical data of the period, the Germans could just as well be anyone. Anticipating victory for the Allies, in the clichéd propaganda terms of the war, Alban does not bother to criticize these terms on political or moral grounds: "lui, le Droit, la Civilisation, il s'en moque bien!" [he doesn't care a bit about right and civilization]. Instead, like his models, Mark Antony and others, he is concerned not to *déchoir* [demean himself] by betraying the high standards of conduct he sets.[36]

Le Songe reveals the author as an heir of Corneille and of Stendhal, or at least of the side of Stendhal (which he mocked withal) that showed itself in Julien Sorel in *Le Rouge et le noir*; Montherlant's hero views everything as a struggle, a test, and demands that the self meet the adversary—rival, sexual opponent, or its own weakness—according to the self's own rules, and win, on pain of losing self-esteem. For Alban, as for Stendhal's Fabrice, the war is an occasion for experience and self-knowledge; it is seen subjectively, not comprehensively. The front is analogous to the sporting field, where he has tested himself in the past, and to the bullring to which, in *Les Bestiaires*, Montherlant later sends his hero for his initiation experience. Going to battle is a luxury: Alban volunteers to do so, out of solidarity with a friend who is at the front, out of impatience with anything smacking of the facile, out of his "appétit du danger" [appetite for danger] and desire to "racheter ses péchés" [atone for his sins] (but he acknowledges only those it pleases him to own— even with God, he wishes to keep the initiative) and join the "saint ordre mâle" [holy virile order].[37] He is not without pity, far from it; but this appears to be his choice, not an obligation. To some degree, he is his own opponent; the war takes place in his soul, as the inclusion of numerous interior monologues in the form of dialogues suggests. One could argue, then, that the book is a classical psychological study, built around pride; its teleology is a private one. Only the fact that Alban is wounded, and does indeed risk death frequently, lends to what he calls the *jeu* (game) its seriousness. What readers of the war and postwar years came to expect from writers on the event was quite different from Montherlant's work, with its somewhat ambiguous individual teleology involving a personal morality that tends to the aesthetic and that is, ultimately, aristocratic, since it concerns his superiority over others, women included, and of one aspect of self over another. Montherlant's style—with its pithy maxims, its classical psychological analysis, a certain preciosity (including poetic inversions), of which he later purged his writing, and its mixture of irony and indulgence toward the hero (whether in interior monologue, summary, or narratorial apostrophe)—reinforces the gulf be-

36. Montherlant, *Le Songe*, 151, 171.
37. Ibid., 16, 40, 104.

tween this war novel and those where the combatants *suffer* (in both senses of the term), undergoing the war, whether seen as senseless or not, on behalf of others.

For certain other writers, war was similarly aesthetic, less in psychological terms—the cultivation of the fine soul—than in terms of spectacle. The spectacular consists of two tendencies, the painterly and the theatrical, sometimes joined, of course. Present-day readers are familiar with the importance of the visual in understanding war and the tendency to pictorialize; televised wars, from the Vietnam conflict (from which broadcast scenes played a role in changing American opinion) to the Gulf War and the conflict in Bosnia, become spectacularized, acquiring entertainment value, on the same level as much other televised material, including cartoons and other fictitious programs. (This does not mean, of course, that the newscast is truly the raw war; data have been selected, arranged, and are often commented on by a voice-over.) In 1914 the spectacle was a local one. Families, dressed in their Sunday clothes, crowded at railroad stations to send off those who would soon be called *poilus*, tossing flowers, pouring out wine, shouting "A Berlin!" (in a *re-vanchiste* echo of the phrase used in the Franco-Prussian War). In Raymond Radiguet's *Le Diable au corps*, in which the Great War appears to the young hero as "quatre ans de grandes vacances" [four years of summer vacation], the narrator evokes the following tableau: "Nous emportions des campanules et nous les lancions aux soldats. Des dames en blouse versaient du vin rouge dans les bidons et en répandaient des litres sur le quai jonché de fleurs" [We carried bluebells and threw them to the soldiers. Women in smocks poured red wine into cans and spilled liters of it onto the platform strewn with flowers].[38]

In early months of the war, the spectacular was given positive value, as the passage from Radiguet suggests. In later months, and after the conflict, as the cataclysm was culturally deconstructed, aesthetic spectacle was generally in the mode of tragedy or irony. An exception is offered by Vaslav Nijinski, who in 1919 in Paris condensed the previous four years into a single aesthetic moment by a performance in which, in his words, he "danced the war." Similarly, the victory celebrations in Paris on Bastille Day 1919, in which troops paraded down the Champs-Elysées in unconscious reference to the

38. Raymond Radiguet, *Le Diable au corps* (1923; reprint, Paris: Livre de Poche, 1964), 8, 14.

glorious battlefield charges that had proven impossible, were a restaging of war as a nationalist spectacle with a positive cultural value. There was to have been a giant cenotaph under the Arc de Triomphe, lit with torches and a brazier on top, decorated with wings from actual French aircraft, and guarded by mounted troops; but the design was judged to be *munichois* (Munich-like) and, before the festivities, the huge rolling monument was destroyed.[39]

A number of well-known writers treated war as spectacle, whether according to modernist aesthetics or others, often incorporating, along with formal innovations, elements of the same technology that becomes monstrous in trench novels. "Ah Dieu! que la guerre est jolie" [Oh how lovely is war] — so begins one of Apollinaire's lyrics from the early months of the war. A severe critic of the conflict and the society that led to it, Drieu La Rochelle had his autobiographical hero establish an ironic comparison between a performance by the Russian ballet and the death of his captain, tossed in the air by a shell, his feet flying. He speaks of his "masque de comédien" (actor's mask) and calls the area peripheral to the battlefield "les coulisses" (the theatre wings), while pointing out the *failure* of war as spectacle or *comédie*. Elsewhere he speaks of history as constructing "de vastes perspectives avec de sales petits bouts de décor" [vast perspectives with dirty little bits of scenery].[40]

The same theater metaphor underlies much of Jean Cocteau's poetic novel *Thomas l'imposteur* (1923), the story of a sixteen-year-old orphan who, being mistaken in the confusion of wartime for a relative of the eminent General Fontenoy and secretary to another general, finds all paths open to him, including those leading to the front — that is, to the excitement, challenge, and spectacle of which he dreams. His *comédie* is dual: as an impostor (since he is not the general's nephew), and a pseudosoldier ("devenu fusilier sans l'être" [having become a rifleman without being one]), he is doubly playacting, even though, childishly, he is to some degree taken in by his own game. Too young to fight, Guillaume Thomas can be only a mascot, a pal, a comedian for those in the trenches. Even his love for a girl at the rear is a fiction. He cannot leave the village to go on patrol with the others: "Il n'était que touriste. Il quittait

---

39. Eksteins, *Rites of Spring*, 144, 273; Silver, *Esprit de corps*, 222–24.

40. Apollinaire, *Œuvres poétiques*, 253; Drieu La Rochelle, *La Comédie de Charleroi*, 22, 89, 92. The final phrase, from Drieu's unpublished journal, is quoted in Reck, *Drieu La Rochelle and the Picture Gallery Novel*, 11.

le théâtre et se retrouvait dans la rue, sans partager la mystérieuse vie des acteurs" [He was only a tourist. He left the theater and found himself again out in the street, without sharing the mysterious life of the actors].[41]

The theater vocabulary in this novel is not confined to Thomas: it appears in connection with others. For the very Stendhalian older heroine, "la guerre lui apparut tout de suite comme le théâtre de la guerre. Théâtre réservé aux hommes" [war looked to her right away like the theater of war. A theater reserved for men]. Others also tend to treat the war as a game or to assume roles, as though the conflict were the work of some master director. "Ces jeunes hommes, les plus braves du monde, jouaient à se battre, sans la moindre haine. Hélas, des jeux pareils finissent mal" [These young men, the bravest in the world, played at fighting, without the least hatred. Alas, such games end badly].[42] One episode deals with a visit near the front lines of a theatrical troupe from Paris: one set of actors is playing to a much greater one. Their reception is spectacular, literally: planes, cannons, helmets, and so forth compose a decor at once theatrical and military. Useless fortifications built near Nieuport—the work of a colonel (named Jocaste) obsessed with the threat of invasions from the sea—are compared to the seven wonders of the ancient world (that is, to objects built for display), and their underground structures are said to be like those of the Châtelet theater in Paris and the corresponding subway station, whose charm they share. Elsewhere, a group of African *tirailleurs*, dancing and singing to their special *nouba* music, wearing African ornaments, crosses the village as in a performance.

The war is not only theater in Cocteau's representation of it; it is also tableau, a painterly (if dynamic) scene, which, like the theater metaphor, tends to undercut the violence and destruction, making them anodine, unreal. (The novel does not consist entirely, however, of a cardboard war; there are moving details of suffering—a German with his hands blown off, a French soldier about to undergo amputation without anesthetic.) The painterly effect is achieved through comparisons: the image, for instance, of soldiers whose color and thinness are likened to those of El Greco's monks. When the troupe of actors, including Thomas's protectrix and her daughter, arrives at the front, the narrator observes, "Ces femmes et lui formaient un groupe de gra-

41. Jean Cocteau, *Thomas l'imposteur* (Paris: Gallimard, 1923), 118, 124.
42. Ibid., 18, 121.

vure empire: Le Retour du Soldat" [The women and he formed a group from an engraving of the Empire period: The Return of the Soldier].[43]

Likewise, the novel's style—and not only in the explicitly theatrical or painterly passages—tends, rather than denying the conflict, to transform it through metaphors, creating scenes where beauty arises from horror. Consider this description: "La lune grandissait ces petites ruines toutes jeunes, et à droite du sable, deux ou trois arbres chloroformés dormaient debout. . . . La nuit, cette eau devenait phosphorescente. Si on y jetait une douille, elle sombrait toute [sic] éclairée comme le *Titanic*. Un projectile y tombant, sa chute allumait au fond un boulevard de magasins splendides" [The moonlight made these new little ruins look larger, and to the right of the sand, two or three chloroformed trees were sleeping on their feet. . . . At night, this water became phosphorescent. If someone threw a cartridge casing in it, it sank all lit up like the Titantic. If a projectile fell into it, its fall lit up at the bottom a boulevard of splendid shops]. This transformation of a battleground is not identical to the sort of aestheticizing of war found in such German writers as Ernst Jünger and Ernst von Salomon, who make of war's principles both a sign and source of national and individual virtue. For Cocteau, war is disguised, not hypostatized into an overreaching value. The episode when Thomas is killed takes place in a framework of loveliness, but without glorification of death: "La nuit froide était constellée de fusées blanches et d'astres. . . . Un dernier rideau se lève. L'enfant et la féerie se confondent" [The cold night was starry with white rockets and heavenly lights. A last curtain rises. The child and the enchanting spectacle are one and the same]. Hit in the chest, he thinks of playing dead: "Mais en lui, la fiction et la réalité ne formaient qu'un" [But in him, fiction and reality were one]; war as stage becomes war as death.[44]

The poetic and theatrical treatment of the war by Cocteau has, like numerous other aspects of his creative output, led to the accusations of superficiality, *légèreté* (or levity), even moral indifference. There is, however, no reason to believe that Cocteau was without sensitivity to the suffering of his nation and its young soldiers or that *Thomas l'imposteur* expresses what one critic calls "un désir pervers d'insulter à la mémoire des combattants de 14–18" [a

43. Ibid., 133.
44. Ibid., 114–15, 171.

perverse desire to insult the memory of the soldiers of 1914–1918]; on the contrary, the novel reveals much feeling as well as Cocteau's sense of the magic, poetic world behind appearances. "La première visite que Guillaume accomplit en première ligne se transforme . . . en une efflorescence de visions féeriques et de métamorphoses enchanteresses, qui traduisent . . . l'exaltation de l'enfant subitement propulsé sur la scène du théâtre de ses rêves" [The first visit that Guillaume makes to the front lines is transformed . . . into an efflorescence of marvelous visions and enchanting metamorphoses, which express . . . the exaltation of the child suddenly propelled onto the stage of his dream theater]. That this literary metamorphosis is less serious than the naturalistic treatments of war found in Barbusse and others may remain, to be sure, a matter of dispute. Cocteau was persuaded, certainly, that the conflict in its horror could be conveyed by spare observations, discreet symbols, telling details, better than by accumulation of repetitious scenes: "Le vrai écrivain," he asserted, "est celui qui écrit mince, musclé. Le reste est graisse ou maigreur" [The true writer is he who writes sparingly, muscularly. The rest is grease or skinniness]. His own approach to writing the war can be contrasted to the *graisse* of a "description complaisante et pathétique du champ de bataille" [complacent and pathos-laden description of the battlefield] of the sort with which postwar readers were "abreuvés et écoeurés" [bombarded and revolted].[45]

Lyricism concerning the war can be found in a number of other writers. One of the most original treatments of the rear comes from Proust, whose rejection of formulaic fiction, on the one hand, and genius at capturing phenomena through close analyses of perceptions and extended metaphors rather than through abstractions, on the other, led him to experience and capture in poetic prose the extraordinary conditions of Paris in wartime. In *Le Temps retrouvé* (1927) he devoted some 100 pages to depicting the changes war had wrought. (This is, of course, but an episode in Proust's great structure; he cannot be considered as a war novelist but only, and marginally, as one of wartime.) Socially speaking, Paris appears transformed: identifying, like a naturalist, the laws of the social organism, he showed how the old barriers

45. Jean-Pierre Chauveau, "Tradition et modernité dans les romans de Cocteau," in *Jean Cocteau aujourd'hui: Actes du Colloque de Montpellier, mai 1989* (Paris: Klincksieck, 1992), 86–87. Cocteau's statement is quoted in this passage.

between classes were breached. Prestige goes not to the oldest families but to the most stridently patriotic ones (thus Charlus, who refuses to be chauvinistic, loses standing) and to those who boast of relations with generals and ministers; departures for the front create vacuums into which parvenus and profiteers rush. Linguistically, the narrator and his friend Saint-Loup observe the transformation of French under the influence of Germanophobic government clichés, war bulletins, and trench slang exported to the rear.

Morally speaking, Proust's narrator identifies a true spirit of patriotism, which he calls that of "Saint-André-des-Champs," in reference to a modest medieval church mentioned many volumes earlier. By this appellation he invokes the medieval traditions (illustrated in ecclesiastical sculpture and architecture) that are the essence of the French humanistic spirit (and here his kinship with Péguy is striking). This patriotism means devotion and self-sacrifice; it is displayed, he says, by countless anonymous citizens at the front and at home. He also identifies, and criticizes, a false patriotism, as superficial as it is ostentatious: the kind that refers to the Germans as Boches and would ban from libraries and concert halls the works of Goethe and Beethoven — or that is simply insincere. Consider in this connection the passage in which Mme Verdurin, opening the morning paper, reads of the sinking of the *Lusitania*: as she deplores aloud the latest atrocity of the barbarians, she bites into a buttery croissant, a luxury not found at the front and scarcely in Paris, and such a smile of satisfaction spreads over her face that her outrage over the sinking is revealed as mere playacting.[46]

The Proustian aesthetic mode of perceiving the war is among the richest in the literature under consideration. Instead of naming things, simply stating them, the narrator evokes wartime phenomena by their effects: for instance, the metamorphosis of the city at night during blackout (recalling his childhood walks after dark and his magic lantern); or Paris transformed by a heavy snow, which cannot be removed for lack of workers and which makes the trees resemble those in Japanese paintings or certain canvases of Raphael. In a long walk through Paris that has an erotic element, he notes the exoticism provided by the uniforms of colonial soldiers on leave, and, with irony, the current high fashions, which incorporate military touches such as tunics and leggings as well as an Egyptian motif, intended to invoke Napo-

46. Proust, *Le Temps retrouvé*, 773, 846.

leon's African campaign. The narrator's space is both historical and psychological, as beauty, in an array of wondrous, sometimes bizarre forms, rises from the social and physical changes of the city, creating an impressionistic drama that he compares to Wagner's.[47]

In Proust's evocation of Paris during the Great War, there is radical change from war writing in France prior to 1914. Aerial warfare, which succeeded the invention of the airplane, entailed reconnaissance flights and air battles—developments of the highest importance, both strategically (as the Spanish civil war and World War II would demonstrate) and in human terms. Proust conveyed this technological change aesthetically: the skies over Paris are transformed by the searchlights and night-flying planes. Cocteau was another artist who found poetic, and poeticized in his turn, the military use of planes. In contrast, when Céline dealt with zeppelins over Paris, he employed his typically bitter, sardonic tone.

It should be noted that, like other manifestations of modernism, such a poetics and its implications were anathema to national socialism. The Nazis would put into effect a contrary aesthetics by the concentration of political power in a unifying myth located in a centralized, symbolic space— Nuremberg and its parade ground along with the Olympic stadium in Berlin are the salient examples—that drew to itself as if centripetally the dispersed energies and space of greater Germania. The challenge for authors dealing with the second great world conflict of the century would be to find forms appropriate to its peculiar features and especially to the sense of historical repetition, whether by renewing older techniques, carrying farther the techniques of modernism, or developing new ones, which would convey the growing twentieth-century angst in the face of history. Yet the images of peace continued to make use of images of war, suggesting that the desire for revenge had not been entirely satisfied, and that war had shaped the minds of those who were to organize the peace.

47. Ibid., 736, 763.

7

VARIATIONS ON A THEME
World War II and Literary Forms

IN THE 1930s, the poet Louis Aragon, a former surrealist, converted to Stalinism, and thus to social realism after it was promulgated in the USSR; nevertheless, he remained one of France's great patriots and was active in the Resistance. In 1942 he wrote in the preface to his collection of verse _Les Yeux d'Elsa_ the following: "_Arma virumque cano_ . . . 'I sing of arms and man': thus begins the _Aeneid_, thus should all poetry begin."[1] This statement, which would seem either to poeticize war or put at the inception of poetic literature the armed struggles of mankind, surely reflects its date as well as its author's political position. Even when writing love poetry (Elsa was his wife), Aragon was then concerned primarily with his suffering nation, its defeat, and its need to free itself from Germany through armed force—as a prelude to the total social revolution that, as a fervent communist, he had imagined and called for in his writings since he composed _Front rouge_ in the 1930s. In other times, neither he nor others would, presumably, have assigned such a privileged position in literature to the theme of war. That he saw World War II— the historical phenomenon—with all the bloodshed it produced, as intrinsically poetic is surely not possible. The classical and chivalric tradition of noble combat and identity gained through valor held no meaning for him; he had seen the previous world war and had come out of it with as much revulsion as most of his contemporaries.

The connection between literature and armed struggle was an integral one for him at the time because of the role he assigned to language as a sign and

---

1. Louis Aragon, _Les Yeux d'Elsa_ (1942; reprint, Paris: Seghers, 1964), 30.

means of French identity. Quoting, in his anonymous preface to *Europe*, Stéphane Mallarmé's well-known line "Donner un sens plus pur aux mots de la tribu" [Give a purer meaning to the words of the tribe], Aragon commented, "Il est bien que les poètes français aient su le faire . . . quand précisément le langage était détourné de son cours, les mots étaient dénaturés, pervertis par ces usurpateurs" [It is good that French poets were able to do so . . . when, precisely, language had been turned aside from its course, words were denatured, perverted by those usurpers]. (Similarly, Pierre Emmanuel wrote that Vichy and the occupants could live only by perverting language, and to "wound" language was to wound mankind.)[2] Literary language was not only to *represent* France—that is, its past—with its lyricism and grandeur; it was to serve as agent, helping (along with other acts such as sabotage) to produce events that would lead to the liberation of France and then to the nation of the future. In other terms, the question of representation of event through language, which arose in the slaughter of World War I, was implicitly restated in terms of *praxis*: could language represent political realities in such a way as to produce action?

It should be noted that, in fact, Aragon's wish for a militant or at least patriotic poetry was fulfilled. The period of the war—more strictly, of the Occupation—produced a sizable body of poetry; indeed, it seems remarkably large, when one considers the difficult conditions of production, and is of high quality. Pierre Seghers's substantial anthology *La Résistance et ses poètes* testifies to the abundance of underground patriotic poetry. This abundance is due partly to chance: France could boast then of a flowering of major poets— Aragon, Emmanuel, René Char, Robert Desnos, Paul Eluard—most of whom had gone through surrealism and evolved thence to a position of *engagement* (commitment). They took it upon themselves to celebrate their suffering nation and the principles of liberty for which, in their eyes, it stood. Other war poetry came from the pens of authors less well known, many poised on the threshold of their careers, who became war poets because that was the situation they faced: Jean Cayrol is one of these. The art critic Jean Cassou, well known in the art milieu, gained fame for his *33 sonnets composés*

2. Both these statements are quoted in Ian Higgins, "France, Soil and Language: Some Resistance Poems by Luc Bérimont and Jean Marcenac," in Kedward and Austin, eds., *Vichy France and the Resistance*, 217.

au secret, written while he was imprisoned for Resistance activity. Perhaps poetry could more easily express the patriotic message than could fiction, and more effectively—at least for readers who would be disturbed by the authorial manipulation that characterizes thesis novels. Verse was also much better suited to the circumstances: it could be written rapidly, on small pieces of paper, easily reproduced, smuggled, even memorized. Aragon's war poems, for instance, were circulated in clandestine form from Lyons and other Resistance centers. At the extreme, paper is not even necessary. Poetry can be transmitted through recitation, and even composed mentally or orally on occasion: Cassou composed his sonnets completely in his head. Some small but important literary magazines in North Africa also printed patriotic poetry and smuggled it into France.

By contrast, one observes that French fiction concerning World War II is, in some ways, disappointing: perhaps, broadly speaking, inferior to that of the century's earlier conflict. Before considering possible reasons for this disparity, I want to look at the meaning of war for the French in 1939. I noted in chapter 3 that the relationship of author to topic, both historically and ideologically, is especially pertinent in fiction of World War II. Although for France the second war was less destructive than the first in human and material terms, the complex political landscape created from the beginning a wider range of relationships between individuals and event: as early as 1939, the meanings that could be given and were given to war with Germany and to the following Occupation were more varied and had more active consequences than meanings assigned to war against Kaiser Wilhelm's imperial state in 1914. The Russian Revolution of 1917 and its sequels, the European economic crisis, the failure of the League of Nations, and the rise of the Nazis had produced a very different Europe from that of the early century. The polarized politics of the thirties, pitting aggressive right-wing groups against those who would join later in the Popular Front—radicals, militant socialists, and especially the French Communist party—meant diverse reactions to the threat of war, especially since among the right-wing groups there were many admirers of Hitler and national socialism. War with Germany could mean, to some, salvation from the rotten Third Republic and the politics of the left; to others, it could mean the transformation of a war-mongering bourgeois nation into the new classless society, through the final cataclysmic explosion of capitalism's internal contradictions. This political landscape was complicated by the German-Soviet Nonaggression Pact (also known as the Molotov-Rip-pentrop Pact) of 1939. By this agreement between Hitler and Stalin, the former obtained the freedom to invade Poland without Soviet interference or protest, while the latter was assured that German aggrandizement would not compromise Soviet security. Orthodox communists had to digest the pact as a necessary tactic, but as the case of Paul Nizan shows, it caused no little anguish during the nearly two years it was operative to those whose communism was associated with a genuine patriotism. These factors all influenced fiction of the Second World War by complicating the ideological ground.

In particular, the conflict carried for many French a horrible sense of *déjà vu*—first of the defeat of the Franco-Prussian War, and then the almost Pyrrhic victory of the Great War, obtained at tremendous cost—a victory so precarious that the war had to be fought all over again in a world that nevertheless called itself civilized, humane. Not only was it clear that the harsh terms of the Versailles treaty had encouraged the development of national socialism; in the eyes of some, the victory had led to false self-confidence. From the military point of view, it sprang in part from the congealing of strategy in the forms it had taken in 1914–1918—that is, a war of defense. "When the Second World War began," observes Stanley Hoffmann, "the French army was hampered by the cult of the defensive and by instructions that were stuck in time around 1918." Even in the application and understanding of tactics, the model furnished interference. R.-L. Bruckberger observes, "La dernière guerre impose ses cruelles et meurtrières images qui faussent toute l'appréciation de ce qui se passe actuellement en ligne" [The last war imposes its cruel and murderous images, which distort all understanding of what is happening right now on the lines].[3]

Politically speaking, the false sense of security had been established by the settlement of 1919, although it had not been carried out as originally planned. André Gide wrote in 1940: "L'on peut penser aujourd'hui qu'il eût bien mieux valu que [la France] fût vaincue en 1918, plutôt que de remporter alors ce faux triomphe qui acheva de l'aveugler et l'endormit dans la décadence" [One may think today that it would have been better for France to be beaten in 1918, rather than to achieve then this false triumph which ended by blind-

<hr/>

3. Stanley Hoffmann, "The Foreign Policy of Charles de Gaulle," in Craig and Loewenheim, *The Diplomats*, 229; R.-L. Bruckberger, *Si grande peine (1940–1948)* (Paris: Grasset, 1967), 26.

ing her and lulling her into decadence]. Elsewhere he observed: "Nous n'aurions pas dû gagner l'autre guerre. Cette fausse victoire nous a trompés. Nous
n'avons pu la supporter. Le relâchement qui l'a suivie nous a perdus. . . . Oui,
nous avons été perdus par la victoire. Mais saurons-nous nous laisser instru-
ire par la défaite?" [We should not have won the other war. That false victory
deceived us. We were not able to bear it. The slackening that followed it
undid us. Yes, we were undone by victory. But will we allow ourselves to
learn by defeat?]. That there was good cause to resist the Germans in 1939
did not suffice to offset a justified cynicism about French policies and, more
broadly, about the possibilities for peace in Europe. After France fell in 1940,
whatever the attitude taken toward defeat, the historical experience was
problematic.[4]

Moreover—and this is surely a factor in the literary production of the period—the sense that heroism and military glory were possible certainly had
diminished in France by 1939, for various reasons, political and social, at the
very time when, as millions of patriotic French saw it, the nation most needed
a strong military commitment. Whether presented directly or indirectly,
whether approved or challenged, heroism had been a major principle of the
earlier war novel, one perhaps necessary in war fiction at least as a *possible*
means of motivating action and evaluating the conflict, even if it is ultimately
rejected. The defeat of 1940—consecrated in an armistice signed by Philippe
Pétain, one of the greatest of World War I generals—deflated most of the remaining images of military grandeur that had persisted in the literary, and
public, imagination. Disappointment, cynicism, and acrimony were common
responses to the war and its sequels; and although they may on occasion be
the source of good war writing, as in the war episodes of Louis-Ferdinand
Céline's *Voyage au bout de la nuit* and his volumes on the end of World War II,
unadulterated resentment and cynicism do not generally favor literary flowering.

Even after the war's end, there was no wave of great war novels. Amid the
ineffective governments of the Fourth Republic, the acrimonious dissension
among political parties that had scarred the 1930s resumed, shedding retrospective light on the war years and directing writers' attention toward deep
domestic divisions. Postwar revelations about the extent of Nazi brutality

4. André Gide, *Journal; Souvenirs* (Paris: Gallimard/Bibliothèque de la Pléiade, 1954), 29, 43.

added to the horrors that the French had already read about or seen for themselves; to these were added in due course reports on the tremendous abuses of Stalinism. At the same time, Europe was again armed, with the United States and Western forces facing off against those of the Soviet bloc, ready, it would appear, for another world conflict—with France in between. The depth of the political rifts presumably stifled some voices and made a *national* war literature unlikely. Moreover, although the war was won by the Allies, France's position in the struggle was ambivalent since the Vichy government was collaborationist, and many writers preferred to put behind them memories of the period. Some writers doubtless preferred to make war films, which presented the conflict in a popular medium. Others, of various political persuasions, who might have produced impressive war fiction had died.

There are, to be sure, outstanding exceptions to the generalization I have drawn concerning the absence of heroism in this era: to begin with, Charles de Gaulle, that icon of resistance whose strategies certainly contained an element of heroism. In addition, many members, known or anonymous, of the Free French movement and of the underground and *maquis* or Forces Françaises de l'Intérieur (FFI) at home merited the label "heroic." However, much of their activity was propagandistic, cloak-and-dagger, and sometimes terrorist; they were not engaged in regular combat until late in the war period. Moreover, the squabbling of Gaullists with other groups—the British and Americans, General Henri Giraud and his partisans, the French Communist party—detracted from their military prestige, and questions of their legitimacy plagued them throughout the period, even among those who deplored the armistice. Postwar publicity subsequently exaggerated the heroics of underground groups.

All of the historical and political factors here identified must have influenced the production of war writing, although it is impossible to judge fully their effect. Factionalism and political polarization likewise affected literary reception. Tendentious works were admired or attacked according to the critics' political views; those not beholden to the Communist party generally agreed that *Les Communistes* was very bad, just as Céline's works were denounced and virtually proscribed because of his anti-Semitism and the widely held view that he was a collaborator. Pierre Drieu La Rochelle's last fiction was consigned to literary damnation along with the man. Antoine de Saint-Exupéry was somewhat suspect as a war writer because he had been close to some Vichy supporters and had not denounced Pétain with the speed and vigor that Gaullists would have wished. André Malraux's war novel was underrated probably as much because of its author's postwar Gaullist politics as because of its meditative, intellectual tone, which foreshadowed Malraux's adoption of art criticism as his principal genre after the war. Some two decades after the war, aesthetic criteria came to assume a greater role in assessments; Céline's stock as a writer is now very high, although he remains controversial. Moreover, some of the most thoughtful war novels were produced well after the conflict itself, as if distance from the event had allowed for greater perspective; two noteworthy examples are Claude Simon's *La Route des Flandres* and Jules Roy's *Le Désert de Retz*.

Despite the ingenuity, perhaps genius, shown by some authors in recounting the catastrophe, it may be argued that literature generally revealed itself to be inadequate to what Céline called the "cataclysm" of World War II. Theodor Adorno's view that no literature was possible after *le monde concentrationnaire* was shared by many, including Elie Wiesel, who for years declined to draw upon his experiences in concentration camps for literary material before writing *Night*. Paradoxically, the complication of the political and ideological ground often led to oversimplification of the ideological and historical scene and to thesis novels; fiction of the period is highly tendentious. Dozens of novels, films, *témoignages*, and historical reconstructions revealed a tendency that has not yet disappeared more than fifty years after the war's end — that of mythifying the defeat, the Free French, the Occupation, or the Resistance — a tendency that in turn has produced the effort to demythify.

—

The previous chapter showed how, starting with World War I and its aftermath, the epistemological functions of the novel, directed traditionally toward understanding, were often transformed, becoming instead the project to illustrate *lack* of understanding, of ability to deal with the historical event. The collapse of fictional coherence that marks several novels of that war and the following one is the structural equivalent of the lack of understanding. Such lack does not mean necessarily, however, failed writing. As Henri Godard, an authoritative commentator, observes, Céline's work is "une des rares oeuvres dans lesquelles la littérature parvienne à se saisir de cet événement historique qui paralyse d'autant plus les imaginations et les plumes qu'il a plus radicalement bouleversé notre monde. . . . L'Histoire semble avoir pris d'elle-même l'allure d'un roman célinien" [one of the few works in which literature succeeds in getting hold of that historic event, which paralyzes imaginations and pens in proportion to its having radically shattered our world. History itself seems to have taken on the appearance of a Céline novel]. Godard goes on to argue that Céline was conscious of being one of the few whose sensibility, imagination, and style allowed them to deal with the apocalypse—seeing the grandiose and horror but also the comic element and beauty within the horror.[5]

Illustrating the derationalization of history, Claude Simon's hero Georges (of whom I say more shortly) speaks of "cette espèce de décomposition de tout comme si non pas une armée mais le monde lui-même tout entier et non pas seulement dans sa réalité physique mais encore dans la représentation que peut s'en faire l'esprit . . . était en train de se dépiauter se désagréger s'en aller en morceaux en eau en rien" [this sort of decomposition of everything as if not an army but the whole world itself and not only in its physical reality but also in the image that the mind can have of it . . . were in the process of being dissected disintegrating coming to pieces turning to water to nothing].[6] The question of the human subject's identity and stability is thus linked to the war experience (in Céline's case, both world wars, as well as his politics of persecution): the subjectivity that modernists had radicalized in their own way from the beginning of the century, while the extreme Left sought to dismantle and devalorize it in the context of socialist thought, dissolves along with the world. Yet the consequent pulverization of war narrative is, paradoxically, connected to its power.

There were, however, other ways of looking at the conflict and shaping it into fictional form; several writers both well known and less so deserve consideration in this respect. Both Saint-Exupéry and Malraux, eschewing the project of recounting the war as such, chose to use the framework of the conflict to explore the possibility of historical meaning, pointing to values that did indeed transcend the conflict and could constitute a foundation for a new philosophy of history and a postwar rebuilding; their meditations on history

5. Céline, *Romans*, 1:ix, xi, xiii.
6. Claude Simon, *La Route des Flandres* (Paris: Editions de Minuit, 1960), 16–17.

tend toward essentialism or mythification. A number of other authors used the war or Resistance novel to suggest moral or political messages for the reconstruction of Europe: for instance, Vercors (Jean Bruller) in *Le Silence de la mer* (1942).

Saint-Exupéry, a civilian pilot when France fell, insisted upon rejoining the air force, although he was thirty-nine years old. His friends, cognizant of his literary gifts, attempted first to dissuade him from returning to military service, then, when that failed, to convince him and the authorities that he should not participate in dangerous flights. He rejected all favoritism and, as a pilot based in northern France, flew numerous reconnaissance missions in May and June 1940, after the Germans crossed the Belgian border. From his experiences he drew *Pilote de guerre* (1942).[7] Written in the first person, it recounts a reconnaissance flight (based on several, which are telescoped) over a region occupied on the ground and dominated in the air by Germans. The flight is both exceptionally dangerous and senseless: he is to bring back information that, when received, will no longer be valid or, even if accurate, will be useless, since French forces are unable to stop the invaders. The fact that the flight is experienced partially in a poetic mode should not signal that the pilot is unaware of danger: rather, the style reflects his psychological defense mechanism and serves to bring to the forefront the central questions of nation and duty. The nation that, in the person of commanding officers, has sent him over German-occupied territory is the beautiful France to which he is devoted, the country of his childhood, his language, his friends, and his values; and the exquisite beauty of its fields and skies, which he notices even as he dodges antiaircraft fire, as well as the French moral tradition, lays claim to his attention and indeed his life.

To his surprise, the flyer succeeds in making his way through the flak to Arras, burning like an inferno below him, and then back. The author's meditations on what France means, in the context of the war, and on the relationships between his activity and the values to which he subscribes, form the concluding section of the book. While not based on invention, the book is fictionlike, shaped around a suspenseful battle and marked by superb characterizations and variety of tone, even as it moves toward a serious, reflective

---

7. See Michel Quesnel, *"Pilote de guerre* ou le refus du romanesque," in *Cahiers du Cerf XX*, no. 2 (Brest: L'Université de Bretagne Occidentale, 1986), 95–125.

humanism. In narrative techniques and style, it is, of course, traditional: Saint-Exupéry's originality consists in a way of seeing, not in technical innovations.

While *Les Noyers de l'Altenburg*, by Malraux, published in Switzerland, is the only surviving part of what was to be a longer work called "La Lutte avec l'ange" [The Struggle with the Angel] and thus in some sense is fragmentary, it forms an aesthetic whole. Malraux recounts how the rest of the manuscript disappeared when the Gestapo ransacked his apartment; however, this explanation for the unfinished state of the work has not been independently verified. I noted in chapter 3 that critics have judged as overintellectual its long discussions set at a colloquium in Altenburg on the definition and meaning of human beings, or what the author calls permanence and metamorphosis of man. The novel's technique is not radical, although it is marked by some of the stylistic traits that made Malraux's earlier fiction stand out: rapid changes of scene, striking chiaroscuro, telegraphic style, and minimizing of psychological analysis.

The action is set early in World War II after the defeat of France. The hero is a prisoner of war, housed temporarily in the cathedral of Chartres, as Malraux had been imprisoned from June through November 1940 in Sens. In this medieval setting, which emphasizes the continuity of history, the hero reflects in a long analepsis on the war and the experiences of his father, Vincent Berger, a quarter-century earlier, as a combatant in the Great War. (Malraux chose the name *Berger* because it is both German and French.) Flashbacks present the horrors of the trenches, of early tank battles, and especially of gas—an abstract weapon producing gruesome physical consequences without blood or wounds. In one of the best-known passages of the book, Malraux recounts the death-agony of a tank and its crew. The recurrence of violence in Europe, particularly the destructive hostility between France and Germany—nations whose achievements are among the finest products of culture—suggests a closed, deterministic historical cycle from which escape is impossible. Such thinking reflects the influence on Malraux of Nietzsche (who figures in a long embedded story in chapter 2 of *Les Noyers*), Leo Frobenius (a model for one character), and Oswald Spengler.

Clearly, for Malraux the second great war, even more than the previous one, posed grave questions concerning not just Western social and political structures in the twentieth century but also the nature of man and the possibility of transcending human self-destructiveness. Tentative answers come through artistic and organic images, especially the connection between the younger Berger's experience and his father's: there *is* continuity, not only biological but also cultural. In particular, the elder Berger leaves to his son his own moral legacy, which is that of belief in fraternity based on the *common* quality of men, irrespective of national differences: he recounts how, when gas spread across the battlefield, horrified German soldiers rushed to the aid of their enemies, the Russians.

While the historical and ideological field explored in *Les Noyers de l'Alten-burg* is not simple, and the meaning of the war, as one type of historical event, is a matter of dispute rather than a given, in Resistance fiction one generally finds a clear-cut oppositional pattern, pitting underground activists against the double enemy, the Germans and their Vichyite henchmen. In works such as those by Elsa Triolet and Joseph Kessel (whose politics differed considerably nonetheless), the conflict may be diverse but the values are not: all the action is directed toward overthrowing the double enemy. Incidental plots are seen as just that; and character, in the moral and literary senses alike, is and must be entirely subordinated to clandestine activity, to the point where, if someone steps out of his role, he is, at best, of no interest, and at worst, a traitor to be liquidated. This simplistic functional field and often minimal characterization mean that Resistance fiction can come very close to propaganda. Questions of internal politics (mainly communists versus non-communists) and of plans for the future, while alluded to, generally play a negligible role in the ideological field and structure; the only basic vector of action is to get rid of the Germans and their allies. The words that Joseph Fabre attributed to Joan of Arc could have been applied aptly to the Occupation: "Il n'y a qu'une querelle à vider" [There's only one quarrel to be settled] — that is, between France and Germany.[8]

It is noteworthy in addition that, like the historical reality they are to portray, Resistance works tend to be episodic, without a sustained, total action (such as Waterloo), built instead around multiple networks, movements, and isolated acts. Kessel claimed even that the episodes that make up *L'Armée des ombres* [The army of shadows] (1943) were collected sometimes at random.[9]

8. Joseph Fabre, *Jeanne d'Arc* (Paris: E. Dentu, 1890), 104.

9. Joseph Kessel, *L'Armée des ombres, chronique de la Résistance* (Algiers: Charlot, 1943), preface.

That book, which he calls a chronicle, although it has the characteristics of fictional prose, and *Le Premier Accroc coûte deux cents francs* [The first hitch costs 200 francs] by Triolet (1945) consist of discrete sections — not quite stories, because they lack shaping and fictional development — that can be read separately but among which ties are knit through recurring characters and motifs as well as the dominant theme. In Kessel's book, the diary form is used for one of the central sections, reflecting the rhythm of day-to-day activity. Composed during the war, these two works reflect the fractured reality of France at the time, divided politically and geographically (the various zones, plus Algeria), with two languages, two views of patriotism, two governments (if one counts the Gaullist government in exile — three if one considers that France was governed in part from Berlin), two economies (the black market and the other), at war but not at war. In short, it was a nation where the most important, the most authentic actions and thoughts were hidden or marginalized. Either of these authors could, presumably, have composed a novel of sustained action, like Roger Frison-Roche's *Les Montagnards de la nuit* (1965). Their choice not to do so may reflect the difficult circumstances of composition, or the conviction that it would be impossible to give a full-scale view of the Resistance.

The question of classifying these and other Resistance works as war fiction, a question that arose briefly in chapter 3, can be examined more closely here. In one sense, the label *war* cannot be challenged: these works deal with one of the participants in World War II, and although the armistice had put an end to France's status as a belligerent, the effects of the fighting and fall of France were ongoing. In another sense, also, they are war literature, since the underground fighters saw their action as war, not merely in a metaphoric sense but in an actual one, as a prolongation of the 1939–1940 conflict against an invader. In their view, the conflict should not be seen as finished: civil disobedience is war against the foreigner. Are the Resistance works *fiction*? Kessel said of *L'Armée des ombres* that every word was true. The acknowledgments recognize the help Kessel received from a Colonel Bourgoin and his paratroops, whose testimony allowed him "d'appuyer une oeuvre d'imagination sur la vérité de l'histoire et la force de l'épopée" [to base a fictional work on the truth of history and the power of epic]. Yet this work, like other Resistance chronicles built on fact, is clearly fictionalized by the choice and arrangement of materials and the handling of plot.

Another volume by Kessel treating the period, *Le Bataillon du ciel* [The sky batallion] (1947), touches only marginally on the Resistance and FFI, since it deals principally with French regulars—paratroops who were dropped into Brittany at the time of the June 1944 landings. Much of the novel consists of combat scenes. Although there are multiple characters, illustrating a variety of French types and roughly constituting a group actant, all presented by a narrator-author using the third person, only one principal story line is used along a single vector of action; the work has thus greater coherence than *L'Armée des ombres*. This coherence is fitting in view of the type of historical action it narrates: first, preparing in England for commando action; then, once the troops parachute onto the continent, carrying out these missions— blowing up tunnels and bridges, blocking roads, killing officers, and stealing plans—single-mindedly and successfully, without regard for anything else. There is room for no ideology save an unexamined patriotism: Vichy politics are not discussed, differences between Great Britain and France concerning the conduct of the war are similarly omitted (only occasional grumbles are heard against the English), and the reasons for which the Germans have fought—practical or ideological—are totally absent. Indeed, the German opponents are mechanical though powerful figures, lacking individual, even human, dimensions.

The conflict in the book comes from three sources: the basic opposition to the enemy, which is a given; the differences among French fighters, whether over questions of tactics or for personal reasons, leading to disputes and error; and struggles within individual characters. The novelist shows how unity of purpose can, generally, bring about unity of action, even against a background of quarrels; great sacrifices are demanded and made. No character struggle is explored in depth, to be sure; this sort of novel does not reveal subtle psychology. Rather, it is to be read, presumably, as a patriotic lesson, set in the very particular circumstances by which Frenchmen trained in England to invade their occupied homeland and free it from foreigners and local accomplices.

The title of Roger Vailland's *Drôle de jeu* [Funny game] (1945), a novel centered on the Resistance (if not a "Resistance novel," according to the author's note), recalls the age-old analogy between war and sport, which I discussed in connection with Henry de Montherlant in chapter 6. In *Drôle de jeu* the game involves not ordinary warfare between two belligerents, but rather elements of civil war—French against French—and uprising against an occupant; the activities are terrorist rather than military. But the novel draws an explicit parallel between war as an activity and Resistance work; the latter *is* war.[10] Moreover, the protagonist, whose *nom de guerre* is, significantly, Marat, associates his activity with the heroic tradition, as well as with eroticism, thus reintroducing, but in the ludic mode, the classical figure of the warrior/hero/ lover. Although there is mention of the quarrel between Gaullists and Giraudists, as well as that between the communist and non-communist underground, and although left-wing politics, taken to be the norm, are discussed in lengthy passages, the protagonist's attitude of *joueur* casts an antipolitical light on the story. It is significant that Vailland (himself a former surrealist, a Resistance participant, and infamous as a lover) delineated connections between surrealism and communism: both are rejections of bourgeois aesthetics and structures and the capitalist system; both look to radical revolution; war and occupation become an arena for reconfiguring, or playing with, the world.

When Simone de Beauvoir's *Le Sang des autres* [Others' blood] was published in 1945, it was greeted as a Resistance novel—which it certainly is; but that viewpoint displeased the author, who looked upon it instead as an examination of the human condition from an existentialist viewpoint. The novel, which covers considerable ground in plot and characters, is constructed around a system of dualities: two narrators, two narrative lines, two diegeses (frame narrative and embedded story)—thus affording a double viewpoint on much of the action and the enriching presence of two strong subjectivities. The historical setting is appropriate, because for Beauvoir, as for Sartre, literature was to convey the *vécu*—the concrete, lived experiences of human beings in their historical situation, which inevitably conditions them even while they enjoy utter ontological freedom. Any contemporary moment, any past one, could illustrate the human situation; but the Occupation was particularly suitable, because in historical form it illustrated what existentialists call *limit* or *borderline* situations: extreme circumstances that call for anguishing decisions, whose consequences may be radical. Beauvoir's choice to follow her two main characters, a man and a woman from different social classes, from the prewar years through the Phoney War and into the

10. Roger Vailland, *Drôle de jeu* (Paris: Gallimard, 1945), 42.

Occupation, then finally into active underground work, allowed her to illustrate, by plot and discourse, social differences and tensions and their relationship to politics and activism.

The theme of responsibility appears in *Le Sang des autres* in multiple guises:
social, ontological, political, and criminal responsibility. The main question
concerning terrorist activity on behalf of politics is posed in the concrete, implicitly nationalistic terms of French versus German occupants: should one
engage in militant, armed resistance, risking others' lives, or is a policy of pas-
sivism more advisable from the national standpoint? The decision of the hero,
Jean, to consent to sending *others* to die is based on two arguments. The pragmatic one, often made during the Occupation years, is that a few lives lost
through terrorism will ultimately save many more. The philosophical one,
which looms larger in the novel, is that "le sang qu'on épargne est aussi inex-
piable que le sang qu'on fait verser" [the blood that one spares cannot be ex-
piated any more than blood one sheds]—an argument grounded on the existentialist premise that all action is equally meaningless, all existences
indifferent, and yet action is necessary. One's only hope for existence, or
what Sartre called this "useless passion," is to use it for a finality with which
one agrees.[11] In this case, the finality is French national autonomy; but, in
conformance to Beauvoir's left-wing political views, the endeavor is seen not
as a restoration of the Third Republic, but as a step to something greater, a
postwar socialist society. This interpretation of the war revives a pattern from
World War I fiction: war as a means to socialist revolution and thus pacification.

Sartre's last two completed novels—*Le Sursis* [The reprieve] (1945) and
La Mort dans l'âme [Sick at heart] (1949)—and an associated fragment, all
war fiction in some sense, are built in part on radical fictional techniques,
according to his desire to create a new kind of fiction, fitting subjective experience amid the social, political, and philosophical realities of his time. His
self-conscious effort to reject aesthetic models while dealing with the major
historical event of the midcentury constitutes a noteworthy attempt to histori-
cize or "situate" (his term) a genre. Underlying the novels are questions concerning how an individual mind registers the threat of coming war, what relationships obtain between individual consciousness and political event, and,

11. Simone de Beauvoir, *Le Sang des autres* (Paris: Gallimard, 1945), 257.

ultimately, what makes history. Sartre's war novels, which have an admirable immediacy and often convey the very feel of experience, distinguish themselves not by epic scenes of battle but by their sense of what war means to those who participate in it and those who, according to Sartre's view of freedom, are responsible for it.

The first work—not a combat novel, but a war novel according to the broad definition I proposed earlier—takes as its subject the Munich agreement of 1938, that is, the threatening conflict and the appeasement measures that postponed it by a year. Sartre avoids the traditional fictional models wherein one main plot line and a handful of characters are dealt with in depth. Instead, following in part models devised by John Dos Passos and Virginia Woolf, in a narrative framework consisting of eight dated sections (23–30 September) he creates dozens of plots and characters, leaping from one set to another without warning, even in the middle of a sentence, with ambiguous use of pronouns such as *he* and *she*. He also makes extensive use of the present tense and stresses simultaneous actions. While this form may seem gratuitous, there is a dual rationale behind it: to suggest the confusion of Europe in 1938, the interdependency of human destiny, and the collectivity, or what he called "detotalized totality"; and to suggest the confused dynamics of political decisions and the immanence, the *presence* of war in human consciousness.

I have observed elsewhere that for Sartre at this time, "war is an intention of consciousness and exists because and wherever one is conscious of it." Desire for war is not implied in this intention, nor is any bellicose act presaged. Rather, the word *war* designates a composite human product that exists in so far as it is intended (in the phenomenological sense) by consciousness, but no farther. It occupies the same ontological status as other events and incidents, small and large; it does not descend into history ready-made, nor is it foreordained by any metaphysical agent, even when it appears humanly inevitable. Although it is a broadly based, collective action, and is thus composed of a multitude of intentions, it has no abstract or supraconscious existence. For these reasons, it is meaningful to say that war in *Le Sursis* figures almost as the protagonist, but as an intention of consciousness inseparable from characters whose thoughts it permeates. Mathieu, the novel's main character, underscores this idea when he ruminates thus: "La guerre: chacun est libre et pourtant les jeux sont faits. Elle est là, elle est partout, c'est la totalité de toutes mes pensées, de toutes les paroles d'Hitler, de tous les actes de Gomez: mais personne n'est là pour faire le total. Elle n'existe que pour Dieu. Mais Dieu n'existe pas. Et pourtant la guerre existe" [War: everyone is free and yet the chips are down. It is there, it is everywhere, it is the totality of all my thoughts, of all Hitler's words, of all Gomez's acts: but no one is there to add them up. It exists only for God. But God does not exist. And yet war exists].[12]

The following volume, *La Mort dans l'âme*, presents the war itself by more traditional techniques. In the first part, the "hero," Mathieu, is involved in fighting on the eastern front in June 1940; his friend Gomez is in exile in New York; other characters are experiencing what it is like to be in a France under attack and, shortly, defeated. Thus, on a smaller scale and with fewer abrupt transitions than in *Le Sursis*, Sartre suggested what war is in different circumstances, to different actors and observers. Characteristically, he conveyed persuasively the feelings, both affective and visceral, of those doing the fighting, removed as always from the centers of power and decision. The focus is on the microlevel; rather than experiencing a general apocalypse, the front-line soldiers, elements of troops mostly in disarray, sense war in the quotidian, chiefly as discomfort, disorder, and fragmented withdrawal, with a minimum of political meaning, despite Hitler's politics of aggression. However, the defeat (prematurely, they believe the armistice has been signed) does make Mathieu aware of his French nationality for the first time — not in the patriotic sense, but as an accident of circumstance. And this realization carries responsibility: "Nous avons perdu la guerre. On nous l'avait confiée et nous l'avons perdue" [We have lost the war. It was put into our safekeeping, and we lost it].[13]

The final scene of part 1, a tense and well-crafted depiction of fighting, shows Mathieu and a buddy in the belfry of a village church, trying to hold off the invading Germans, although they are aware that most of the eastern front has been lost. Sometimes taken to epitomize the exercise of Sartrean freedom, Mathieu's pointless action (it is clear that the Germans will soon overrun the village anyhow) is, according to the author, an entirely negative act and the opposite of true freedom: it is the meaningless exercise of hostility

12. Catharine Savage Brosman, *Jean-Paul Sartre* (Boston: Twayne, 1983), 61; Jean-Paul Sartre, *Le Sursis* (Paris: Gallimard, 1945), 258.

13. Jean-Paul Sartre, *La Mort dans l'âme* (Paris: Gallimard, 1949), 37.

inspired by resentment the hero feels for all he has not accomplished in the past.[14] This authorial interpretation is, of course, open to question. Objectively speaking, the action can be viewed as useful, since, by tying up a number of German troops, it delays their progress if only briefly and eliminates (by killing them) some enemy soldiers who otherwise would be available for combat during later battles. According to this interpretation, which is consistent with much of Sartre's thought, Mathieu's motives are less important than the actual consequences of his action. It can be argued further that such acts are exactly what patriotism is made of.

Part 2 and its sequel, "Drôle d'amitié" [Strange friendship], published separately, deal with prisoners of war; they thus belong to the internment literature of World War II—to which Cayrol, Claude Simon, and Wiesel also contributed—variously featuring French prisons, stalags, camps for deportees, or extermination camps. In the second part, the experiences of another character are represented: Brunet, who is captured by the Germans. The defeat is now a given; the struggle will be to regain France and then to redefine and reorganize it—according to the socialist (that is, communist) vision that Sartre had adopted by the time he composed the novel. Questions of means versus ends dominate, with the Nazi-Soviet pact in the background. How can French patriotism be defined by communists when their own national political party has subscribed to the Soviet pact with the enemy? And how can French will to overthrow the occupant be aroused, given the lack of resolve during the previous decade, the endless political quarrels, and French willingness to deal with the Nazis and live under their yoke? The ultimate denunciation of the pact and of current Communist party policy by the most orthodox hero, and the acknowledgment of the politicization of all, lead to an escape attempt that fails but nonetheless affirms the characters' freedom.

Céline, who has the highest literary standing of writers who were collaborationists or Vichy sympathizers, is one of the major recorders of the war in the imaginative mode, although the time period he depicts is brief. Brilliantly idiosyncratic, his trilogy D'un château l'autre [From castle to castle], Nord [North], and Rigodon [Rigadoon] deals with the final months of the war.

14. Michel Contat and Michel Rybalka, A Bibliographical Life, vol. 1 of The Writings of Jean-Paul Sartre, trans. Richard C. McCleary (Evanston, Ill.: Northwestern University Press, 1974), 115.

Called *romans*, these works are nevertheless wholly transparent chronicles of his own experiences, featuring himself (a clearly identified Céline), his wife Lili, their cat Bébert, and a variety of historical characters, mostly under their own names. Fictional elements are not entirely lacking: there is shaping of the story line, although it is highly episodic; characters are drawn deftly; conversations are reported that may or may not have taken place as such. But the triology would appear to be and indeed is presented as a prima facie record of the author's own experiences, joined to what Godard calls a "prétention historique" [historical claim]. (The collaborationist writer Lucien Rebatet, who was likewise in Sigmaringen—a Vichy French enclave in the Black Forest of Germany, where Céline lived out the last months of the conflict—attested to the fidelity of Céline's depiction.[15]) The stylistic innovations Céline had introduced in *Voyage au bout de la nuit* are carried further: wartime slang is joined to a jerky, elliptical, ungrammatical French, reflecting conversational language and the flowing, impressionistic style of interior monologue.

Céline's success at expressing what Godard calls images "à la mesure" of the war's near-apocalyptic quality seems to be the fruit of two visions: a historical one—that is, the worldview that both produced and was a product of the war—and a personal one. His pessimism and bitterness, already thoroughly established before the conflict, were increased by the conditions under which he lived in Sigmaringen. There he was galled by the attitude toward him of other French residents—some of whom, particularly Pierre Laval, he despised—and by Germans, whom he did not care for generally and also dreaded, since they too were in positions of power along with the transplanted collaborationist authorities. "Dieu sait si les Allemands sont louches, surtout les *von*! . . . onctueux, aimables et atroces!" [God knows that Germans are shady, especially the *vons*! . . . unctuous, pleasant and atrocious!]. He retained from earlier experiences a dislike for the German character: "Méchants qu'ils étaient acharnés déjà! . . . les mêmes sauvages qu'en 14!" [Malicious as they were already relentless! . . . the same savages as in 1914!]. His situation, his political views, and his persecution complex resulted in his having very sharp eyes for his surroundings and the events, which, if one is to judge by his statements, he read more clearly than other French exiles. Accused, in his words, of having sold out the *département* of Pas-de-Calais, after

15. Céline, *Romans*, 2:979–80.

he had volunteered for military duty and worked in a hospital during the 1940 exodus of refugees, he was extremely sensitive to the politics and plottings around him and to the way power (industrial, political, partisan, family) was related to the war, its conduct, and its aftermath.[16]

Céline the witness reads the disaster as total, both militarily and culturally, in the conditions around him. The skies are alive with RAF bombers; the streets and hotels, having fallen into an abominable state of sanitation, teem with disoriented people from all over, bereft of food and provisions, whom the war has displaced and who are mutual enemies; the castle of Sigmaringen resembles a *Cour des Miracles*, that is, an assembly of thieves and thugs. The events as reported by the BBC and the German press and as circulated by rumor among the streams of refugees continually arriving all contribute to his dark perspective. One of the reproaches leveled at Céline by his contemporaries was that, at the war's outbreak, he was not optimistic, seeing the "Boches" as likely victors. If witnesses are to be believed, he was similarly clairvoyant in 1944 with respect to the fate of Germany toward the war's end. In a fascinating episode recounting a dinner with Otto Abetz, he asks the former ambassador to Vichy France what he will do when the army of General Leclerc arrives in the Black Forest; Abetz, nonplused, speaks of the German secret weapon and "maquis brun" (Nazi resistance), and of the enduring value of national socialist ideas, whereas Céline knows that the Germans' game is up and that it is the victors who write the history of wars. Godard quotes Céline as writing at the time: "Les Allemands sont archifoutus. . . . y comprennent rien à ce qui se passe. . . . Valsez, fantoches, à la ballade des fusillés" [The Germans are damned done for. . . . don't understand anything about what's going on. . . . Waltz, puppets, to the ballad of the firing squad].[17]

Céline felt no sense of loss for the Germans, but both personally and culturally he saw devastation everywhere. His own pessimism and hostility thus encountering what he perceived as historical ruin, he included the Germans in a powerful vision of nihilism, expressed in a quick, cutting, almost visceral vocabulary. The war-torn world was, to his thinking, the consequence of policies he had inveighed against in earlier texts. But it was more: a product of the temperament of the human race. "En vrai, un continent sans guerre s'en-

16. Ibid., 61, 158, 276.
17. Ibid., 221, 227–28, 990.

nuie . . . sitôt les clairons, c'est la fête!" [In truth, a continent without a war is bored . . . as soon as the bugles sound, celebration!]. The history of Europe in the twentieth century shows a pattern of destruction and madness that can be altered only by a radical change, a sort of *tabula-rasa*. "L'Europe s'en relèvera jamais de cette folle maladie 'transe et zut'! tout en l'air! . . . le pli est pris! il faudra la bombe atomique qu'elle redevienne normale et vivable" [Europe will never get over this crazy sickness "terror and damn"! everything in a mess! . . . the habit is formed! it will take the atomic bomb for it to become normal and livable]. Reflecting on the city of Ulm, leveled by bombing, he gives evidence both of concern for those in other German cities, including some refugees (women and children) and himself, and of a nihilistic—or perhaps moralistic—vision of total retribution: "Ulm absolument rasé, ils ne vont pas recommencer tout de suite! . . . j'espère . . . une petite chance qu'ils nous loupent! Plus d'Ulm! . . . le monde sera seulement tranquille toutes les villes rasées! je dis! c'est elles qui rendent le monde furieux, qui font monter les colères, les villes! . . . tout le monde à l'air! le cul à la glace! vous parlez d'une hibernation! cette cure pour l'humanité folle!" [Ulm completely razed, they're not going to start again right away! . . . I hope . . . Slim chance that they'll miss us! No more Ulm! . . . The world will be calm only when all cities have been razed! I say so! It's they that make the world mad, that get up your anger, cities! Everybody out! Rumps on the ice! Talk about a hibernation! This cure for lunatic humanity!].[18]

Jules Roy, who was discussed briefly in chapter 5, is considered, after Saint-Exupéry, the finest aviation writer in France as well as a military philosopher. Roy was a career officer from 1927 to 1953, and in the air force starting in 1937. As a Pétainist, like almost all air force officers, when France fell he flew his plane to Algeria from its base near Grenoble and remained with the Pétainist armies until after the Anglo-American invasions of November 1942. He then turned against the Vichy government and its military arm and lent his support to oppositional movements, training recruits at various bases in North Africa. In 1943 Roy flew to England, where he became a bombardier and copilot on Lancaster and Halifax bombers in the French section of the Royal Air Force. In that capacity, he flew thirty-seven missions over occupied territory, most of them over the Rhine valley.

18. Ibid., 163, 243, 286.

In 1946 his novel *La Vallée heureuse* [The happy valley], concerning action over the Rhine, won the Prix Renaudot and earned him a wide following in literary circles and among general readers; he was, however, reprimanded by certain hierarchical superiors for having portrayed the experience of fear among flyers. In 1951 he published his RAF diary, *Retour de l'enfer* [Return from hell], and in 1954 a short novel, *Le Navigateur*. Both it and *La Vallée heureuse* include a midair crash between two RAF bombers in which he was involved; he survived but most of the crews perished. Both representations emphasize the experience of combat, both its psychological aspects, for the individual flyer and the unit of the crew, and the action itself, involving tactics of approach, bombing, evasion, and return.

Many years later Roy returned to the subject of the war in two full-length novels (*Danse du ventre au-dessus des canons* [Belly-dance above the cannons] and *Le Désert de Retz*), a short narrative (*Pour le lieutenant Karl*), and memoirs. While retracing the same sort of RAF action that appears in the earlier books, they approach the subject differently: in a more mature, thoughtful style, the narratives look beyond the aviators' experience and questions of tactics in order to explore the rationale for the war and its strategies. What was a given in 1943 is no longer unquestioned; a sense of guilt is perceptible. The flying machine, which Roy had poeticized in pages written before his war service, and which in his earlier war books appeared as an instrument of an unexamined armed struggle, assumes ambivalence in the later works.

Roy addressed two problems in particular in this later fiction. One is the irony of fate that has made the Germans and the French try to destroy each other repeatedly, despite—or perhaps because of—their common racial origins. (The Franks were, after all, a Germanic tribe.) This question interests Roy particularly because, on his father's side, the blood line is as much German as French; he himself is tall and blue-eyed. The killing of one's brother— the *same*—poses terrible problems of conscience. (In his works concerning the Algerian war and colonialism, he extends the idea of *brother* widely to embrace virtually all mankind.) The second matter is the bombing of cities, ordered by Bomber Command but questioned by some even then, and the subject of much reconsideration since. Roy's aviator heroes agonize over the destruction they wreak on civilians in the great firestorms over German cities.

This questioning is not surprising, some thirty years or more after the event, in the light of such changes in Europe as the Franco-German rapprochement through NATO and the Common Market. Modern war is generally an ideological face-off, pursued *à outrance* (Clausewitz's unlimited warfare), each of the two sides asserting its rights over the other without qualification; the lines of right and wrong appear perforce simple and unnuanced, distorting the ethical complexities, which then emerge with clarity later. (This is one reason why many ordinary war novels strike one as simplistic; the vectors of action and thought are few and leave little room for ethical maneuvering.) During a war, a participant or any member of a belligerent nation is, short of choosing objector status, obliged to follow these lines of right and wrong, if not in thought, at least in action; moreover, the lines are supported by a weighty national rhetoric and the suppositions behind it—not to mention the necessities of military thinking. Well after the war's end, though, it is impossible to ignore complexities and nuances not admissible during the conflict; the emphasis shifts from the action of war to its meaning.

Claude Simon's artistically radical novel *La Route des Flandres*, in which postmodernist techniques are combined with refusal of historical meaning, has already been mentioned in this study. While the novel's style and themes somewhat resemble those of William Faulkner, the plot is still more complex than most of Faulkner's, rich though they are, because Simon deals not only with a hero and his family, past and present, but also with war—a particular battle and its aftermath, and the phenomenon of war as a whole. It is true that some concerns in the work are not dependent upon the setting or theme of war; but the settings—for the most part during the war, or immediately thereafter—the action, and the title, as well as the thematic center, justify the term *war novel*.

La Route des Flandres recounts the fighting in Flanders in May 1940 and subsequent captivity of French soldiers in a German camp, experiences which are those of the author, but elaborated through various fictional strategies and a highly developed verbal and visual imagination. Simon served in the Thirty-first Regiment of Dragoons, which actually used horses in Flanders against the onslaught of German armor and aviation on the west bank of the river Meuse.[19] His novel is dominated by cynicism toward history, a cynicism arising from the war but doubtless increased by what occurred in the period

19. See Higgins, *The Second World War in Literature*, 59, 121, 125–27, for the autobiographical background.

from 1945 to 1960: postwar revelations about the extent of Nazi brutality, added to what was already known; reports on the tremendous abuses of Stalinism; the *épuration*, bitter political struggles, revelations about collaboration and collusion; the rearmament of Europe and another world conflict looming; then, in the 1950s, the Indochinese and Algerian wars.

Even more than Sartre's novels, Simon's text conveys the breakdown of meaning in midcentury Europe and the impossibility for the individual to control or see a pattern in events. History, associated with progress by thinkers of the Enlightenment and their heirs through most of the nineteenth century and into the twentieth, has lost its rationality, replaced by Nietzsche's eternal return, seen negatively, or by total chaos, an implosion of meaning into a dark hole. Historical repetition is illustrated by the pattern of French retreats: the withdrawals first from Moscow, then from Waterloo foreshadowed the disaster of the Franco-Prussian War, the German invasions of 1914, and Dunkirk. (It is noteworthy that the passage depicting the retreat of the wounded in Erckmann-Chatrian's *Histoire d'un conscrit de 1813* bears numerous resemblances to trench novels of 1914 and to Simon's evocation of disaster in 1940, the chief difference being that the nineteenth-century authors, while affording graphic scenes of amputated limbs and other suffering, eschewed coarse language.) Christian eschatology no longer holds the Western imagination; liberalism—the legacy of the Age of Reason and the French Revolution—is bankrupt; belief in a Hegelian or Marxist philosophy of history, seen as a rational product of a dialectical process, is dead.

In Simon's novelistic space, moreover, culture is a lie. The war took place in a world that deemed itself civilized, humane, where music, libraries, art, philosophy were promoted by great expenditures. All the libraries of Europe did not prevent the tortures of millions; nor are the humanistic platitudes dished out by the hero Georges's father of use to prisoners who need shoes and soap.

Georges, as a prisoner-of-war, speaks here about his reply to a recent letter from his father that detailed the bombing of the Leipzig library:

> . . . à quoi j'ai répondu par retour que si le contenu des milliers de bouquins de cette irremplaçable bibliothèque avait éte précisément impuissant à empêcher que se produisent des choses comme le bombardement qui l'a détruite, je ne voyais pas très bien quelle perte représentait pour

l'humanité la disparition sous les bombes au phosphore de ces milliers de bouquins et de papelards manifestement dépourvus de la moindre utilité. Suivait la liste détaillée des valeurs sûres, des objets de première nécessité dont nous avons beaucoup plus besoin ici que de tout le contenu de la célèbre bibliothèque de Leipzig, à savoir: chaussettes, caleçons, lainages, savon, cigarettes, saucisson, chocolat, sucre, conserves, gal . . . [. . . to which I replied in return that if the contents of the thousands of books of that irreplaceable library had been, precisely, powerless to prevent such things as the bombing that destroyed it, I didn't see very well what loss for humanity was represented by the disappearance under phosphorous bombs of those thousands of books and papers obviously without the least utility. There followed the detailed list of sure assets, of basic things that we need here much more than all the contents of the famous library of Leipzig, to wit: socks, underpants, woollen garments, soap, cigarettes, hard sausage, chocolate, sugar, canned goods, ca . . .][20]

As chapter 6 in this study shows, such cultural bankrupcy had been declared during and after the Great War. As the dadaists and surrealists saw in the 1920s, the very possibility of language to regulate human conduct, contribute to understanding, and create meaning had been undermined. While promises of change (the League of Nations, surrealism, socialism, the Spanish Republic, the Popular Front) provided in the 1920s and 1930s what appeared to be new departures, the cataclysm of 1939–1945 was a dreadful repetition of the previous one.

Simon's views on the failure of civilization and the struggle against barbarism had already been expressed by others. For instance, this theme is prominent in Malraux's 1948 statement on the death of man and in Vercors's story "L'Impuissance" (1944), where a Frenchman's anguish over the bloodshed of war—particularly the massacre at Oradour—and the sufferings of those in torture-chambers and camps is expressed in his violent rejection of literature, history, and painting as mendacious. In a rage, Vercors's protagonist attempts to light what is in effect a funeral pyre of culture: his entire library and art collection piled up in the garden. Simon's reiteration of the theme is, how-

20. Claude Simon, *La Route des Flandres* (Paris: Editions de Minuit, 1960), 224–25.

ever, expressed also by fictional technique, by which multiple voices in a radical, decentered style explore the relationship between artistic meaning and
meaninglessness. It is as if Simon took up the challenge formulated by Jack
Kolbert on the subject of Wiesel's work: "How could one use language, a re-
fined and orderly system of signs developed by civilized society, to express
experiences that were totally antithetical to civilization, events that were in
all regards supreme manifestations of chaos and disorder?"[21]

La Route des Flandres begins simply, "Il tenait une lettre à la main . . ." [He
was holding a letter in his hand]. As in *Le Sursis*, pronouns often have no clear
antecedent and refer sometimes in the same sentence to more than one character; this procedure suggests the breakdown of psychological wholeness and
the interchangeability of subjectivities. The predominant tense is the imperfect, suggesting "what was going on" but not "what was concluded"—as if
the thread of history continually unwound without visible progress. Simon
makes extraordinary use of the present participle, multiplied over and over:
"progressiveness" without progress, circular stasis. In opposition to the logical, well-ordered discourse for which French literary writing is famous, the
sentences are almost without punctuation and run on sometimes for pages.
Almost all of the novel takes place as stream-of-consciousness in the mind
of Georges as a recovery of the past, involving present-tense narration and
flashback and flashforward (analepses and prolepses); but there are also long
pages of dialogue. Furthermore, the hero is split into three voices: referred
to alternately as *je*, *il*, and *Georges*, he has an uncertain identity and occupies
alternately the position of central consciousness or experiencing subject, and
that of object—the *object* of history. This multiplying of points of view has
the effect, as in cubism, of fragmenting and undermining the identity of the
subject.

In addition, incidents recur in a meaningless repetition, imitating the futile
repetitions of history. The novel was composed, Simon wrote, according to a
cloverleaf pattern. At its crux is a dead horse—a consecrated icon of French
warfare—which Georges sees on a road in Belgium during the terrible retreat, when the routed army is in complete disorder. He passes by the same

21. [Jean Bruller] Vercors, *Les Armes de la nuit* (Paris: Editions de Minuit, 1946), 127–34;
Jack Kolbert, "Elie Wiesel," in Catharine Savage Brosman, ed., *French Novelists Since 1960, Dictionary of Literary Biography*, vol. 83 (Detroit: Gale Research, 1989), 324–25.

road, the same decomposing horse three times more, each time more disoriented and dazed with fatigue; and each time, the disgusting image gives the
lie to any sense of progress or escape. In addition to this major structural repetition, many incidents recur, now in Georges's voice, now in that of his fel-
low-soldier Iglesia, later his companion in prison camp. The repetition is justified in part by the obsessive reliving by the prisoners of their past, as they
recount, with variations and sometimes arguments, scraps of experience; but
it also suggests the inability of the psyche to go beyond the war experience
and to determine historical truth. "Comment savoir, comment savoir?" [How
can one know?] is Georges's obsessive question.

In short, plot and characters, alternately multiplied and rewritten or undermined, have broken down; style is out of control; and the work goes nowhere, being very nearly circular and constantly calling into question its own
meaning. The four cavalrymen who are Georges's companions are metamor-
phosed into the Four Horsemen of the Apocalypse, riding on a meaningless
path of destruction through a history that has escaped from both divine and
human control. This vision is an ironic one, doubly so, if one agrees with the
definitions of irony offered by Hayden White as (1) recognition of the eternal
return of the same human folly in different disguises, and (2) recognition of
the impossibility of establishing objective historical truths. Irony, using language, nevertheless turns on (or against) language: "Irony represents a stage
in the evolution of consciousness in which the language itself has become an
object of reflection and the sense of the inadequacy of language to the full
representation of its object has become perceived as a problem."[22]

Marguerite Duras's *La Douleur* [Sorrow] (1985), a novella concerning the
war's end, is the principal work in a collection by the same title. Despite its
publication date, the novella was composed much earlier, according to an author's paratextual note; internal evidence points to the late forties as the earliest possible period of composition for some portions. It is a powerful, though
not flawless, rendering of affective experience connected to a returning deportee and of the physical and moral misery of those who had been interned.
Duras's characteristic style and composition—praised by her countless admirers, irritating to other readers—find here, perhaps more than in any other
text, their justification. Lack of full identification of characters; syntactic, lex-

22. White, *Tropics of Discourse*, 207.

ical, and structural repetition; imprecision of place and time, elliptical or incomplete statements; unprepared, arbitrary analepses and prolepses; psychological murkiness: such Durassian features all contribute to narrative
indeterminacy and suit well the narrator's state of mind. It may be said that
they *constitute* her mind. Lack of clear memory, which on occasion confuses,
somewhat implausibly, characters in other books by Duras, is persuasive in
this case; precise verbalization of feelings cannot be expected in the circumstances. Rehearsal and mental reliving of scenes are convincing on the part
of one obsessed with fear. The irrationality of the war itself as well as her own
mind is well conveyed by such phrases as: "Je hurlais, de cela je me souviens.
La guerre sortait dans des hurlements" [I howled, that I remember. War
came out in howls].[23]

Composed as a diary, with more or less precise dating of its sections, the
narration is in the voice of a woman—a pseudo-Duras, addressed sometimes
as Marguerite—who is waiting in Paris for what she hopes will be the return
of her husband, Robert L., from Dachau in spring 1945. The dominant tense
is the present. The distance between narrating voice and event narrated is
usually very small—the conversations and thoughts of the day or the previous day; but on occasion it stretches, and the past tense used gives a feeling
of considerable elapsed time, coloring the event differently (as in "Je ne sais
plus quel jour c'était, si c'était encore un jour d'avril, non c'était un jour de
mai" [I no longer know what day it was, whether it was still April, no it was
a day in May]). At the end the tenses and narrative tone suggest a composition time well past the last internal date, summer 1946. There may be slippage
between the voice of the diary and another doubling it, which speaks of "re-
transcribing" lines written earlier that have escaped from her; this second
voice can know more than the first, which is mainly based in the events of
spring 1945. Both voices are usually in the grammatical first person; however,
Duras moves in some passages toward distancing the narrator from the first
person, when the general, anonymous *on* (translated by Barbara Bray as
"you") seems to represent her consciousness. More strikingly, Duras dupli-
cates (somewhat in the manner of Simon, though presumably without knowledge of his technique in *La Route des Flandres*) the *I* with a third-person character, *she*: "Qu'est-ce qu'elle attend en vérité? Quelle autre attente attend-

23. Marguerite Duras, *La Douleur* (Paris: P.O.L., 1985), 64.

elle?" [What is she waiting for, in truth? What other wait is she waiting for?][24]

The novella's later sections constitute a powerful imaginative effort to reconstruct what Robert L. feels and sees—to suffer with him; the speaker's projection into an *on* serves, paradoxically, to bring the imaginative reconstruction closer rather than to distance it. Conversely, the sections with past tenses and narrative distance dilute the sense of sympathetic suffering. When the reader learns, tardily, that the narrator plans to tell Robert L. that she wishes to leave him for D., the intensity of the previous identification with the victim in Dachau is called into question. In this passage, as the narrator modulates into *she*, it is not to effect a powerful sympathetic relationship with Robert L., but, on the contrary, to deny it: "Je n'existe plus. Alors du moment que je n'existe plus, pourquoi attendre Robert L.? Autant en attendre un autre si ça fait plaisir d'attendre? Plus rien de commun entre cet homme et elle" [I no longer exist. So, since I no longer exist, why wait for Robert L.? Might as well wait for another if she wants to wait? No longer anything in common between that man and her].[25]

In such passages, typical Durassian ambiguity and indeterminacy creep in, no longer conveying the contradictory feelings of hope and dread of one waiting for a returning deportee (who may be dead and not return at all), but rather incongruous sentimental uncertainties. The narrator-author feels estranged from all culture: "Il n'y a plus la place en moi pour la première ligne des livres qui sont écrits. Tous les livres sont en retard. . . . Derrière nous s'étale la civilisation en cendres, et toute la pensée, celle depuis des siècles amassée" [There is no longer any room in me for the first line of the books that are written. All books are late. . . . Behind us civilization spreads out in ashes, with all thought, all that has accumulated for centuries]. It is the fault of the Germans, in the first instance: "Comment être encore Allemand? On cherche des équivalences ailleurs, dans d'autres temps. Il n'y a rien. . . . Une des plus grandes nations civilisées du monde, la capitale de la musique de tous les temps vient d'assassiner onze millions d'êtres humains à la façon méthodique, parfaite, d'une industrie d'état" [How can one still be a German? One looks for equivalent things elsewhere, in other times. There is nothing. One

24. Ibid., 46, 61.
25. Ibid., 46.

of the greatest civilized nations in the world, the all-time musical capital has just murdered eleven million human beings in the methodical, perfected manner of a state industry]. But the narrator argues, in a Sartrean vein, that the crime must be assumed by all: "Si ce crime nazi n'est pas élargi à l'échelle du monde entier, s'il n'est pas entendu [sic] à l'échelle collective, l'homme concentrationnaire de Belsen qui est mort seul avec une âme collective et une conscience de classe . . . a été trahi. . . . La seule réponse à faire à ce crime est d'en faire un crime de tous" [But if this Nazi crime is not extended to the scale of the whole world, if it is not heard on the collective scale, the man in the concentration camp in Belsen who died alone with a collective soul and class consciousness . . . has been betrayed. . . . The only response to make to this crime is to make it everyone's crime].[26]

These works by Simon and Duras, as well as others, support Jay Winter's claim that "the rupture of language and imagery which followed the Second World War" was profound and enduring. Julia Kristeva has similarly argued that the power of symbolic expression to give meaning to war was destroyed by that conflict; and others, including Cayrol, Adorno, Wiesel, and George Steiner, have stressed either the failure or the inappropriateness of formal and linguistic expressions of a cataclysm of that scale. As Robert Antelme (Duras's husband at the time of the war) pointed out, victims and prisoners themselves—of whom he was one—could not then express their experience; it was, even to them, unimaginable.[27] Broadly speaking, the development of the New Novel and the Theater of the Absurd in the 1950s and later can, like surrealism three decades before, be attributed at least in part to the postwar breakdown in literary forms and loss of belief in meaning, although these generic developments have roots in certain modernist forms of the 1920s and 1930s, even earlier. Multiple pressures gave rise to the post-1950 tendency to replace imagined self and character and linear narrative structure—or at least the sense of *time*, moving forward, moving toward conclusion, fulfillment— with blurred or noncentered psyche and personage, dispersed event, arbitrary or even contradictory sequence, abolition of boundaries, and absence of conclusion; but this erosion of ground, in the philosophical and imaginative sense, sprang in part from the literal erosion of ground in two world wars and the apocalyptic destruction of material and cultural wealth that they caused.

26. Ibid., 44, 60–61.
27. Robert Antelme, *L'Espèce humaine*, 2d edition (1957; reprint, Paris: Gallimard, 1978), 9.

Narratologically speaking, the sender (nationalist creed, homeland, cultural values, Western civilization) has been found bankrupt and denounced, the receiver (those same values or nation) similarly so, and the identity of subject and object undermined. What many French saw as the failures of Cold War politics did not remedy the matter. Similarly, the growing popularity of structural linguistics and the rise of anthropological structuralism, followed by poststructuralism, with their skepticism concerning meaning and their relativistic bent, undercut further the foundations of meaning on which orderly fiction depends. Great fiction there may be after 1960; great war fiction may have come to its ending with Simon's *La Route des Flandres* and its Four Horsemen and hammering implication of failure, echoed by Duras in *La Douleur*, "Comment savoir?"[28]

28. Winter, *Sites of Memory*, 8; Julia Kristeva, *Black Sun: Depression and Melancholia*, trans. Leon R. Roudiez (New York: Columbia University Press, 1982), 223; Duras, *La Douleur*, 46.

8

REPETITION AND RUPTURE
The Legacy of Modern French Wars

SARTRE POINTED OUT in *La Nausée* that, whereas life is lived forwards, fiction is recounted backwards: that is to say, everything is subordinated to an end, which alone justifies the preceding elements. The inconclusiveness of much human activity lacking a clear-cut *telos*, the arbitrary endings of death, and, by the dialectic of praxis, the transformation of ends into means for still further ends, are among the ways in which historical happenings resist narration. On the general plane, because history remains unfinished, its meaning is in suspension, depending, as it does, on one's consciousness of it and one's own historicization. Even if the *immediate* outcome of an event is known, its ultimate outcome is *not* known, since each event is prologue to others. Sartre is only one of many modern thinkers to note the problem, which he examined also in *L'Etre et le néant*: "Ainsi faudrait-il une histoire humaine *finie* pour que tel événement, par exemple la prise de la Bastille, reçût un sens définitif. . . . Celui qui voudrait en décider aujourd'hui oublierait que l'historien est lui-même *historique*, c'est-à-dire qu'il s'historialise en éclairant 'l'histoire' à la lumière de ses projets et de ceux de sa société. Ainsi faut-il dire que le sens du passé social est perpétuellement *en sursis*" [Thus it would require a *finite* human history for a certain event, for instance, the taking of the Bastille, to acquire a definitive meaning. Anyone who would wish to decide upon it today would forget that the historian is himself *historical*, that is to say that he historicizes himself by illuminating "history" in the light of his projects and those of society. Thus one must say that the meaning of the past is perpetually *suspended*].[1]

---

1. Jean-Paul Sartre, *L'Etre et le néant* (Paris: Gallimard, 1943), 582.

This view of historical development and the epistemological difficulties attendant upon understanding it varies considerably from that of the New Historicists, which I discussed briefly in the preface. The former does not deny the historian's ability to be in touch with the past (through documents and other evidence — that is, through language), but rather views present assessment as incomplete, contingent upon a final and definite understanding which cannot be reached. Both views, however, posit a gulf between, on the one hand, lived experience of the past (the stuff of history) and even present experience (at least for Sartre), and, on the other, its conceptualization and writing. Yet novelists, poets, filmmakers, graphic artists, and historians, all concerned with expression as well as comprehension, have continued to be drawn to the subject of war, whether that of their own period or another, and, acting as though understanding were possible, have attempted to render the war experience and thus, in some sense, explain it and generalize from it. The theoretical problems involved in dealing with the past and the future and in entertaining such notions as historical cause and responsibility, stasis versus change, and progress versus decadence are either ignored, put within brackets as unknowable or unsolvable, or set aside as irrelevant. This dodging of the theoretical is particularly true in imaginative narrative, which, at its most fundamental level, can be considered a trope for the linear experience of one human life — the irreducible experience of the single thinking and feeling subject moving through time. What fiction does particularly well is to show not events themselves, but how human beings think about them; to provide elements for establishing the meaning of the past as it can be known — the meaning for those who lived it, those who wrote it, and those who read it from their individual viewpoints, appropriate it or subvert it, and help join past to future.

From the study of their nation's wars as depicted by French writers and other artists from the Napoleonic period through mid-twentieth century, one can draw a number of conclusions, some aesthetic, others moral and historical. On the one hand, striking similarity, even identity, frequently obtains among responses from author to author, artist to artist, war to war. This resonance holds for both the disasters of war and the thrills and achievements that conflict brings — war's horrors and its strange appeal. The wars of Napoleon, the Franco-Prussian War, and the two great conflicts of the twentieth century simply *sound* alike when they are put into imaginative prose and treated as experience—and this despite the changes in magnitude and in the kind of fighting introduced. In his *Once There Was a War*, John Steinbeck reminds readers that in ancient Greece it was said that a war was necessary every twenty years, so that each generation of men could know what it was like; one can assume that for each, the discovery was the same, both the terror and the joys.[2] In the comparatively short period—approximately 150 years—from the Revolutionary and Napoleonic Wars through World War II, the historical situation in France and the nationalistic attitudes that arose in that nation and then spread elsewhere on the continent remained similar enough to sound the same notes throughout the period under review; to the fundamental predicament of all wars (kill or be killed) are added thus, in literary renderings of them, cultural and political patterns repeated from the beginning of the nineteenth century through the mid-twentieth.

The most striking element of recurrence in the modern French experience is, of course, the repeated struggle against troops from Germanic nations—first the Prussian enemy (along with the English) at Waterloo, then a pan-Germanic adversary in 1870, 1914, and 1939—and the repeated invasion and occupation of French territory by this adversary, abetted on occasion by its allies. To this experience, with its numerous adjuncts and variants—not excluding wars of conquest and bellicose attitudes on the part of the French also—narrative and graphic works, with their vocabulary of symbols and attitudes, show time and again similar responses, while at the same time evolving in formal terms and genres. Particularly on the experiential level—that plane of individual feeling, thought, and action which Romantic and post-Romantic literature has taken for its own—the responses to war and the language and symbols in which they are couched remain nearly constant. It must be so, if one agrees that, whether or not combat is central to the work, war implies destruction and death. Death, which Henry James called the "distinguished thing," appears instead, terribly ordinary, plain, and unremarkable—except, of course, for the person who undergoes it; so that depictions of the ultimate destruction of war will always make central the commonplaces of suffering and dying, which have not changed since the Greek epics and tragedies, however much modes of feeling and expression have been modified.

If, however, one compares France at the end of the eighteenth century

2. John Steinbeck, *Once There Was a War* (1959; reprint, London: Corgi Books, 1973), 7–8.

with France in the second half of the twentieth, one sees vast political and cultural changes. Despite similarity of material conditions of war and existential responses to it, along with persistence of nationalist and militant symbols, attitudes taken toward these experiences and the nation on whose behalf they are undergone display changes and perhaps evolution. While this study does not investigate works dealing with the two colonial wars in which France was embroiled after 1945, a few words on the legacies of 1945 and the period of decolonization may confirm some of the points made in foregoing chapters and at the same time reveal new attitudes.

The national humiliation and trauma of defeat at Dienbienphu in May 1954—the first time that France, or indeed any European power, had been defeated on a wide scale by an Oriental army—and the even more profoundly disturbing and divisive experience of the Algerian conflict, followed by loss of the African territory, can be connected to the conflict of 1939–1945, and especially to the social and political struggles that preceded and followed it. Already in the 1920s and 1930s there were anticolonial currents, notably, on the part of the autochthonous residents themselves. Anticolonialism was expressed in such movements as the Etoile nord-africaine (founded in 1926, headed in the 1930s by Messali Hadj) and, briefly, an autonomy movement within the Algerian branch of the French Communist party before a change in Comintern policy turned it away from nationalistic and local concerns. To numerous centrists as well as thinkers of the Left, the liberation of France in 1944–1945 implied a necessary redefinition of the colonial status of Indochina and especially of Algeria, although the latter occupied a special situation and was geographically, administratively, and demographically closer to France. As Jules Roy argued, in the post-World War II period, those who had fought against the Nazis to *liberate* France were uncomfortable at seeing themselves as occupants of territories that, however Europeanized they might be in some ways, were nonetheless part of a colonial empire.

In the late 1940s and early 1950s, moreover, most of the French had little stomach for any war; the efforts of the army in Indochina to contain and extinguish the nationalist liberation movement were, to most French citizens, out of sight and out of mind. While public attitude toward Algeria entailed the widespread belief that it was an integral part of the nation (it had been declared part of France in 1848), by early 1957, barely two years past the date usually taken to mark the start of this undeclared war (November 1954), this belief had lost force. Many French, aware of the Algerian conflict's high cost in appropriations and young men, were becoming reluctant to support it; by 1960, along with left-wingers, thousands and thousands of moderates believed the war should be brought to a close, preferably in such a way as to retain French influence in the territory, but, if necessary, at any price, including granting its total autonomy. The "Letter of 121," published in *Les Temps Modernes* in August 1960 and signed by eminent intellectuals and artists (many of whom were also public figures), merely gave widespread and illegal expression to views shared by many: that Algeria was not worth the price of war or that, on principle, colonialism must be brought to an end, even if that meant loss of three French *départements* in which over a million European settlers lived. While radicals of the Left who called for immediate liquidation of French hegemony in Algeria were not satisfied immediately, Gaullist policy, based on expediency (as well as on de Gaulle's personal dislike for Algeria) and supported by many moderates, eventually sacrificed the territory after temporizing.

Behind these colonial wars and the attitudes toward them, one can see not only the politics of World War II but, perhaps even more organically, the Great War. James J. Cooke has argued that the first and most crucial watershed between the domination of French empire and its dissolution was neither the aftermath of World War II—not even the harshly repressed native uprisings in Sétif in Algeria (May 1945), which coincided significantly with the victory of democracy in Europe—nor, earlier, the Colonial Exposition of 1930 and nascent autonomy movements mentioned above. Rather, the crucial moment was the aftermath of World War I, that is, the moment when the colonial soldiers from North Africa who served in substantial numbers in France as well as their fellow colonized discovered that the democratic rights for the defense of which the war had ostensibly been fought would not be extended widely in the empire: their brethren had died for values of fraternity and equality in which they could not share.[3] While it remains difficult for historians to assess the precise consequences of the participation of Algerian combatants in World War I, the 1920s were in fact the decade when indigenous movements appeared on the literary horizon as well as the political one, and the European war was frequently denounced.

3. James J. Cooke, "Nationalism in Algeria" (Paper delivered at Tulane University, 18 October 1996).

After 1945 contradictions between liberal principles and illiberal fact were even more marked. The contrast between very limited civil and political rights for indigenous inhabitants — often hypocritically granted and imperfectly implemented — and the democratic values for which France stood acted as a stimulant to colonial rebellion, along with the economic exploitation that Albert Camus and others had denounced before the war. The idea of liberation, dramatized in the patriotic literature under the Occupation, was appropriated by anticolonialists and recast in terms both local and universal. The call to arms was taken up by native writers who would shortly become more and more radicalized. For their liberal supporters in France, the idea of the war novel or other literary depiction of armed struggle became associated necessarily with anticolonialism. A striking illustration of this is offered by Sartre's play *Les Séquestrés d'Altona* (1959), a drama set in post–World War II Germany and referring, on the surface, to German attitudes and conduct, but, by Sartre's admission, concerned at its depths with France and Algeria: France had become the oppressor, the torturer, the guilty one.[4]

Repetition, both historical and literary, was thus interrupted. In the war's aftermath, an alliance was soon made and eventually strengthened between France and its historical enemy, Germany; while there were many repressions by the Soviet bloc, no further warfare among nations was conducted in Western Europe; French troops in Indochina, who were mainly colonials, career officers, and Legionnaires, seemed very far away; the Cold War, while a clear threat to French security and prosperity and a cause of enormous and costly dissension within France, was not fought in any real sense; and when the Algerian conflict began, the grounds for and characteristics of the fighting as well as the identity of the belligerents gave to the struggle an entirely different face from that of the wars France had fought in the previous hundred and fifty years. Whether they were conservatives anxious to hold Algeria indefinitely on the same constitutional and economic bases ("Algérie française!"), or liberals or radicals desirous of revising the status of the territory — autonomy of some sort, perhaps complete independence — or merely weary of war, French writers faced in the 1950s and early 1960s an entirely different field of battle: an undeclared conflict "that did not dare say its

4. Oreste F. Pucciani, "An Interview with Jean-Paul Sartre," *Tulane Drama Review*, 5 (March 1961): 13.

name," setting French against French, a war both foreign and civil, both urban (within Algiers and, threateningly so, in France) and rural, involving regulars and guerrillas. The battle novels of the previous wars, from Napoleon onward, could not be revived; the ideas of heroism, attacked throughout the century, though tenacious, lost all remaining luster when it became clear in the battle of Algiers that terrorism and torture were the chief tactics on both sides. Journalism siphoned off the efforts of many writers; few found in the conflict material for fiction. The myth of nationalism in its militant form, powerful from the Revolution onward and instrumental in bringing about wars and in their development, was so undermined that its defenders (prime among them the Organisation armée secrète) could properly be called fanatics and behaved accordingly, making threats, throwing bombs, and plotting within the army itself to overthrow the elected government.

While a small body of what may be called imperialist fiction was produced during the two colonial conflicts and their aftermath — Jean Lartéguy's *Les Centurions* is an example — other works called into question the bases of colonial occupation or the conduct of colonial wars. Jules Roy's novel about Indochina, *Les Belles Croisades* [Fine crusades] (1959), and numerous works by others concerning Algeria — Camus's posthumous unfinished novel, *Le Premier Homme*, Roy's *Le Tonnerre et les anges* [Thunder and angels] (1975), and works by Emmanuel Roblès and Jean Pélégri — though imbued with nostalgia for the lost territory, all betray uneasiness, if not guilt, about the politics of French imperialism or the military operations carried out to defend it. Acts of individual heroism notwithstanding, the French flag was tainted, the sacrifice of young men senseless, the idea of war corrupted. Ghosts of 1914–1918 had returned to denounce the very notion of nationalism. Many of these denunciations were, and remain, highly partisan: in a nation with a Communist vote of approximately 20% in elections time after time and with a powerful Socialist party that dominated politics for fourteen years, a strong vein of left-wing pacifism and internationalism remains. Yet it is obvious that, under the Gaullists (1958–1981) and even under François Mitterrand's Socialist government, militarism did not disappear, and, like other powers, France has used its armed forces on a small scale in recent years to support its economic interests and, in some cases, to contribute to international peace-keeping enterprises. Not surprisingly, these undertakings have not produced a significant war literature.

During the same years, the reexamination of World War II, especially the question of collaboration with the Nazi occupants and the world of concentration camps, has occupied the French to no small degree; fiction, documentaries, and especially films, including Jean Cayrol's *Nuit et brouillard* [Night and fog] (1956), Marcel Ophuls's *Le Chagrin et la pitié* (1969), and Claude Lanzmann's *Shoah* (1985), have contributed to this reexamination. The Resistance is not forgotten, despite widespread recognition that many more French collaborated with the occupant than long believed and participated in dreadful deeds. One would expect that in the early decades of the twenty-first century there will be further developments in the fictional and cinematographic treatment of wars of the preceding two hundred years—including, doubtless, romanticized as well as critical versions of everything from Napoleon to the Indochinese conflict. The models of war novels, like the wars themselves, await those who would revive them; may no dreadful, unimaginable war of the future destroy the art that has borne witness to the sacrifice, senseless or meaningful, of millions.

BIBLIOGRAPHY

PRIMARY SOURCES

Alain (Emile Chartier). *Mars; ou, La Guerre jugée*. 1921. Reprint. Paris: Gallimard, 1995.

Antelme, Robert. *L'Espèce humaine*. 2d ed. 1957. Reprint. Paris: Gallimard, 1978.

Apollinaire, Guillaume. *Œuvres poétiques*. Edited by Marcel Adéma and Michel Décaudin. Paris: Gallimard/Bibliothèque de la Pléiade, 1965.

Aragon, Louis. *Les Communistes*. 6 vols. Paris: Bibliothèque Française, 1949–1951.

———. *Le Crève-coeur*. New York: Pantheon, 1943; London: La France Libre, 1944.

———. *Les Yeux d'Elsa*. 1942. Reprint. Paris: Seghers, 1964.

Aragon, Poet of the French Resistance. Translated from the French by Rolfe Humphreys, Hannah Josephson, Malcolm Cowley, and others; edited by Hannah Josephson and Malcolm Cowley. New York: Duell, Sloan & Pearce, 1945.

Aubigné, Agrippa d'. *Les Tragiques*. 1616. Reprint. Paris: Droz, 1932.

Aymé, Marcel. *Le Chemin des écoliers*. Paris: Gallimard, 1946.

———. *Uranus*. Paris: Gallimard, 1948.

Ballanche, Pierre Simon. *Le Vieillard et le jeune homme*. Edited by Arlette Michel. Paris: Garnier, 1981.

Balzac, Honoré de. *Les Chouans*. Edited by Maurice Regard. Paris: Garnier, n.d.

———. *La Comédie humaine*. Vols. 9 and 12. Edited by Pierre-Georges Castex. Paris: Gallimard/Bibliothèque de la Pléiade, 1978, 1981.

Barbusse, Henri. *Le Feu: Journal d'une escouade*. Paris: Flammarion, 1916.

Barrès, Maurice. *Autour de Jeanne d'Arc*. Paris: E. Champion, 1916.

———. *Colette Baudoche*. Paris: Juven, 1909.

———. *Les Déracinés*. Paris: E. Fasquelle, 1897.

———. *Les Traits éternels de la France*. Edited by Fernand Baldensperger. New Haven: Yale University Press, 1918.

Beauvoir, Simone de. *Les Mandarins*. Paris: Gallimard, 1954.

———. *Le Sang des autres*. Paris: Gallimard, 1945.

Benjamin, René. *Gaspard*. Paris: Arthème Fayard, 1915.

Bernanos, Georges. *Jehanne relapse et sainte*. Paris: Plon, 1934.

Bloy, Léon. *L'Ame de Napoléon*. Paris: Mercure de France, 1912.

———. *Jeanne d'Arc et l'Allemagne*. Paris: Crès, 1915.

Boisdeffre, Pierre de. *Les Fins dernières*. Paris: La Table Ronde, 1952.

Bruckberger, R.-L. *Si grande peine (1940–1948)*. Paris: Grasset, 1967.

Camus, Albert. *Essais*. Paris: Gallimard/Bibliothèque de la Pléiade, 1965.

———. *Le Premier Homme*. Paris: Gallimard, 1994.

Cassou, Jean. *Trente-trois sonnets composés au secret*. Paris: Editions de Minuit, 1944.

Cayrol, Jean. *On vous parle*. Neuchâtel: La Baconnière/Paris: Seuil, 1947.

Céline, Louis-Ferdinand. *Romans*. 2 vols. Edited by Henri Godard. Paris: Gallimard/ Bibliothèque de la Pléiade, 1974, 1981.

Clausewitz, Carl von. *On War*. Translated by Colonel J. J. Graham. 3 vols. London: Kegan Paul, Trench, Trubner, 1940.

Cocteau, Jean. *Thomas l'imposteur*. Paris: Gallimard, 1923.

Curtis, Jean-Louis. *Les Forêts de la nuit*. Paris: Julliard, 1947.

Daudet, Alphonse. *Œuvres*. Vol. 1. Edited by Roger Ripoll. Paris: Gallimard/Bibliothèque de la Pléiade, 1986.

Déroulède, Paul. *Chants du soldat*, with illustrations based on watercolors by Eugène Chaperon and Charles Morel. Paris: Modern-Bibiliothèque/Arthème Fayard, 1909.

Dorgelès, Roland. *Les Croix de bois*. Paris: Albin Michel, 1919.

Drieu La Rochelle, Pierre. *Les Chiens de paille*. Paris: Gallimard, 1944.

———. *La Comédie de Charleroi*. Paris: Nouvelle Revue Française, 1934.

Duhamel, Georges. *Chronique des saisons amères, 1940–1943*. Paris: Paul Hartmann, 1944.

———. *Civilisation, 1914–1917*. Paris: Mercure de France, 1918.

———. *Vie des martyrs, 1914–1916*. Paris: Mercure de France, 1917.

Duras, Marguerite. *La Douleur*. Paris: P.O.L., 1985. Translated by Barbara Bray as *The War: A Memoir*. New York: New Press, 1986.

Erckmann-Chatrian [Emile Erckmann and Alexandre Chatrian]. *Le Brigadier Frédéric*. Paris: J. Hetzel, 1874.

———. *Le Conscrit de 1813; Waterloo*. 1864, 1865. Reprint. Paris: Jean-Jacques Pauvert, 1962.

Fiel, Marthe. *Sur le sol d'Alsace*. Paris: Charpentier, 1911.

Frison-Roche, Roger. *Les Montagnards de la nuit*. Paris: Arthaud, 1968.

Gary, Romain. *Education européenne*. Paris: Calmann-Lévy, 1945.

Gide, André. *Journal; Souvenirs*. Paris: Gallimard/Bibliothèque de la Pléiade, 1954.

———. *Paludes*. Paris: Librairie de l'Art Indépendant, 1895.

Giono, Jean. *Le Grand Troupeau*. Paris: Gallimard, 1931.

Giraudoux, Jean. *La Guerre de Troie n'aura pas lieu*. Paris: Grasset, 1935.

Gracq, Julien. *Un Balcon en forêt*. Paris: José Corti, 1958.

Guibert, [Jacques] comte de. *Ecrits militaires, 1772–1790*. Paris: Copernic, 1977.

Hugo, Victor. *Les Misérables*. Edited by Maurice Allem. Paris: Gallimard/Bibliothèque de la Pléiade, 1951.

Kessel, Joseph. *L'Armée des ombres, chronique de la Résistance*. Algiers: Charlot, 1943.

———. *Le Bataillon du ciel*. Paris: Julliard, 1947.

———. *L'Equipage*. Paris: Gallimard, 1923.

Lacaze, André. *Le Tunnel*. Paris: Julliard, 1979.

Lartéguy, Jean. *Les Centurions*. Paris: Presses de la Cité, 1960.

Ligne, Charles-Joseph, Prince de. *Œuvres choisies du Prince de Ligne*. Edited by Basil Guy. Saratoga, Calif.: Anma Libri, 1978.

Maistre, Joseph de. *Œuvres complètes*. Vol. 5. Lyons: Librairie Générale Catholique et Classique, 1892.

Malraux, André. *La Condition humaine*. Paris: Gallimard, 1933.

———. *The Creative Act*. Vol. 2 of *The Psychology of Art*. Translated from the French by Stuart Gilbert. London: A. Zwemmer, 1949.

———. *L'Espoir*. Paris: Gallimard, 1937.

———. *Lazare*. Paris: Gallimard, 1974.

———. *Œuvres complètes*. Paris: Gallimard, 1989.

———. *Les Noyers de l'Altenburg*. Paris: Gallimard, 1948.

———. *The Voices of Silence*. Translated from the French by Stuart Gilbert. Garden City, N.Y.: Doubleday, 1953.

Martin du Gard, Roger. *Journal*. Vol. 1. Edited by Claude Sicard. Paris: Gallimard, 1992.

———. *Les Thibault*. In *Œuvres complètes*. 2 vols. Paris: Gallimard/Bibliothèque de la Pléiade, 1955.

Maupassant, Guy de. *Contes et nouvelles*. Edited by Louis Forestier. Vol. 1. Paris: Gallimard/Bibliothèque de la Pléiade, 1974.

Maurois, André. *Nouveaux Discours du Docteur O'Grady*. Paris: Grasset, 1950.

———. *Les Silences du Colonel Bramble*. Paris: Grasset, 1918.

Mercadet, Léon. *La Brigade Alsace-Lorraine*. Paris: Grasset, 1984.

Merle, Robert. *La Mort est mon métier*. Paris: Gallimard, 1952.

———. *Week-end à Zuydcoote*. Paris: Gallimard, 1949.

Monluc, Blaise de. *Commentaires*. Edited by Paul Courteault. Paris: Gallimard/Bibliothèque de la Pléiade, 1964.

———. *The Hapsburg-Valois Wars and the French Wars of Religion*. Edited by Ian Roy. Hamden, Conn.: Archon Books, 1972.

Montesquieu, Charles-Louis Secondat de. *Œuvres complètes*. 2 vols. Paris: Gallimard/Bibliothèque de la Pléiade, 1949, 1951.

Montherlant, Henry de. *Les Olympiques*. 2 vols. Paris: Grasset, 1924.

———. *La Relève du matin*. 1920. Reprint. Paris: Grasset, 1933.

———. *Le Songe*. Paris: Grasset, 1922.

Nimier, Roger. *Le Hussard bleu*. Paris: Gallimard, 1950.

Paulhan, Jean. *Le Guerrier appliqué*. 1930. Reprint. Paris: Gallimard, 1982.

Péguy, Charles. *Jeanne d'Arc*. 1897. Reprint. Paris: Gallimard, 1948.

———. *Œuvres poétiques*. Paris: Gallimard/Bibliothèque de la Pléiade, 1957.

Perec, Georges. *W ou le souvenir d'enfance*. Paris: Denoël, 1975.

Proust, Marcel. *Du côté de chez Swann*. In vol. 1 of *A la recherche du temps perdu*. Paris: Gallimard/Bibliothèque de la Pléiade, 1954.

———. *Le Temps retrouvé*. In vol. 3 of *A la recherche du temps perdu*. Paris: Gallimard/Bibliothèque de la Pléiade, 1954.

Psichari, Ernest. *L'Appel des armes*. Paris: G. Oudin, n.d.

Radiguet, Raymond. *Le Diable au corps*. 1923. Reprint. Paris: Livre de Poche, 1964.

Renan, Ernest. *Discours et conférences*. Paris: Calmann-Lévy, 1887.

Rivière, Jacques. *L'Allemand: Souvenirs et réflexions d'un prisonnier de guerre*. Paris: Gallimard, 1918.

Romains, Jules. *Le Drapeau noir*. Vol. 14 of *Les Hommes de bonne volonté*. Paris: Flammarion, 1937.

———. *Prélude à Verdun*. Vol. 15 of *Les Hommes de bonne volonté*. Paris: Flammarion, 1938.

———. *Verdun*. Vol. 16 of *Les Hommes de bonne volonté*. Paris: Flammarion, 1938.

Rousseau, Jean-Jacques. *Œuvres complètes*. Vol. 3. Paris: Gallimard/Bibliothèque de la Pléiade, 1964.

Roy, Jules. *Les Belles Croisades*. Paris: Gallimard, 1959.

———. *Les Cerises d'Icherridène*. Paris: Grasset, 1969.

———. *Danse du ventre au-dessus des canons*. Paris: Flammarion, 1976.

———. *Le Désert de Retz*. Paris: Grasset, 1978.

———. *La Guerre d'Algérie*. Paris: Julliard, 1960.

———. *Le Métier des armes*. Paris: Gallimard, 1948.

———. *Le Navigateur*. Paris: Gallimard, 1954.

———. *Pour le lieutenant Karl*. Paris: Christian Bourgois, 1977.

———. *Retour de l'enfer*. Paris: Gallimard, 1951.

———. *Le Tonnerre et les anges*. Paris: Grasset, 1975.

———. *La Vallée heureuse*. Paris: Charlot, 1946.

Sachs, Maurice. *La Chasse à courre*. Paris: Gallimard, 1949.

Saint-Exupéry, Antoine de. *Pilote de guerre*. New York: Editions de la Maison Française/Paris: Gallimard, 1942.

Sardou, Victorien, and Emile Moreau. *Madame Sans-Gêne*. Paris: L'Illustration, 1907.

Sartre, Jean-Paul. *Critique de la raison dialectique*. Paris: Gallimard, 1960.

———. *Le Diable et le Bon Dieu*. Paris: Gallimard, 1951.

———. "Drôle d'amitié." *Les Temps Modernes*, nos. 49, 50 (November, December 1949), pp. 769–806, 1009–39.

———. *L'Etre et le néant*. Paris: Gallimard, 1943.

———. *La Mort dans l'âme*. Paris: Gallimard, 1949.

———. *La Nausée*. Paris: Gallimard, 1938.

———. *Œuvres romanesques*. Paris: Gallimard, 1981.

———. *Qu'est-ce que la littérature?* 1948. Reprint. Paris: Gallimard, 1985.

———. *Les Séquestrés d'Altona*. Paris: Gallimard, 1960.

———. *Le Sursis*. Paris: Gallimard, 1945.

Seghers, Pierre. *La Résistance et ses poètes: France, 1940–1945*. 2d ed. Paris: Seghers, 1974.

Simon, Claude. *La Route des Flandres*. Paris: Editions de Minuit, 1960.

Simon, Pierre-Henri. *Histoire d'un bonheur*. Paris: Editions du Seuil, 1965.

Staël, Germaine de. *An Extraordinary Woman: Selected Writings of Germaine de Staël*. Translated with an introduction by Vivian Folkenflik. New York: Columbia University Press, 1987.

———. *Considérations sur les principaux événemens de la Révolution française*. 3 vols. Paris: Delaunay, 1818.

———. *Madame de Staël on Politics, Literature, and National Character*. Translated and edited with an introduction by Morroe Berger. Garden City, N.Y.: Doubleday, 1964.

Stendhal. *La Chartreuse de Parme*. Edited by Henri Martineau. Paris: Garnier, 1961.

———. *Lucien Leuwen*. Edited by Henry Debraye. Paris: Champion, 1926–1927.

———. *Le Rouge et le noir*. Edited by Henri Martineau. Paris: Garnier, 1960.

Thiers, Adolphe. *Histoire du consulat et de l'empire*. 21 vols. Paris: Paulin, 1845–74.

Tournier, Michel. *Le Roi des aulnes*. Paris: Gallimard, 1970.

Triolet, Elsa. *Le Premier Accroc coûte deux cents francs*. Paris: Egloff, 1945. Translated by Francis Golffing as *A Fine of 200 Francs*. New York: Reynal & Hitchcock, 1947.

Vailland, Roger. *Drôle de jeu*. Paris: Gallimard, 1945. (Livre de Poche edition.)

Valéry, Paul. *Œuvres*. Vol. 1. Edited by Jean Hytier. Paris: Gallimard/Bibliothèque de la Pléiade, 1957.

Vauvenargues, Luc de Clapiers, marquis de. *Œuvres*. Edited by D.-L. Gilbert. Paris: Furne, 1857.

Vercors (Jean Bruller). *Les Armes de la nuit*. Paris: Editions de Minuit, 1946.

———. *Le Silence de la mer*. 1942. Reprint. Paris: Albin Michel, 1951.

Vigny, Alfred de. *Œuvres complètes*. 2 vols. Edited by Fernand Baldensperger. Paris: Gallimard/Bibliothèque de la Pléiade, 1948, 1950.

———. *Servitude et grandeur militaires*. Edited by Auguste Dorchain. Paris: Garnier [1955].

———. *Servitude et grandeur militaires*. Edited by John Cruickshank. London: University of London Press, 1966.

———. *Stello; Daphné*. Edited by Annie Prassoloff. Paris: Gallimard, 1986.

Voltaire (François-Marie Arouet). *Essai sur les moeurs*. Vol. 2. Edited by René Pomeau. Paris: Garnier, 1963.

———. *La Henriade*. In *Œuvres complètes de Voltaire*. Vol. 8. Paris: Garnier, 1877.

———. *Mélanges*. Edited by Emmanuel Berl. Paris: Gallimard/Bibliothèque de la Pléiade, 1961.

———. *Œuvres complètes*. Vol. 48. Oxford: Voltaire Foundation, 1984.

———. *Poème de Fontenoy*. In *Œuvres complètes de Voltaire*. Vol. 8. Paris: Garnier, 1877.

———. *Political Writings*. Edited and translated by David Williams. Cambridge: Cambridge University Press, 1994.

Wiesel, Elie. *La Nuit*. Paris: Editions de Minuit, 1958.

Zola, Emile. *Œuvres complètes*. Vol. 6. Edited by Henri Mitterand. Paris: Cercle du Livre Précieux, 1967.

SECONDARY SOURCES

Adas, Michael. *Machines as the Measure of Men: Science, Technology, and Ideologies of Western Dominance*. Ithaca: Cornell University Press, 1989.

Adorno, Theodor W. *Noten zur Literatur*. Frankfurt-am-Main: Suhrkamp, 1981.

Agulhon, Maurice. *Marianne au combat: L'Imagerie et la symbolique républicaines de 1789 à 1880*. Paris: Flammarion, 1979.

All the Banners Wave: Art and War in the Romantic Era 1792–1851. Providence: Department of Art, Brown University, 1982.

Allem, Maurice. Introduction to Honoré de Balzac, *Le Médecin de campagne*. Paris: Garnier, 1956.

Anselmo, Frank A. "Alsace-Lorraine and the Patriotic Novels of the French Nationalist Revival from 1905 to 1914." Ph.D. diss., Tulane University, 1995.

Aristotle. *The Politics*. Edited and translated by Ernest Barker. New York: Oxford University Press, 1962.

Atack, Margaret. *Literature and the French Resistance: Cultural Politics and Narrative Forms, 1940–1950*. Manchester: Manchester University Press, 1989.

Bann, Stephen. *The Clothing of Clio: A Study of the Representation of History in Nineteenth-Century Britain and France*. Cambridge: Cambridge University Press, 1984.

Bardèche, Maurice. *Léon Bloy*. Paris: La Table Ronde, 1989.

Barnes, Julian. *Evermore*. London: Penguin Books, 1996.

Baroja, J.-C. *Le Mythe du caractère national*. Lyons: Federop, 1975.

Basinger, Jeanine. *The World War II Combat Film: Anatomy of a Genre*. New York: Columbia University Press, 1986.

Bem, Jeanne. "*Châtiments* ou l'histoire de France, comme enchaînement de parricides." In *Victor Hugo 1*, edited by Michel Grimaud, 39–51. Paris: Lettres Modernes/Minard, 1984.

Bevan, David, ed. *Literature and War*. Amsterdam and Atlanta: Rodopi, 1990.

Bonadeo, Alfredo. *Mark of the Beast: Death and Degradation in the Literature of the Great War*. Lexington: University Press of Kentucky, 1989.

Bonnefoy, Claude. "Quand le roman téléscope l'histoire." *Gulliver*, [n.d.]: 37.

Brooks, Peter. *Reading for the Plot: Design and Intention in Narrative*. New York: Knopf, 1984.

Brosman, Catharine Savage. *Art as Testimony: The Work of Jules Roy*. Gainesville: University of Florida Press, 1989.

———. *Jean-Paul Sartre*. Boston: Twayne, 1983.

———. *Reading Behind the Lines*. New Orleans: Graduate School of Tulane University, 1990. Reprinted in *Sewanee Review*, 100 (Winter 1992): 69–97.

———, ed. *French Novelists, 1930–1960*. Vol. 72 of *Dictionary of Literary Biography*. Detroit and London: Gale Research, 1989.

———, ed. *French Novelists Since 1960*. Vol. 83 of *Dictionary of Literary Biography*. Detroit: Gale Research, 1989.

Cahiers du Cerf XX, nos. 1 & 2. Brest: L'Université de Bretagne Occidentale, 1985, 1986.

Carroll, David. *French Literary Fascism: Nationalism, Anti-Semitism, and the Ideology of Culture*. Princeton: Princeton University Press, 1995.

Ceadel, Martin. *Thinking About Peace and War*. Oxford and New York: Oxford University Press, 1987.

Chambers, John Whiteclay II. " 'All Quiet on the Western Front' (1930): The Antiwar Film and the Image of the First World War." *Historical Journal of Film, Radio and Television*, 14, no. 4 (1994): 377–411.

Chauveau, Jean-Pierre. "Tradition et modernité dans les romans de Cocteau." In *Jean Cocteau aujourd'hui: Actes du Colloque de Montpellier, mai 1989*, 79–89. Paris: Klincksieck, 1992.

Churchill, Winston. *Thoughts and Adventures*. New York: Norton, 1991.

Clay, Jean, and Josette Contreras. *The Louvre*. Secaucus, N.J.: Chartwell Books, 1980.

Clifford, James. "On Collecting Art and Culture." In *The Cultural Studies Reader*, edited by Simon During. London and New York: Routledge, 1994.

Cobley, Evelyn. *Representing War: Form and Ideology in First World War Narratives*. Toronto: University of Toronto Press, 1993.

Cohen, Joseph. *Journey to the Trenches: The Life of Isaac Rosenberg, 1890–1918*. London: Robson Books, 1975.

Cone, Michèle C. *Artists Under Vichy: A Case of Prejudice and Persecution*. Princeton: Princeton University Press, 1992.

Contat, Michel, and Michel Rybalka. *A Bibliographical Life*, vol. 1 of *The Writings of Jean-Paul Sartre*. Translated by Richard C. McCleary. Evanston, Ill.: Northwestern University Press, 1974.

Cooke, James J. "Nationalism in Algeria." Paper delivered at Tulane University, 18 October 1996.

Coombes, John E. *Writing from the Left: Socialism, Liberalism and the Popular Front*. New York and London: Harvester Wheatsheaf, 1989.

Cooper, Helen M., Adrienne Auslander Munich, and Susan Merrill Squier. *Arms and the Woman: War, Gender, and Literary Representation*. Chapel Hill: University of North Carolina Press, 1989.

Cooperman, Stanley. *World War I and the American Novel*. Baltimore: Johns Hopkins University Press, 1967.

Craig, Gordon A., and Francis L. Loewenheim, eds. *The Diplomats: 1939–1979*. Princeton: Princeton University Press, 1994.

Crane, Stephen. *The Red Badge of Courage*. 1895. Reprint. New York: Modern Library, 1925.

Cruickshank, John. *Variations on Catastrophe*. Oxford: Clarendon Press, 1982.

Dasenbrock, Reed Way. "Paul de Man: The Modernist as Fascist." *South Central Review* 6 (Summer 1989): 6–18.

Davis, Grady Scott. *Warcraft and the Fragility of Virtue: An Essay in Aristotelian Ethics*. Moscow: University of Idaho Press, 1992.

Debon, Claude. *Guillaume Apollinaire après "Alcools."* Paris: Lettres Modernes/Minard, 1981.

Delon, Michel. "Germaine de Staël and Other Possible Scenarios of the Revolution." In *Germaine de Staël: Crossing the Borders*, edited by Madelyn Gutwirth, Avriel Goldberger, and Karyna Szmurlo, 22–33. New Brunswick: Rutgers University Press, 1991.

de la Gorce, Paul-Marie. *The French Army: A Military-Political History*. Translated by Kenneth Douglas. London: Weidenfeld & Nicolson, 1963.

Des Pres, Terrence. *Praises and Dispraises: Poetry and Politics, the 20th Century*. New York: Penguin, 1988.

Dhoop, Pascale. "André Gide et l'idée de la nation." Ph.D. diss., Tulane University, 1995.

The Doctrine of Saint-Simon: An Exposition. Translated by Georg G. Iggers, with preface by G. D. H. Cole. Boston: Beacon Press, 1958.

Dommanget, Maurice, et al. *Babeuf et les problèmes du babouvisme*. Paris: Editions Sociales, 1963.

Eksteins, Modris. *Rites of Spring: The Great War and the Birth of the Modern Age*. Boston: Houghton Mifflin, 1989.

Emboden, William A. *The Visual Art of Jean Cocteau*. New York: International Archive of Art/H. N. Abrams, 1989.

Explication des ouvrages de peinture, sculpture, gravure, lithographie et architecture des artistes vivans, exposés au Musée royal des arts, le 4 novembre 1827. [1827.] Reprint. New York: Garland, 1977.

Fabre, Joseph. *Jeanne d'Arc*. Paris: E. Dentu, 1890.

Fazia Amoia, Alba della. *Edmond Rostand*. Boston: Twayne, 1977.

Field, Frank. *Three French Writers of the Great War*. Cambridge: Cambridge University Press, 1975.

Fornari, Franco. *The Psychoanalysis of War*. Garden City, N.Y.: Anchor Books, 1974.

Fort, Bernadette, ed. *Fictions of the French Revolution*. Evanston: Northwestern University Press, 1991.

Foster, Mary Lecron, and Robert A. Rubenstein, eds. *Peace and War: Cross-Cultural Perspectives*. New Brunswick: Transaction Publishers, 1986.

French Painting, 1774–1830: The Age of Revolution. Detroit Institute of Arts and Metropolitan Museum of Art. Detroit: Wayne State University Press, 1975.

Furet, François, and Jacques Ozouf. *Reading and Writing: Literacy in France from Calvin to Jules Ferry*. Cambridge: Cambridge University Press, 1982.

Fussell, Paul. *The Great War and Modern Memory*. New York: Oxford University Press, 1975.

Gallie, W. B. *Philosophers of Peace and War*. Cambridge: Cambridge University Press, 1978.

Gat, Azar. *The Origins of Military Thought from the Enlightenment to Clausewitz*. Oxford: Clarendon Press, 1989.

Gay, Peter. *Voltaire's Politics*. Princeton: Princeton University Press, 1959.

Genette, Gérard. *Figures III*. Paris: Editions du Seuil, 1972. Partially translated by Jane E. Lewin as *Narrative Discourse: An Essay in Method*. Ithaca: Cornell University Press, 1980.

Gildea, Robert. *The Past in French History*. New Haven and London: Yale University Press, 1994.

Glidden, Hope H. "La Poésie du chiffre: Le Roy Ladurie and the *Annales* School of Historiography." *Stanford French Review* 5 (Winter 1981): 277–94.

Glucksmann, André. *Le Discours de la guerre*. Paris: L'Herne, 1967.

Godechot, J. "Nation, patrie, nationalisme et patriotisme," *Annales Historiques de la Révolution Française*, no. 206 (1971): 481–501.

Gollwitzer, Heinz. *Europe in the Age of Imperialism, 1880–1914*. London: Thames & Hudson, 1969.

Gordon, Melanie. "'Leben wie Gott in Frankreich': German Identity and the Myth of France, 1919–1945." Ph.D. diss., Tulane University, 1998.

Gray, J. Glenn. *The Warriors: Reflections on Men in Battle*. New York: Harper Colophon Books, 1970.

Greimas, A. J. *Sémantique structurale*. Paris: Larousse, 1966. Translated by Daniele McDowell, Ronald Schleifer, and Alan Velie as *Structural Semantics*. Lincoln: University of Nebraska Press, 1983.

Haig, Stirling. "The Grand Illusion: Vigny's *Servitude et grandeur militaires*." In Stirling Haig, *The Madame Bovary Blues*, 43–60. Baton Rouge: Louisiana State University Press, 1987.

Halbwachs, Maurice. *On Collective Memory*. Chicago: University of Chicago Press, 1992.

Hampson, Norman. *The First European Revolution: 1776–1815*. New York: Norton, 1969.

Hasselbach, Karlheinz. "Politics from the Spirit of Poetics: The Aesthetic Perspective of Ernst Jünger's *Der Arbeiter*." *Orbis Litterarum* 49 (1994): 272–92.

Heffernan, James A.W., ed. *Representing the French Revolution: Literature, Historiography, and Art*. Hanover and London: University Press of New England, 1992.

Heraclitus. *Fragments*. Text and translation with commentary by M. T. Robinson. Toronto: University of Toronto Press, 1987.

Higgins, Ian. *Anthology of Second World War French Poetry*. London: Methuen Educational, 1982.

———, ed. *The Second World War in Literature*. Edinburgh and London: Scottish Academic Press, 1986.

Hirsch, E. D., Jr. *Validity in Interpretation*. New Haven: Yale University Press, 1967.

Hobbes, Thomas. *Leviathan*. Edited by C. B. Macpherson. Baltimore: Penguin Books, 1968.

Holsinger, M. Paul, and Mary Anne Schofield. *Visions of War: World War II in Popular Literature and Culture*. Bowling Green, Ohio: Bowling Green State University Popular Press, 1992.

Hudson, Warren. Written statement to the author, 7 December 1990.

Huizinga, Johan. *Homo Ludens*. London: Routledge & Kegan Paul, 1949.

Hutton, John. *Neo-Impressionism and the Search for Solid Ground: Art, Science, and Anarchism in Fin-de-Siècle France*. Baton Rouge: Louisiana State University Press, 1994.

Hynes, Samuel. *A War Imagined: The First World War and English Culture*. New York: Atheneum, 1991.

Jay, Martin. *Force Fields: Exercises in Cultural Criticism*. New York and London: Routledge, 1992.

Jean Cocteau. Edited by Pierre Chanel, with preface by André Fraigneau. Paris: Chêne/Stock, 1975.

Jeanné, Egide. *L'Image de la Pucelle d'Orléans dans la littérature historique française depuis Voltaire*. Liège: Vaillant-Carmanne, 1935.

Johnson, James Turner. *Ideology, Reason, and the Limitation of War: Religious and Secular Concepts, 1200–1740*. Princeton: Princeton University Press, 1975.

———. *Just War Tradition and the Restraint of War: A Moral and Historical Inquiry*. Princeton: Princeton University Press, 1981.

Jones, Anson. *The Art of War in the Western World*. Urbana: University of Illinois Press, 1987.

Jünger, Ernst. *Das Wäldchen 125: Eine Chronik aus dem Grabenkämpfen 1918*. 1926. Translated as *Copse 125: A Chronicle from the Trench Warfare of 1918*. 1930. Reprint. New York: Howard Fertig, 1988.

Kant, Immanuel. *Critique of Judgment*. Translated by J. H. Bernard. New York: Hafner, 1951.

———. *Kant's Political Writings*. Edited by H. Reiss. Cambridge: Cambridge University Press, 1970.

———. *Perpetual Peace*. Translated by Lewis White Beck. Indianapolis: Library of Liberal Arts, 1957.

Keating, L. Clark. *Critic of Civilization: Georges Duhamel and His Writings*. Lexington: University of Kentucky Press, 1965.

Kedward, Roderick, and Roger Austin, eds. *Vichy France and the Resistance: Culture and Ideology*. London and Sydney: Croom Helm, 1985.

Keegan, John. *The Face of Battle*. New York: Viking, 1976.

———. *A History of Warfare*. New York: Knopf, 1993.

———. *The Second World War*. New York: Viking, 1990.

———, and Richard Holmes. *Soldiers*. London: Hamish Hamilton, 1985.

Klein, Holger, ed. *The First World War in Fiction*. London: Macmillan, 1976.

Kolko, Gabriel. *Century of War*. New York: The New Press, 1994.

Kristeva, Julia. *Black Sun: Depression and Melancholia*. Translated by Leon R. Roudiez. New York: Columbia University Press, 1982.

———. *Semiotikè: Recherches pour une sémanalyse*. Paris: Seuil, 1970.

Krob, Adam Nelson. "Hegel's Community: Synthesizing the Romantic and the Liberal." Ph.D. diss., Duke University, 1997.

Kuh, Katharine. *Break-Up: The Core of Modern Art*. Greenwich, Conn.: New York Graphic Society, 1965.

Laffin, John. *The Western Front Illustrated, 1914–1918*. Wolfeboro Falls, N.H.: Alan Sutton, 1991.

Lane, Arthur E. *An Adequate Response: The War Poetry of Wilfred Owen and Siegfried Sassoon*. Detroit: Wayne State University Press, 1972.

Lawrence, D. H. *Lady Chatterley's Lover*. 1928. Reprint. New York: Grove Press, 1959.

Lebovics, Herman. *True France: The Wars Over Culture and Identity, 1900–1945*. Ithaca: Cornell University Press, 1992.

Lebrun, Richard A. *Joseph de Maistre: An Intellectual Militant*. Kingston and Montreal: McGill-Queen's University Press, 1988.

Leiner, Wolfgang. *Das Deutschland Bild in der französischen Literatur*. Darmstadt: Wissenschaftliche Buchgesellschaft, 1989.

Lévêque, Jean-Jacques. *L'Art et la Révolution française, 1789–1804*. Neuchâtel: Ides et Calendes, 1987.

Lhoste, Pierre. "Jules Roy: Mes mots de passe." *Nouvelles Littéraires* 2201 (17 November 1969): 1, 7.

Lindenberger, Herbert. "Toward a New History in Literary Study." *Profession 84*. New York: Modern Language Association, 1984.

La Littérature française sous l'Occupation. Actes du Colloque international de Reims. Rheims: Presses Universitaires de Reims, 1984.

Lukàcs, Gyorgy. *Realism in Our Time*. Preface by George Steiner. Translated by John Mander and Necke Mander. New York: Harper & Row, 1964.

Lukacs, John. *The End of the Twentieth Century and the End of the Modern Age*. New York: Ticknor & Fields, 1993.

McCarthy, Cormac. *Blood Meridian*. New York: Random House, 1985.

McClay, Wilfred M. Review of Keith Windschuttle, *The Killing of History: How a Discipline Is Being Murdered by Literary Critics and Social Theorists*. *Academic Questions* 11 (Winter 1997–98): 90–94.

McClelland, J. S., ed. *The French Right (from de Maistre to Maurras)*. London: Jonathan Cape, 1970.

Manchester, William. *Visions of Glory, 1874–1932*. Vol. 1 of *The Last Lion: Winston Spencer Churchill*. Boston: Little Brown, 1983.

Margolis, Nadia. *Joan of Arc in History, Literature, and Film: A Select Annotated Bibliography*. New York: Garland, 1990.

Marrinan, Michael. *Painting Politics for Louis-Philippe: Art and Ideology in Orleanist France, 1830–1848*. New Haven: Yale University Press, 1988.

Mérimée, Prosper. *Portraits historiques et littéraires*. Edited by Pierre Jourda. Paris: Honoré Champion, 1928.

Merlant, Joachim. *De Montaigne à Vauvenargues*. Geneva: Slatkine, 1969.

Meyer, Henry. *Voltaire on War and Peace*. Studies on Voltaire and the Eighteenth Century, 144. Banbury, Oxfordshire: Voltaire Foundation, 1976.

Miller, Wayne Charles. *An Armed America: Its Face in Fiction; A History of the American Military Novel*. New York and London: New York University Press/University of London Press, 1970.

Nietzsche, Friedrich. *Thus Spoke Zarathustra*. In *The Portable Nietzsche*. Translated by Walter Kaufmann. New York: Viking, 1954.

Nora, Pierre, ed. *Les Lieux de mémoire*. 3 vols. Paris: Gallimard, 1984–1992.

Norman, Michael. *These Good Men: Friendships Forged from War*. New York: Crown Publishers, 1989.

O'Brien, Tim. *The Things They Carried*. Boston: Houghton Mifflin, 1990.

Obuchowski, Chester W. *Mars on Trial: War as Seen by French Writers of the Twentieth Century*. Madrid: Studia Humanitatis, 1978.

Olney, James. *Metaphors of Self: The Meaning of Autobiography*. Princeton: Princeton University Press, 1972.

Paris, Michael. *The Novels of World War Two: An Annotated Bibliography of World War II Fiction*. London: Library Association, 1990.

Perkins, Merle L. *Voltaire's Concept of International Order*. Studies on Voltaire and the Eighteenth Century, 36. Geneva: Institut et Musée Voltaire, 1965.

Pernoud, Régine, and Marie-Véronique Clin. *Jeanne d'Arc*. Paris: Fayard, 1986.

Peyre, Henri. *What Is Romanticism?* Translated by Roda Roberts. University, Ala.: University of Alabama Press, 1977.

Pfaff, William. *The Wrath of Nations: Civilization and the Furies of Nationalism*. New York: Simon & Schuster, 1993.

Phillips, Henry. "Theatricality in the Tragedies of Corneille." Paper delivered at the University of Sheffield, 1 May 1996.

Popper, K. R. "Utopia and Violence." *Hibbert Journal*, 46 (January 1948): 97–116.

Porter, Bruce D. *War and the Rise of the State: The Military Foundations of Modern Politics*. New York: Free Press, 1994.

Pucciani, Oreste F. "An Interview with Jean-Paul Sartre." *Tulane Drama Review*, 5 (March 1961): 12–18.

Ralston, David B. *The Army of the Republic: The Place of the Military in the Political Evolution of France, 1871–1914.* Cambridge: Massachusetts Institute of Technology Press, 1967.

Ramazani, Vaheed. *The Free Indirect Mode: Flaubert and the Poetics of Irony.* Charlottesville: University Press of Virginia, 1988.

———. "Historical Cliché: Irony and Sublime in *L'Education sentimentale.*" *PMLA* 108 (January 1993): 121–35.

Rapoport, Anatol. *The Origins of Violence: Approaches to the Study of Conflict.* New Brunswick: Transaction Publishers, 1995.

Reck, Rima Drell. *Drieu La Rochelle and the Picture Gallery Novel.* Baton Rouge: Louisiana State University Press, 1990.

———. Review of Robert L. Herbert, *Impressionism: Art, Leisure, and Parisian Society. French Review* 67 (May 1994): 1089–90.

Redman, Harry, Jr. *The Roland Legend in Nineteenth-Century French Literature.* Lexington: University Press of Kentucky, 1991.

Reid, Panthea. *Art and Affection: A Life of Virginia Woolf.* New York and Oxford: Oxford University Press, 1996.

Remenyi, Joseph. "The Psychology of War Literature." *Sewanee Review* 52, no. 1 (1944): 137–47.

Riegel, Léon. *Guerre et littérature.* Paris: Klincksieck, 1978.

Rieuneau, Maurice. *Guerre et révolution dans le roman français.* Paris: Klincksieck, 1974.

Ruskin, John. *The Crown of Wild Olive: Four Lectures on Industry and War.* No. 3, "War." New York: C. E. Merrill, 1891.

Saint-Paulien. *Napoléon Balzac et l'empire de "La Comédie humaine."* Paris: Albin Michel, 1979.

Schwarz, Daniel R. *Reconfiguring Modernism: Explorations in the Relationships Between Modern Art and Modern Literature.* New York: St. Martin's Press, 1997.

Silver, Kenneth E. *Esprit de Corps: The Art of the Parisian Avant-Garde and the First World War.* Princeton: Princeton University Press, 1989.

Simpson, Lewis P. *The Fable of the Southern Writer.* Baton Rouge: Louisiana State University Press, 1994.

Smith, Helen Zenna. *Not So Quiet . . . : Stepdaughters of War.* 1930. Reprint. New York: Feminist Press at the City University of New York, 1989.

Spufford, Francis. "The War That Never Stopped." *TLS,* 22 March 1996, pp. 11–12.

Steinbeck, John. *Once There Was a War.* 1959. Reprint. London: Corgi Books, 1973.

Stora, Benjamin. *Histoire de l'Algérie coloniale.* Paris: La Découverte, 1991.

Suleiman, Susan Rubin. *Authoritarian Fictions: The Ideological Novel as a Literary Genre.* New York: Columbia University Press, 1983.

Sulzberger, C. L. *World War II.* Boston: Houghton Mifflin, 1987.

Targan, Barry. "True Grit." *Sewanee Review,* 103 (Fall 1995): 581–92.

Taylor, Gary. *Cultural Selection.* New York: Basic Books, 1996.

Thompson, J. M. *Robespierre.* Oxford: Basil Blackwell, 1988.

Thomson, David. *Europe Since Napoleon.* London: Longmans, 1957.

Tylee, Claire M. *The Great War and Women's Consciousness: Images of Militarism and Womanhood in Women's Writings, 1914–1964.* Iowa City: University of Iowa Press, 1990.

Vasquez, John A. *The War Puzzle*. Cambridge: Cambridge University Press, 1993.

Walzer, Michael. *Just and Unjust Wars*. New York: Basic Books, 1977.

Warner, Marina. *Monuments and Maidens: The Allegory of the Female Form*. New York: Atheneum, 1985.

Weber, Eugen. *The Nationalist Revival in France, 1905–1914*. Berkeley and Los Angeles: University of California Press, 1959, 1968.

———. *France Fin de siècle*. Cambridge: The Belknap Press, 1986.

White, Hayden V. *Metahistory: The Historical Imagination in Nineteenth-Century Europe*. Baltimore: Johns Hopkins University Press, 1973.

———. *Tropics of Discourse*. Baltimore: Johns Hopkins University Press, 1978.

Whitman, Walt. *Leaves of Grass*. Edited by Emory Holloway. Garden City, N.Y.: Doubleday, 1926.

Winter, Jay. *The Experience of World War I*. New York: Oxford University Press, 1989.

———. *The Great War and the British People*. London: Macmillan, 1986.

———. *Sites of Memory, Sites of Mourning*. New York: Cambridge University Press, 1995.

Wintermute, Alan, et al. *1789: French Art During the Revolution*. New York: Colnaghi, 1989.

Zielonka, Anthony. *Alphonse Esquiros (1812–1876): A Study of His Works*. Paris and Geneva: Champion/Slatkine, 1985.

Zoppi, Gilbert. "Jeanne d'Arc et les républicains." In *L'Esprit républicain; Colloque d'Orléans 4 et 5 septembre 1970*, 313–19. Paris: Klincksieck, 1972.

INDEX

INDEX

Apollinaire, Guillaume, xvi, 29, 35, 37, 44, 141, 142, 169
Aragon, Louis, xiii, 43, 54, 76, 82, 175–76, 177
Arc de Triomphe, 46, 55, 169
Arc de Triomphe du Carrousel, 55
Archetypes. *See* Myth
Architecture, 173, 174. *See also* Arc de Triomphe; Arc de Triomphe du Carrousel; Memorials; Nazis
Aristotle, xxii, 6
Armaments. *See* Artillery; Weapons
Armistice. *See* Fall of France (1940); Victory of 1918
Arras, 183
Arrows. See *Faisceaux d'armes* or *faisceaux de licteur*
Artillery, 35, 37, 41, 146
Artois, 149
Asia, 67. *See also* Indochinese war
Atack, Margaret, xii
Augustine, Saint, 7
Auschwitz, 84
Austerlitz, 55, 101
Autobiographical elements, 79, 193, 196, 197
Autodiegetic narrator, 114
Avant-garde. *See* Modernism
Aviation fiction. *See* Aerial warfare
Aymé, Marcel, 83

Babeuf, François-Emile (Gracchus), 16, 17, 22
Babylon, 123, 136
Badinguet, 121. *See also* Napoleon III
Bakhtin, Mikhail, 28
Baldensperger, Fernand, 18
Ballanche, Pierre Simon, 103
Balzac, Honoré de, xviii, 56, 62, 64, 66, 71, 80, 87–91, 93, 95
Banners. *See* Flags; Iconography
Banville, Théodore de, 112
Baptism by fire, 74, 95
Barbier, Jules, 52
Barbusse, Henri, 66, 75, 79–80, 82, 103, 153–54, 157, 160, 172

Bardèche, Maurice, 87
Barnes, Julian, xii
Baroja, J.-C., 105
Barrès, Maurice, 5, 57–58, 115, 125, 126, 144–45, 146
Barrière, Pierre, 87
Barthélemy, Auguste, 56
Basinger, Jeanine, xvi
Bastille, 25, 72, 206
Bastille Day, 168
Battle Cry (Uris), 5
Battle for France (1940), 78, 83, 183, 191. *See also* Fall of France (1940); Flanders
Battle of Algiers, 212
Battle of Britain, 78
Bayard, 147
Bayeux, 26
Bazaine, Achille, marshal, 31, 110, 112
BBC (British Broadcasting Corporation), 194
Beauvoir, Simone de, xviii, 81, 83, 188–89
Beckett, Samuel, 63
Beethoven, Ludwig van, 173
Belgium, 96, 161, 183, 200. *See also* Flanders
Belsen, 204
Bem, Jeanne, 13
Benjamin, René, 80, 81, 135, 153, 157, 160
Béranger, Pierre-Jean, 56, 86
Berezina, 38, 91
Berlin, Isaiah, 18
Berlin, 34, 168, 174, 186
Bernanos, Georges, 53–54
Bernhardt, Sarah, 53
Bevan, David, xii
Beylisme, 94
Bible, 15, 16, 28, 74, 75, 103, 136, 160. *See also* Apocalypse
Biblical view of history, 4. *See also* Apocalyptic vision
Bildungsroman, 95
Bismarck, Otto von, 75, 121